Miria Matembe

Other titles in Fountain Series in Gender Studies

Miria Matembe

Gender, Politics, and
Constitution Making in Uganda

Miria R.K. Matembe
with Nancy R. Dorsey

Fountain Publishers

Fountain Publishers Ltd
P.O. Box 488
Kampala
E-mail:fountain@starcom.co.ug
Website:www.fountainpublishers.com

ISBN 9970 02 337 3

Cataloguing-in-Publication Data

Matembe, Miria R.K.
Gender, Politics and Constitution Making
Kampala : Fountain Publishers, 2002
____ p. ____ cm.

ISBN 9970 02 337 3
Includes Index
I. Gender - Uganda. II. Politics - Uganda
III. Constitution making - Uganda   VI. Autobiography - Matembe

922.2'096761

Dedication

Dedicated to all women and men of good will struggling to make the lives of women more meaningful and worth living.

Dedication

Contents

Abbreviations

ACFODE	Action for Development
ANC	African National Congress
AWID	Association of Women in International Development
CA	Constituent Assembly
CAD	Constituent Assembly Delegate
CBO	Community Based Organisation
CEDAW	Convention against all forms of Discrimination Against Women
CM	Council Member
CV	Curriculum Vitae
DANIDA	Danish Development Agency
DFID	Department for International Development
DPP	Director of Public Prosecutions
FIDA	Women lawyers' association
FOWODE	Forum for Women in Democracy
ISIS-WICCE	Women International Cross Cultural Exchange
KKK	Ku-Klux-Klan
LAP	Legal Aid Project
LC	Local Council
MDWA	Mbarara District Women's Development Association
NAACP	National Association for the Advancement of Coloured People
NAWOU	National Association of Women Organisations in Uganda
NCW	National Council of Women
NGO	Non-Governmental Organisation

NOTU	National Organisation of Trades Unions
NPC	National Political Commissar
NRA	National Resistance Army
NRC	National Resistance Council
NRM	National Resistance Movement
RC	Resistance Council
SDA	Special District Administrator
SWSA	Social Work and Social Administration (department of)
TASO	The Aids Support Organisation
UCC	Uganda Constitutional Commission
UGRC	Uganda Gender Resource Centre
UPC	Uganda Peoples Congress
UPM	Uganda Patriotic Movement
UWA	Uganda Women's Association
UWESO	Uganda Women's Effort to Save Orphans
UWFCT	Uganda Women's Finance and Credit Trust
UWONET	Uganda Women Network
UNECA	United Nations Economic Commission for Africa
UNIFEM	United Nations Development Fund for Women

Acknowledgments

I must first of all thank God the Almighty for creating me into the person that I am a woman of course, of enthusiasm, commitment and passion. I surely delight in my enormous energy and determination to move things. I am glad I am a woman of destiny. Thank you, Lord, for enabling me to realise my dream and may the glory be yours for ever.

I need to thank my mother Eseza for nurturing and moulding me into what I am. I shall live to treasure the sweet memories of the special love she had for me. She built my confidence for she is the one who made me believe that I am 'the best of the lot'. Thank you, mother, and may the good Lord continue to rest your soul in eternal peace.

I cannot find the real words to thank my special friend and sister Nancy Dorsey, the Editor of this book, who not only inspired me to write it but who literally pushed me into writing it. Although quite a number of women colleagues had encouraged me to condense my life experience into a permanent record, Nancy was not satisfied with mere encouragement. When she realised that I was too busy to sit down and write, she devised a scheme, which certainly worked, resulting in this book. She decided that I should get time, at least an evening or two after my hectic schedule in the office and relax at her Makerere flat to tell her my story as she recorded it.

Nancy and I found this idea not only useful but very exciting, enjoyable and relaxing. It was Nancy's recordings which we later transcribed to form the basis of this book. I wish to express my sincere gratitude to you, Nancy, for being a special mentor. The number of journeys you travelled, at cost, from the United

States of America, to work on our project, the hours, days and months you dedicated to this project, are all appreciated, as are the anxiety and concerns and, at times, stress you endured while on our project. The cost in terms of money and time was so enormous, and all because of me! I love you sweet, Nancy, 'my literally partner', for being a true and sincere friend, all the way from America, and for your commitment to ensure that there is one additional writer on the list of the African female writers. May the good Lord, who has already rewarded us with the success of our project, continue to bless you in mighty.

There are many women and men who have, in one way or another, contributed to my life without whom I would probably have had no story to tell. Among these men and women, I wish to note, with gratitude, my father's efforts in making sure that both his daughters and sons went to school. I must thank my brother Jechoas Kotungire for the tremendous role he played in my life. If it were not for him, I would never have continued with education beyond primary school. My brother Kotu, as he is commonly known, loved me so much and used to visit me, in every school I went to. His attitude towards me motivated me to work so hard because I was scared of letting him down. My political 'drivers' and planners, Jolly Mugisha, Anna Talemwa and Joy Kiconco, without whom I would have had no story to tell about my contribution to the Constituent Assembly and Parliament. You three great women in my life, I thank you so much and pray for you always that my God whom I trust may reward you immensely. Jolly, thank you for contributing to this book.

Special thanks go to Maxin Ankrah and Maude Mugisha, my co-founders of ACFODE and allies in the struggle. I thank them for contributing to this book.

I cannot forget my good friend Mary Maitum, with whom we toiled to ensure that the constitutional Commission's draft constitution was gender sensitive. I wish to thank my sister, Margaret Kyakunda Mubanda, for her love and spiritual support. She keeps me in her prayers always.

My dear friend sister and neighbour, Doreen Muyingo, who is always there for me; Beth Bamwine and Joy Kafura-Kabatsi, childhood friend who has become a real sister, I thank you all so much for what you have been in my life. I cannot forget my special aunt Olive Mirama Myhren and my childhood friend Edith Mirembe who both contributed financially and materially to my welfare during my education time. I always remember and treasure those contributions without which my life story would not have been the same. Kitty Tweyanze, my Secretary, when I was Chairperson of ACFODE, also deserves a mention in this book.

Let me also thank the men and women in my life that have guided my intellectual, and spiritual growth. Among these, is the late George W. Kabugo, whose words inspired a great confidence in me and an urge to move to greater heights, shall live to remember. George played a big role that has led me to succeed in all these challenging political tasks. I had the opportunity to meet and work with George at the Chartered Institute of Bankers between 1983-89. George used to tell me again and again, 'There is so much in you that I wish to develop.' When I look back to those years and see what I have achieved, I cannot fail to thank him for his determination and ability to develop in me that which he desired. Sarah Timarwa, my long time friend and spiritual mentor, I must recognise you for all that you have been in my life. I treasure your love and encouragement.

In a special way, I wish to thank His Lordship Justice George Kanyeihamba and Rev. John Mary Waliggo for their support and for contributing to this book. It was a pleasure for me to know how they perceive me.

I wish to express my deep gratitude to my husband, Nekemia, for all the support he has given me and for contributing an article to this book.

May I also thank my sons Godwin, Gideon and Gilbert Grace who have had to miss mother's care and presence while I was busy doing all the work recorded in this book. I thank them for their understanding.

May I in a big way thank the Netherlands government which through its embassy in Uganda, contributed funds towards the publication of this book. I am thankful to His Excellency Ambassador Matthieu A. Peters for presenting my request to his government.

Last but not least, I wish to express my gratitude to the National Resistance Movement government under the leadership of His Excellency Yoweri Kaguta Museveni for creating the conducive environment that enabled me to realise my dreams.

May God bless you all.

M.R.K.M.
June 2002

Foreword

Sarah E. Ntiro *

The autobiography of Mrs Miria Rukoza Koburunga Matembe, Member of Parliament for Mbarara District in south western Uganda and Minister of State for Ethics and Integrity in the Uganda government, deliberately breaks through the traditional silence of a Ugandan woman to talk openly about herself and to document her achievements for publication.

Miria conceived the idea of bringing out a book telling her life story long before the 2002 theme of celebrating the International Women's Day on 8 May, 2002 which was called 'Break the Silence: Stop Violence against Women.' She wanted girls and women to read her life story and use it as a source of inspiration, comparison and encouragement.

Miria is a self-confessed village girl activist of a peasant extraction, a born-again Christian and a tireless and bold champion of the Uganda women's cause. She became a renowned, astute legislator, a well-informed and highly motivated feminist, a role model whose spectacular success has been recognised locally, nationally and as an international heroine. All this before she becomes fifty years old.

Her journey to fame started when her parents sent her to primary school in her home village, in Rutoma, Kashari, Ankole in south western Uganda. Then she proceeded to Bweranyangi Girls Secondary School, Bushenyi, Ankole, where she spent

---

*Sarah Ntiro is one of the pioneers of the Women's Movement in Uganda and indeed in East Africa. She was the first woman graduate in Mathematics in East and Central Africa. She was also one of three African women to enter the Uganda Legislative Council (Legico) in 1958. She is a prominent player in the struggle for gender equality in East Africa.

four years and continued to Namasagali College in eastern Uganda to complete her secondary education.

She was a highly organised, focused and enthusiastic learner throughout her school days with her dream of becoming a lawyer vividly in her mind always.

In 1972 Miria entered Makerere University to study Law. Studying Law was her childhood dream. As a small girl, she had observed many women suffering at the hands of their male relatives. She, herself, suffered social injustices simply because she was a girl. Her achievements were not recognised. In fact, they were often taken for granted or completely ignored. She was not amused by this treatment and she resolved to become a lawyer, when she grew up, in order to solve women's problems and stop their suffering. She hoped that her becoming a lawyer would ensure their enjoyment of a peaceful and prosperous life.

A number of forces have shaped Miria's life and contributed significantly to her growth, development and success.

First and foremost, was her family. She is a product of a monogamous marriage where the meagre family resources were shared for the general good of the family. But there were inequalities, which Miria noticed at a very early age. She tried fighting against some of them during her early childhood. Others she promised herself to fight against after qualifying as a lawyer.

Eseza Kajwengye Rukoza, her mother, was a born again Christian and a rock of stability in Miria's trials and tribulations, until her death in 1992. She firmly believed in her daughter's ability to achieve her set goals and to realise her dreams. She had the courage of a mother in making her daughter what she had to be. She was a counsellor, a collaborator and mediator between Miria and her father.

Samuel Rukoza, her father, was the traditional, conservative and undisputed head of an African household. His negative attitude towards his fourth child, his clever, argumentative daughter, who did not fit in the stereotype of feminine gentle behaviour, was always stressful. But it must have contributed to the sharpening of Miria's skills in dealing with male chauvinism as an adult woman.

Miria's siblings, five brothers and three sisters are part and parcel of her life. They have always called her 'Koburunga' her given name, affectionately at their home.

Another force which has enormously influenced Miria's career making a life long impact on her, is her Christian faith. She was baptised in her village church as an infant and called Miria. She was confirmed in her faith at Bweranyangi as an adolescent. She belongs to the Mother's Union in the Anglican Communion and today she often preaches in church services. Her Christian belief must be the rock on which she stands to condemn, boldly, all wrongdoing, social injustices of all kinds and which gives her courage and conviction to do her challenging work as Minister of Ethics and Integrity. Her belief that all people are God's children encourages her to take responsibility to devise strategies intended to relieve their suffering.

Last, but not least, is her committed and supportive husband and their four sons. They have kept her on an even keel in her turbulent political career.

Life at Makerere University gave Miria an opportunity to meet interesting people with whom she has made lifelong relationships. At first, there were her five maternal uncles who, by their own volition, volunteered to protect her against the vagaries of men and alcohol in Kampala. She also met a young woman medical student called Specioza Wandira who has continued to be Miria's friend and political ally as Dr Specioza Wandira Kazibwe, Member of Parliament for Kigulu South and Vice President Uganda. But most of all, that is the time she met her future husband, Nekemia Matembe.

Not all people who meet Miria are fascinated and overwhelmed by her public image. They condemn her deep strong voice and the forceful way she uses it, and her tall figure, as being unfeminine and unwomanly. The media in Uganda, with its tabloid approach, has done its best to pull her down. But she is resilient and determined to defend and maintain her public image, which she has, so painstakingly created, for herself. They resent her non-conformist approach to social injustices, which she articulates in colourful language. Miria has a love/hate relationship with the Uganda media. It has got to the point where she does not have to ask them to come and report what she is doing. They seek her out and report whatever sensational stories they can get about her. The more sensational the reporting the more attention it attracts and sells, even when the salient issues raised are omitted. With time, that relationship has stabilised to some sort of mutual respect and co-existence.

But, 'Who is this Hon. Mrs Miria Matembe?' Or as the press would have it, 'Who is this Matembe?'

To many of us, who have come to know her over the years, we would say that Miria has an open mind. She is a continuos learner who is willing and ready to learn on the job, new technologies and new methods of operation and to absorb new but relevant terminologies, all for the enhancement of her work. She even took off time to study for a Master's degree in Law and Development so as to re-tool herself for new challenges in the quest for women's empowerment.

An infectious sense of humour is one of Miria's attributes. She laughs heartily at genuinely funny jokes and even laughs at herself when she is in the wrong. She has the gift of addressing serious issues with a lot of humour, which encourages people to listen to her attentively.

Contrary to what her detractors might imagine, Miria is a keen listener who demands explanations and clarifications when, initially, she does not understand a point. This kind of humility helps her to admit her ignorance and encourages her to want to be more enlightened. Also, it breaks down some of the resistance to her unexpected demands. She knows when to withdraw and act behind the scenes, if that is the best strategy for that particular activity.

Miria loves people and her ability to make friends at places of work, of socialisation and in voluntary organisations has created around her a circle of genuine friends who argue with her, advise her, help her to think through problems and comfort and console her when the public is attacking her. Miria's love for women is extremely amazing and she will not hesitate to embrace any opportunity available, or create it if need be, in order to address what she commonly refers to as the subject closest to her heart, 'the Gender Question.'

I recall sometime in 1990 when Miria went to Lira in northern Uganda, as a commissioner of the Uganda Constitutional Commission to mobilise and sensitise the people about the constitution-making exercise, she managed to fit in the Commission's programme a visit to Lira District Hospital, particularly the Maternity Ward. To her horror and disgust the mothers were delivering their babies on a cold, bare cement floor. She was outraged. She was angered and felt very sorry for the mothers and the babies. She came away determined to take action. Immediately, she returned to Kampala, ACFODE members were summoned to an emergency meeting to discuss the Lira District Hospital Maternity Ward situation. A fund raising meeting was held there and then and, within a few weeks, money was available to buy furniture, furnishings, beds, cots and beddings, etc, for that Maternity Ward. All items marked 'Donated by ACFODE' not by Hon. Miria Matembe were handed over, at the City Square in Kampala, to the relevant Lira District authorities for the users of the Lira District Hospital Maternity Ward.

We also know that Miria is a woman of contradictions. While she openly condemns male chauvinism, patriarchy, etc, she uses, as part of her identity, her father's name Rukoza and she is popularly known as Matembe, her husband's name.

She condemns domesticity as an insidious evil, which, over the centuries, has prevented women from participating fully · in public affairs. Yet, she relishes hosting her friends, colleagues, relatives, constituents and foreign visitors to her home both in Kampala and Ankole.

I remember, in 1992, when Miria's mother died, large crowd of mourners converged on her home in Rutoma. Miria was there to welcome each mourner. She was wearing what I call domestic and an in-doors attire. She made sure we were all comfortable in a venue not designed to accommodate huge crowds. She personally supervised the serving of lunch to every mourner and then she disappeared for a little while, only to return in a different role. She was then dressed as a political activist standing behind a microphone giving the main eulogy for her departed mother. What a transformation!

She is dead serious at public and religious affairs functions but she believes in having good innocent fun at social events, especially at dances. I can cite many other examples, but that suffice to say those contradictions have a sound and rational basis.

It would appear, from her book, that the most productive period of Miria's life, especially in matters of good governance, is from 1985 to 1995. That is when she came into her own as a political activist. Somewhere during this period, Miria discovered that being a lawyer only would never empower her enough to make policies that would benefit women. She had to go into politics. She entered into local government politics, sensitising her colleagues and other audiences on gender issues and monitoring the implementation of the NRM policies at all levels. Then she entered national politics and got elected as a Member of Parliament representing Mbarara District.

She got deeply involved in constitution making as a commissioner in the Uganda Constitutional Commission and as an elected delegate to the Constituent Assembly. All this is chronicled in detail in this book. She did not neglect the crucial role civil society plays in good governance management in the nation. There, her entry point was being a member of ACFODE (Action for Development) and later its chairperson. All this activity stimulated and re-kindled her literary creativity and she wrote plays in which she sometimes acted and poems, which she often recited in public gatherings, in order to illustrate her messages on gender equality. Wearing all those hats, she made a dramatic entry on the political scene which we are now celebrating in this book.

Miria's area of operation has not been confined to Uganda only. It has had an East African and Pan-African dimension.

1. In 1993 Miria made her mark in FEMNET (the African Women's Communication and Information Network) based in Nairobi and she is a founder member of Women in Law and Development in Africa (WILDA).

2. Miria has played an outstanding role as a member of the secretariat of the Pan-African Movement, which among other things organised the seventh Pan-African Congress in Kampala in 1994. That congress stands out from the six preceding ones in that African women met at Makerere University, Kampala Uganda in the run up to the congress. Miria made a rousing closing speech, which was met by a thunderous standing ovation. Among the people who attended this meeting which led to the birth of the Pan-African Women's Liberation Organisation (PAWLO) was:

   - Dr Fatuma Mahmoud (Sudan), the current President of PAWLO.
   - Dr Betty Shabbaz (RIP) widow of the late Malcomx (USA)
   - Mrs Gracia Machel (Mozambique), now Mrs Gracia Mandela,
   - Ms Esi Sutherland, Deputy Minister of Education (Ghana)
   - There has also been valuable interaction between Miria and a number of distinguished African Women in the African Women's Movement since the 1990s.

   Some of the questions her many admirers and well wishers are asking today are:

   - Is Miria completely satisfied with the result of her achievements?
   - What is she going to do beyond 2006?

   - Will she use similar strategies and structures, in her on-going crusade, to achieve her goal of promoting women's human rights?

   This is the challenge Miria is facing between now and the year 2006.

   Meanwhile, I very much hope that women, girls and all men of goodwill, who enjoy reading women's success stories, will read Miria Matembe's book of her life history and emulate her phenomenal example, to transform their lives. If a village girl with a clear vision and the will to work hard can become an international role model, so can·they.

Introduction

Nancy R. Dorsey

Writing African history that includes the female half of the population has hardly begun. For example, a major historical work, the 8-volume *General History of Africa* published by UNESCO in 1981, says next to nothing about the women who contributed to the development of the continent. With the advent of the International Women's Movement, with the arrival of Women's Studies programmes and libraries, with considerable new research being done about women from women's perspectives, there is growing interest in publishing stories about women's lives and experiences.

There is no doubt that the work of Miria R.K. Matembe has been a key factor in the gains made for women in Uganda since stability returned to the country in 1986. Matembe has been widely recognised for the leadership role she has played. For International Women's Day 1997, ISIS - Women International Cross Cultural Exchange (ISIS-WICCE) held a programme to honour Ugandan women leaders. Matembe was chosen by a cross-section of Ugandan women as one of two 'Women Achievers of 1997.'

In 1998 the lifetime achievements of Miria Matembe captured the world's attention when she was named as an international heroine by the 100 Heroines Project in the USA. This project was held in conjunction with the celebration of the 150 anniversary of the first American women's rights convention held in 1848 in Seneca Fall, New York. The Heroines were chosen based on three criteria:

1. They act courageously to achieve equal rights and freedom for women.

2. They risk their social acceptance, financial security, health, or even their lives on behalf of women.
3. They serve as role models for women and girls.

In *The New Vision's* Uganda's Top 100 Women competition in March in 1999, Matembe scored the highest in the Women Activist category, having twice as many votes as the second place finisher. It is clear that when it comes to talk about women, Ugandans know one name above all others – Matembe.

A book about Matembe's commitment and dedication to the cause of women will not only be a major addition to the historical record of the continent, it will also be available to inspire African girls, and other girls around the world, to adopt serious goals and to overcome difficulties. The book will also chronicle the ups and downs of a political life and the strategies that played a key role in the remarkable changes in gender relations that have taken place in Uganda in the recent past.

Miria Matembe is an electric and unforgettable public figure. The first time I saw her in her performance mode was in 1993 at the AWID (Association of Women in International Development) conference in Washington, DC. I was one of an interesting mix of graduate students in attendance, ten of us from six or seven countries, all of us doing development studies at Ohio State University in Columbus, Ohio. We shared a long mini-van ride to the three-day conference to join the other conference participants, over 2000 attendees, almost all women, from more than 70 countries.

Miria was one of three keynote speakers. I remember her presentation very well. Opening the morning session, she appeared confidently in a spotlight on the stage of the large hotel auditorium. A tall, distinguished woman, she wore a bright coloured gomesi, a full length, elegant dress traditional to Uganda. Miria is very much at home on a stage or at a podium - performing. In her deep, resonant voice, she presented one of her poems, 'Women of Uganda.' (This poem is on page 91). With passion and pathos, she recited from memory the poem, consisting of several verses. The poetic images describe the hardships Ugandan women face every day in their lives of never ending work and overwhelming responsibility, for which they experience little recognition and from which they receive little respite. When Miria finished the poem, there was silence for a few moments. Then the auditorium exploded with applause and, like a tide, people rose to their feet in a standing ovation. Next, without a single note, Miria gave a well-constructed description of women's problems in Uganda, and followed that gloomy picture with a vision of better things that were even then occurring in her country. When she concluded her remarks, the audience was on its feet again to give her a second standing ovation.

Prior to this conference, I had been in Uganda twice. I had met several prominent women leaders there and had scrutinised the newspapers for coverage of gender issues. Stories about 'Matembe' appeared prominently in the media. Now, here in the United States capital, it was interesting to watch the impact this dynamic Ugandan woman had on a diverse group of development practitioners from around the world. After her presentation Miria was the focus of a good amount of interest. In the halls of the conference hotel, people recognised her and moved to speak a few words to her, touching her hand as they spoke to her. Miria was magnetic in attracting attention and contact. Florence Wakoko, one of my colleagues from Ohio State, had worked with Miria in ACFODE (Action for Development) and, to my surprise and pleasure, I found myself sharing lunch with Miria and Florence that same day. That was the beginning of my fascination with this incredible woman.

In 1995, armed with my new PhD degree, I took a lecturing position in the Department of Women Studies at Makerere University in Kampala, Uganda where I stayed for four years. During that time Miria and I met occasionally. I observed that, whether she was addressing a large crowd in a public setting or a few people in a social gathering, she used stories about her own life to advocate justice and equality for women and girls. This technique was very effective. Her stories were fresh, interesting and relevant. One day I told Miria that she should write the story of her life since there are so few books published about women in politics. She replied that others had made that same suggestion. In the following year or so, we had that same conversational interchange several times. Nancy: 'You should write a book about your life.' Miria: 'I know, but I'm busy with many other things.' At some point, it occurred to me that her stories could serve as the basis for the book she needed to write. Perhaps the book would write itself.

In 1998, Miria and I began to 'write' her book. This is how it happened. We would meet at my flat on Makerere's campus and tape record her stories. From that point, transcriptions of the tapes served as a text from which to work. Miria's speeches, papers and her MA dissertation provided important supplemental material. We found that bits and pieces of her writing integrated well into the taped interviews. Of course, her speeches and writing (and her life story) have a single theme, the problem of gender inequality and the solution to that problem - the emancipation of women and girls.

It is important to describe our objectives for the book and the working relationship that emerged. True to ideas about feminist writing, we worked to produce Miria's story, in her own words, with as little editing as possible. As Miria said, 'When someone reads the book, I want them to say, "Yes, that's Matembe."' From the beginning, my main editing job has been to let Miria tell her story in her own voice, with as little interference as possible. Since Miria is an outstanding communicator, this has not been a difficult task. She has good command of English, her second language, which she uses with skill and flair, in her own unique style.

Guided by a preliminary outline, it became my task to take the text created from the transcriptions and written materials and to organise it into a coherent whole. Miria regularly reviewed the manuscript as it started to take shape. It took a number of meetings to get the project off the ground as we worked out what form this collaboration would take. More stories were told and recorded. Sometimes I would stop Miria in mid-sentence so that we could get her words on tape. Both of us were serious about achieving this fine balancing act of creating a narrative that Miria was comfortable with and that was also well organised and readable. Every effort was made to retain Miria's unique use of language and imagery. What had Miria seen, experienced and felt? What was the story she wanted to tell?

Another issue was to maintain the conversational tone as much as possible. We didn't want this to be an academic exercise, but one woman's personal testimony about her journey through life. Footnotes and academic references were kept to a minimum. In her life and work, Miria struggles to be accessible to people, especially women. We wanted her life story to project that same tone and flavour. Miria has been a prominent actor in highly significant historical events taking place in Uganda and beyond. How could we offer a clear representation of the role she played in these things, from her own perspective? Our collaboration moved to email after I returned to the US in 1999. Two trips to Uganda in 2000 and 2001 made it possible for me to work in close contact with Miria, as we moved the manuscript forward.

As Miria and I worked together, I observed myself playing different roles in the writing process. In many instances, I was simply the listener to Miria's stories. Part of my academic training has been learning to be a good listener. In research one has questions that beg for answers. Someone knows something the researcher wants to know. If the inquirer talks a lot, it interferes with the flow of information which is the end product one is working to get. We found that there were patterns in Miria's stories that parallel what other women leaders and activists have experienced in this period of women gaining ground, and together we explored some of the issues involved.

As Miria recalled her life, vivid pictures emerged. Something happened, someone said or did this, Miria replied or acted in a certain way, and that incident carried a certain meaning to her. When I didn't fully understand what she was trying to convey, we would discuss the matter, sometimes at length, sometimes on several different occasions. This point is important, so I'll include an example. Miria has very strong feelings about her father. As we worked she would describe something that had happened between them, and after minor editing, I would give her a printout of that part. Somehow the sections about her relationship with her father would leave her unsatisfied. It seems that during this period, she was privately revisiting this troublesome relationship and struggling to come to terms with it. It took a considerable amount of work before this relationship settled comfortably into the flow of Miria's story. Looking back, I can see that it may be that my loving relationship with my own father was a bit of a hindrance to the process. I found myself wanting her to soften what she said about her father, and, after all, I was in a position to control the flow of words. At the same time, Miria was determined to tell the truth about the harsh treatment her father directed her way. What happened between Miria and her father had a tremendous impact on her development. This difficult relationship helped to define who she became. She was not willing to back away from what she knew to be true about that relationship. In one sense, she was writing her story for other women and girls, and she refused to lose that focus. The point is, it took us a good amount of time and effort to get down on paper the words she wanted to use to record this complicated relationship.

Before moving on, I want to return to Miria's unique ability as a public actor. Those who have seen her in her public role have already formed a strong impression of her. Undoubtedly some have recognised and acknowledged her enormous talent, while others have chosen to be offended by such an 'unwomanly' public presentation by a woman. It could be that some people may not have decided as yet just where they stand on the Matembe phenomenon. It is to those who have never had the opportunity to see her in action that I direct the following.

Miria Matembe is a master of the role she has taken on, a fearless advocate for women. She is a star performer, an eloquent speaker who fills the public space allotted to her, and quickly takes charge of an audience. Yes, while she has the floor, the audience is truly hers, as she fully engages a group with her timely, intense message, 'Let me tell you about women, because nobody knows better than I do what women's lives are like. You must listen to what I say. I speak for women, especially for those women who can't speak for themselves. And, it is time for something better.'

Miria is what a public speaker should be. She is confident and 'good on her feet.' She has a strong, well-modulated voice, and she speaks loud enough for all to hear. She displays an intelligent use of language, such as colourful local proverbs and expressions for emphasis. With wit and humour – she loves joking – she charms and disarms people. She influences and persuades.

Miria's life story is as fascinating as she is. How did a shy girl from a poor rural family develop this art of politics so beautifully? It is too bad that no one was there to record her development as a public speaker when she first started to go wherever anyone would listen to her, while she sharpened the tools of her trade. Miria is aware of the power at her command and wonders about it. Somehow her dream has given her the strength and courage she needs to be this Matembe she has created in the face of public abuse and ridicule.

As with many important historical figures, Miria was in the right place at the right time to fully use her talents. (One can only grieve for Kenyan women whose dictatorial government even today squelches their efforts to gain equal rights and opportunities.) The times were right for Miria to emerge as a leader, and to play that role to the full. When she recognised the possibilities, Miria literally went to war. She had weapons, and she has learned how to use them ever more effectively. Never mind a little blood in the process, hers and others. Miria knows how to be ladylike, but being a lady did not get her what she wanted. It is no wonder she has been so controversial. Miria has continually said things that women are not supposed to say, things that even if women think them, most are afraid to say them out loud. Many women who have stepped out to speak the truth about the persistent biases against them just because they are female find they are not able to stand the firestorm their words and actions bring upon them. When attacked, they back off. Not Miria! She couldn't retreat. Her dream drove her, so she suffered the blows. For her, taking the blows was less painful than betraying her vision.

Miria's relationship with the media has been a heavy cross to bear. The press in Uganda more often than not chooses a quick headline over serious journalism, and it appears they regularly use Matembe for target practice. Often one statement she makes is taken out of context, headlines are created, and papers sell. This tabloid approach, with little or no basis in fact, sells papers. Yes, battering Matembe sells papers in Uganda. There is no doubt that many people have formed their opinions about her from this negative press. The media have created a mystique around this woman Matembe. When she has challenged what they have printed about her, they have even used that against her.

Miria is definitely not the Matembe portrayed in the media. She is at once more and less: more serious, more worthy of respect, more important as an historical figure; less controversial, less deviant, less foolish. Another point here is that an attack on Matembe is an attack on women who believe they are equals with men, women who aspire, women who take themselves seriously as thinkers and doers. An attack on Matembe is an attack on reasonable requests for fairness and justice, on a progressive agenda for Uganda. An attack on her is something to talk about for all the wannabes in the local drinking places where they are drinking up their money rather than developing their families, their communities, their nation.

It is time to discuss the unique structure of the book. While the book was taking shape, Miria and I speculated about how it might be received. One worry she had was that the book might prove to be just one more chance for her detractors to bash and batter her. We wondered, was there any way to include something in the book written by some of the people who had worked with her and knew what she had accomplished? Important people, respected people who could add credibility to her story. Subsequently, I interviewed several people who provided interesting insights about Miria's life and work. The next question was, how should we integrate this material into the book?

After due consideration, we decided to include these testimonies of others in the main text, rather then to add them as appendices at the end of the book. If these lively additions were placed at the end, some readers might never get that far. A more innovative construction made sense to us. And so it is that, following Chapter 2, which describes Miria's development as a political activist, comes the eye-witness account of Jolly Mugisha, Gender Officer for Mbarara District. Mugisha has worked side by side with Miria for several years in her work as Women's Representative in Parliament for the district.

Chapter 3 chronicles Miria's involvement in the formation and activity of a prominent women's NGO, Action for Development (ACFODE). As a supplement to Chapter 3, there is an extensive dialogue about the founding of this ground-breaking organisation between Miria and two other founding members, Maxine Ankrah and Maude Mugisha.

Miria's work as one of two women on the Uganda Constitutional Commission (UCC) is the main subject of Chapter 4. Following this, Father John Mary Waliggo, Secretary of the UCC, gives his views of Miria's service on the Commission.

In the second phase of the constitutional process, the elected Constituent Assembly (CA) debated the draft constitution and promulgated the new Constitution on 8 October 1995. Chapter 5 is Miria's account of her participation in that august body. Hon. George Kanyeihamba, who is now a Supreme Court Justice, served with Miria in the Constituent Assembly. His description of his work with Miria follows her account.

People have always been curious about Miria's husband. Because she is such a different kind of woman, since she has broken many of the rules about what a traditional woman does, people want to know about this marriage. At the end of Chapter 8, Nekemiah Matembe (Nicky) describes how he met Miria, why he chose to marry her, and what it is like to be Matembe married to Matembe. These five transcripts add to the richness of Miria's story.

In conclusion, let me say that I am aware of my own biases on the subject of this formidable woman. By now the reader is aware of my admiration and respect for Miria. I see her as a mountain mover, an earthquake happening, a battering ram, a big mouth who will not be silenced, an unreasonable voice of reason. It has been a great privilege to work with her. It is an honour to know her.

Select Chronology

1953	Birth
1960	Started school
1962	Uganda became independent
1967	Joined Secondary School
1971	Amin overthrows the Obote government
1972	Entered Makerere University
1975	Married Nekemia Matembe
1976	Graduated from Makerere with Honours Degree
1977	Graduated from the Law Development Centre, Kampala with Post Graduate Diploma in Legal Practice
1978	Worked briefly as State Attorney – Ministry of Justice before joining Uganda College of Commerce as a lecturer
1979	Amin was overthrown by UNLF
1980	Obote elected president second time
1983	Joined Bank of Uganda as a lecturer seconded to the Chartered Institute of Bankers
1985	The 2nd Women's International Conference held in Nairobi as Obote's second government fell to Okello Lutwa
1985	Founding of ACFODE
1986	Museveni's National Resistance Movement takes power. Publication of Ten Point Programme. Election of Resistance Councils & Committees. Elected as Secretary for Women's Affairs, Luzira Parish Elected Vice Chairperson – Nakawa Division

1987   Elected Secretary for Mass Mobilisation and
        Education Kampala District
        Travels outside Uganda for the first time to
        attend a seminar on Women and Politics in
        Zimbabwe
1989   Elected Woman District Representative to the
        National Resistance Council
        Founding of Mbarara District Women
        Development Association
        Appointed commissioner to the Uganda
        Constitutional Commission
        Led Government delegation to the 4th Regional
        Conference on the Integration of Women in
        Development Association
1992   Attended a course on the Human Rights of Women
        in Austria
1994   Elected to the Constituent Assembly
1996   Elected to Parliament
1997   Received 2nd Women Achiever's Award from ISIS
        WICCE
1998   Graduated with a Master's Degree in Law and
        Development from the University of Warwick
        Received an International Award of Woman
        Heroine from New York
        Appointed Minister for Ethics and Integrity
2001   Re-elected to Parliament and re-appointed
        Minister in the same portfolio

CHAPTER 1

Rural Childhood, Childhood Dreams

Much has been written about the problem of education for the girl child in Africa. The story of my own struggle to get an education appears to resemble that of many other girls growing up on the African continent. My parents had nine children, five boys and four girls. I always had a special relationship with my brother Sam (now deceased), the third born child in the family who was two years older than me, the fourth in line. However, I saw very early that Sam was given priority over me when it came to going to school. For instance, when my mother had to go to the market to sell produce on market days, I was expected to stay at home and keep the little ones while Sam went to school. Sometimes there would not be enough money for school fees for both of us, but somehow my father would be able to find the fees for my brother quickly while I would have to stay home for a week or two. And yet, I was expected to do as well as Sam did in school.

I grew up seeing this discrimination. I remember questioning this situation at a very early age. In fact, my interest and commitment to gender equality came from this kind of personal experience. In the rural area where I lived, I could see how discriminated against I was because I was a girl, although, in my case, I was given the opportunity to go to school.

Another thing that disturbed me, as I grew up, was how many women, where I lived, were mistreated. Sometimes they

1

would come to our home when their husbands beat them. My aunt, my father's sister, was in this kind of situation. She married a very difficult man who drank a lot. This man would 'go to Buganda.' In those days in my childhood, if a man left home to work somewhere, it was said he had 'gone to Buganda'. 'Going to Buganda' was a general expression used to describe someone who left his village and went out in search of a job as an unskilled labourer, possibly to town. This man, my uncle, would stay away for so many years that people would say, 'He's lost.' When he did come back, he generally came with nothing, no money, no clothes for the family, nothing, and then he would beat my aunt and chase her away from home. I want to make this clear. This was a woman who was staying in this home, maintaining the family by growing all the food, and somehow managing to raise the children alone. Ordinarily, a man like this, when he came home after being away for so long, would be expected to bring home a significant contribution to the household and to be grateful to this woman who had managed to maintain the home alone in his absence. And yet, imagine! He just beat her up and chased her away! Many times this poor woman came to take refuge with us.

I really loved this aunt and I was very happy when she came to stay with us. What hurt me was that after three or four days my father, her own brother with whom she had taken refuge, would turn against her and start abusing her. He would say, 'You useless woman. You have even failed to manage your home. That's why your husband is chasing you away.'

During my many years of struggling for women's rights, I have remembered my aunt's pitiful answer. 'Look,' she would say, 'I am not useless. I brought bride price to this home.' And another day she would say, 'I'm not useless. I have produced sons to this man. I'm not useless.' These two statements show clearly the realities of women's place in Ugandan society, although at that time I did not fully understand all the implications. It was only later that I came to know that many women in the rural areas look at themselves this way, and that people in their own communities actually regard them as *useless*. If a person is told that enough - that you are useless - before long you come to believe it. Despite all the important work women do, despite the fact that women hold human life in their hands, that they produce the babies and rear them to maturity, and also produce most of the food the family eats - imagine, useless! With their productive and reproductive work, certainly women play a major role in maintaining the society in which they live, but they are told they are useless. In defence, they say, 'But I brought cows,' because that's the thing they are told gives them value. They see the sons they deliver - of course it's not the daughters - as the thing that gives them value. They only see their value in terms of the bride price their family receives from the bridegroom's family and the number of sons they deliver. Since many women believe that bringing bride price to the family gives them value, it is no wonder that even today many women do not favour the abolition of this cultural practice.

I grew up questioning these things. I thought, now these things must change. That's when I started to think that I must study law. I had come to learn something about the legal system. In our local area when crimes were committed, suspects would be brought to court and the lawyers would 'plead for them'. In this way, I learned that lawyers plead for people. So I thought, when I grow up - and this was right from primary school, I think I was about 12 years old - I will become a lawyer so that I can plead for the women. I can talk and question why women are treated like they are. This idea was formed at a very early age.

Then when I reached Primary 7, our family began to have some serious money problems. Sam and I were scheduled to sit the terminal exams that determined which students went on to secondary school. At that time we were both in P7 at Rutoma Primary School in Kashari. I had caught up with Sam as he had repeated Primary 6. Now, of course we studied hard and went to sit for the exams. The results were that I got first grade and my brother got second grade. This meant that Sam missed the marks necessary to enter secondary school. At this stage my mother, a born-again Christian, who always had very traditional ideas about appropriate roles for boys and girls, said something interesting.

She said, 'You know, my daughter, I must confess to you. I wanted you to pass, but I knew that if you wanted to go to secondary school, I could not afford the school fees for two.' She said she was very worried about the two of us passing. So she prayed, 'God, let these children pass so they can go to secondary school. But should either of them fail, let it be this girl who fails so that I can send the boy to secondary school.' Of course, this conformed to the traditional pattern where boys were expected to carry on the family line while girls moved out, leaving their families when they married. This was my mother's prayer since she knew that if I passed she had no good excuse for not letting me go on to secondary school. She told me, 'I'm sorry I prayed like that, but I'm happy God has rewarded you.' So in 1967 I entered Bweranyangi Girls' Secondary School in Bushenyi.

The next year my brother repeated Primary 7 and when he took the exams, this time he made grade one. As I've said, our family didn't have much money in those years. One day my mother came to Miss Hall, the Headmistress at Bweranyangi, and said, 'Madam Hall, I don't have enough money to pay school fees for two children. I have come to ask you if you will help Miria get into a teacher training college.' The situation was that any girl or boy who finished primary school could go at government expense to a teacher training college to become a primary school teacher.

When I heard about this, I thought in my heart, this is extremely unfair, and unreasonable, too. Here I was, a student who had never repeated any class, whereas my brother had repeated two classes. I caught up with him, I did exams with him, and I left him behind. I had shown signs of being a top student and now I was expected to leave secondary school and go to a teacher training college so I could become a primary school teacher. I was expected to give way to my brother who, because he was a boy, was more entitled to secondary school education than I was. All of this conformed to the expectations of society that girls who got educated should only become

teachers or nurses. The injustice of this was breaking my heart.
I could see this turn of events shattering my dream of studying
law and pleading for women. I told the Headmistress, - I had
started to cry, 'Excuse me, Madam, I am not leaving secondary
school. I am not going.'

The Headmistress said, 'You see, you have to be fair. You
have to be considerate. Your mother cannot manage.'

I said, 'But if she cannot manage, why doesn't that boy go to
teacher training college? I am already here and I'm doing so
well. Surely I can go on.' The Headmistress did not agree with
me.

I was thirteen years old at that time and very determined. I
had heard that there were bursaries available for peasant
children, for orphans, and for those whose parents were not
able to pay. So I asked Miss Hall, 'Where do people get
bursaries? Can't I look for a bursary?'

She replied, 'Well, you can go to see the District Education
Officer. You can get information about bursaries there.'

As soon as I arrived home, I said to my mother, 'Why don't
you take me to the Chief Education Officer in Mbarara so I can
ask for a bursary?'

My mother said, 'My dear, I don't know how to speak English.
How can we go to this man? How can I talk to him?'

I said, 'If you know the way, you take me there. For me, I'll
speak the English.'

So my mother and I went to Mbarara town. I remember I
was in my school uniform, a very small girl at that time. When
we reached the district education office, we entered and sat
down in the waiting room. We watched as a variety of visitors
came in and out of the big man's office. We didn't know the
procedure, that you could just go and open the door and tell
the man what you wanted. It didn't occur to us that we could
approach this important man so easily. So we stayed there for
quite a long time, with other people coming and going. When
it came to lunchtime, this man opened the door and I could
see inside his office. He was talking to a visitor who was leaving
and I saw there was nobody else in the office. So I jumped up,

telling my mother to come, too. Then this man looked at my mother and asked her what she wanted.

Since my mother didn't speak English, I didn't wait for her to reply. I spoke right up, 'Sir,' I said, 'I want fees. I want school fees.' This man looked at me, thought a bit and then invited us into his office. I don't know what kind of English I was speaking. In a rural primary school, you normally don't speak very good English. But in my poor English I talked rapidly, hoping to attract this man's sympathy. I remember telling him, 'Sir, I passed. I have been attending secondary school where I am now in Senior 2 but my mother doesn't have enough money. She has asked me to leave school so she can send my brother to secondary school, my brother who has been repeating classes. That means that, for me, I must miss out and take a teacher training course.' I took a breath and kept talking, 'But sir, for me I'm interested in studying law, and if I take a teacher training course, I'll not study my law.'

The man looked at us a few moments. He then asked my name and what school I attended. After I gave him this information, he told us to go home. 'We shall see,' he said as we left.

After about a week, the Headmistress came excitedly into my classroom to say, 'Congratulations, Miria, good news for you. You've got the bursary.' The truth is that the government awarded me a very large bursary which was enough for me to complete my six years of secondary education, although a teaching job I got during holidays after O-level provided some of the needed funds for my last two years.

In 1971, having completed four years at Bweranyangi Secondary School, I began higher secondary school (HSC) at Namasagali College in Kamuli where new opportunities awaited me. The students at Kamuli studied British history, and the class work included parliamentary debates. Now imagine, a subject would be introduced and we were expected to debate it. A student would stand up and make statements, while imitating the manner of British parliamentarians of the time as he or she argued. Our British teacher taught us how to stand up and argue in that school classroom and to take this exercise and ourselves seriously.

My dreams about being a lawyer now included a vision of some day having a place in Parliament in my own country where I would debate the important issues. I remember thinking, OK, now when I study law, I'll be able to go to Parliament. I will learn what the law says about this unfair situation for women. If I find that the law is not promoting women's rights, then I will go to Parliament and argue like these British parliamentarians, you know, like the one-time Prime Minister, Lord Callaghan. I can't remember all those names, but you know, that rich history, those impressive speeches, I knew it very, very well. I was one of the top students in history in HSC, partly because I was quoting those important people and using their words. At the same time, I was developing an ability to speak in public and dreaming about the day I would use that ability in the struggle for women's rights.

I should mention that, although I had a clear vision about my future life as a lawyer, my father continued to have very different ideas. He was well aware of my plans, that when I finished HSC I would go to Makerere University in Kampala and study law. One day when I was discussing these plans, he attempted to block my way. 'No, not my daughter,' he said. 'You can't do this, not a girl in my house. You must study nursing or teaching. You go and study to be a nurse at Mulago (where nurses' training was centred in Kampala). Otherwise you will no longer be my daughter.' It seemed that he was threatening to disown me.

But by that time I was so determined to study law that nothing, in fact nobody, was going to stand in my way. Of course, the fact that I had proved myself in school and had passed the national exams successfully gave me confidence. I remember thinking along these lines. This man, even in secondary school, he did not pay my fees. When students go to Makerere, the government pays their fees, which at that time included accommodation, food, and some allowances. It may sound harsh now, but I concluded that I didn't really need my father's money or his consent. So, I thought angrily, for me,

I will study my law. I can't help it if he doesn't agree. Under the conditions at the university I might even do better because I will not be depending on him. And if he decides to cut ties with me, that might be beneficial to me in the long run. Later on, after finishing my education, I will be free. I will be free of the responsibilities towards his family. I don't care if he opposes my plans. He is the one who will miss out, because if he opposes me, who is the loser? I won't lose anything. I said to myself, I'm going to study law. As for my father, I kept quiet.

When finally the call came and I confirmed to my father that I had been called to take law at Makerere, he resumed his opposition and his arguments. He again told me, 'You just cannot study law.'

At this point I decided to take a different approach. I said, 'Okay, sir, I really have no say in this matter, because it is the university that allocates students what they are to study. I think you can go to Makerere and talk to the Vice-Chancellor about me not taking law, and request for a change of the course.' Now picture this simple, rural man who didn't know where Makerere was, much less have the ability to travel to Makerere, and to enter the Vice-Chancellor's office in order to discuss his daughter's course of study. I think the matter proved just too difficult to him, and so he just kept quiet. I knew that this was very complicated for him, and beyond his ability to cope.

As I think about what it meant to be this man's daughter, other incidents come to mind. During my vacation after HSC while I was waiting to go to the university, I spent seven months as a licensed teacher at Rwantsinga Primary School in Kashari. At the end of each month, my father would come on his bicycle with one bunch of matooke (the local cooking banana which serves as the basic food for the area), and a container (we call it a milk pot) that held about one litre of milk. He would say, 'Koburunga (my original name), I've come to see you. This is your milk and this is your matooke. Now, give me my money (meaning my salary, all of it for the whole month). This money is mine because I have to pay school fees for your brother.'

But now, what is this, I wondered. My situation as a teacher at the school wasn't bad. The school provided my accommodation and a salary which was sufficient for me to buy food and other necessities. Now my father enters the picture. Imagine, one bunch of matooke and a pot of milk to feed me for a whole month! However, I had no choice. I had to part with the money. Good enough, the people there were very kind to me. Actually they loved me like a daughter. They would bring me things to eat, matooke and chicken, or they would invite me to eat lunch or dinner at their homes. So I depended on that charity although I was working and earning a salary.

The next time my father came for money, I tried to convince him that I should keep some of it, but he would not allow that. Finally, I told him, 'But look, I need this money to do shopping when I go to the university. After all, I need to buy a few nice clothes that will meet the standard of the university.' He told me not to worry. He promised me that when I went to the university, he would sell his bull so that I could buy what I needed.

When the time came for me to go to Makerere, I reminded him of his promise to sell a bull and give me money for shopping. I thought I should buy some things when I went to Makerere University. After all, Makerere was a prestigious national institution. Of course, I wanted to look good when I went there. I wanted to have better clothes. In my view, going to Makerere and going to study law - something so few girls did - showed that I had reached the level of success that my father had talked about so much. Having reached that level, I felt that it was right to have some better things. I wanted some new clothes, some better clothes, and some better shoes than those I wore as a girl from the village. My things were old and they were not fashionable enough to suit city life, Makerere University being in Kampala city. And, of course, I also wanted to buy a watch.

Certainly a watch was a luxury in the world where I lived. But I was going to a new world, a far-away world, the university world, where university students wore watches. And my father had promised. I wasn't even expecting my father to buy the watch. I had earned enough money to buy clothes, shoes, a handbag and a watch. I had achieved the mythical/magical 'level' my father had described by being accepted as a student at Makerere, and I had earned enough money to buy what seemed to me like the necessities of university life. To put it simply, I didn't want to go to the university looking like a peasant girl from the village. Village girls like me didn't have nice clothes or a watch, but students going to Makerere did have watches, perhaps in recognition of their achievements.

My father asked me, 'What do you want?'

I said, 'I want some dresses.'

'But,' he said, 'you have some, look at those you are wearing.'

I said, 'I also want a handbag.'

He said, 'But you have one.' You see what was happening. Next, I told him that I wanted to buy a watch since I did not have one. You know what he told me? He said, 'You, Koburunga, remember I told you never to put yourself at a level you have not yet reached. Do not put yourself at a standard which you have not yet acquired.' In the Runyankore vernacular, he was saying, '*Nkakuzibira okweta ahaidara ryotakahikireho.*' I must admit that over the years I have really thought deeply about this latest restriction. I wondered just when I might achieve enough to satisfy my father so that I could put on a watch.

I had attained this level through hard work and using my intelligence, and by earning money. By denying me the watch, he seemed to be saying that I had not reached that level of success, in contradiction to all the evidence. I was not asking him for his money for the watch. He had said, don't even desire what you can't afford, and don't put yourself at a level you have not reached and I had abided by his rules. But here I was, having money which I earned. This meant that I could afford to buy some things, and I had reached 'the level.' Surely this man was not being fair. Why couldn't he think lovingly of me and act kindly to me? I didn't like his decision.

Some of my feelings about my father are really tied up with this issue of a watch. I realise now that to me wearing a watch was a symbol that someone had 'arrived' among the successful. In the world I lived in at that time, clearly I was successful: a top student, a graduate from HSC, someone going to Makerere University. It was very irritating that my father was denying me this symbol of that success, especially so, since I had earned my own money. With the money I earned I could have bought myself a watch, and yet he was denying me this pleasure.

Anyway, my father never bought me the watch and he didn't sell the bull. Good enough, I was able to use my last month's salary to buy a few things, as I recall, two blouses, two skirts and some shoes. Of course, I could not afford a watch, but I was to have a happy surprise there. My late uncle Lazarus Tabaro had a business partnership with a friend, a man called Peter Kyangungu. Whenever I would go to visit my uncle, this man was very happy to greet me. 'How are you?' he would ask me.

My uncle would say, 'My daughter here is a very sharp girl.' This man, too, started treating me like his daughter although he was just a friend of my uncle.

When I announced that I was going to the university to study law, this friend of my uncle was very happy and excited. He told me, 'I will buy you a present. In fact, I am going to buy you a watch. When my son went to the university, I bought him a watch. Therefore I will also buy you a watch.' Can you imagine, this was just a friend of my uncle! He did buy me a watch. God usually meets me at my times of need. So, finally, I went to Makerere to study law.

When I reached Makerere, we were getting an allowance called 'boom'. Unfortunately for us, we got it the first year and then Idi Amin, the President of Uganda at that time, abolished it. But I remember even that money which I got for my boom used to go to pay fees for my brother who was in Lubiri Secondary School. Let me say one thing here in relation to that matter. Here I was, poor really, with only meagre means, but I never went with 'sugar daddies' to supply my needs like many girls used to do. In fact some girls continue to do this today.[1] I sincerely credit my parents for this moral upbringing. Although my father was very harsh, surely he bound us together as a family, and he bound us to a system of real ethical values and integrity. We worked hard. We shared what we had. No one was allowed to put himself or herself ahead of the family. His uncompromising rule was that we should never desire what our parents could not afford to buy for us. We were told, 'Do not even admire it.' We were to be satisfied with what they could give us.

When I reached Makerere, that was the time when Amin had taken over the property of many Asians he had either killed or banished from the country.[2] Some of that property, and consequently wealth, had been given to Amin's henchmen. Some of these newly rich men who got all that wealth for no good reason started appearing at the university in search of Makerere girls, good-looking girls, to go with them. Although I had little money, I was never even slightly tempted to join in that game. First of all, I was very serious about my studies in the Faculty of Law and, secondly, I had high moral standards taught by my parents. It is hard to understand how some Makerere female students, who are among the best students in Uganda, would sell themselves for a little bit of money. I made it through the university with very meagre resources. I was not ready to be lured into any nonsense so that I could buy a few things to make my life more comfortable. Life is certainly more than the things we possess.

These girls who go to a sugar daddy to get something they think is missing should have a mother like I had. This wise woman provided me with a really potent weapon to use in the struggle to maintain my virtue. Let me tell you about 'the swamp'. When I was going to Bweranyangi Secondary School, I was 13 or 14, a teenager. On my first few trips to school, my mother accompanied me since I was so young. On the way to the school, there was a good distance where we travelled on foot. Part of this journey was through a swampy area, a huge swampy area full of water and papyrus. The first time we took this route, as we were crossing the road in the swamp, my mother suddenly said, 'You know, Koburunga, if you ever get pregnant, never come back home. Throw yourself into this swamp.'

Her words really shocked me. I turned my gaze to the swamp, this little girl of 13 looking at this forbidding area full of who knows what. I saw some wrecked cars that had fallen into the swamp, and I imagined snakes, crocodiles, and other scary things hiding in the dark waters. On other occasions my mother repeated her message, 'If one day you become pregnant while you are in school here, don't ever come home. Just throw yourself in this swamp.' I clearly remember looking at the swamp, and thinking, 'Me? Not me in this swamp.' I never doubted that my parents were serious about this. I truly believed that if I went home pregnant, they would kill me or I would be thrown into the swamp. This terrifying image kept me safe, I'm telling you. Every time I was on that road, I looked at that swamp, and said to myself, 'Not me.'

So when I was at home on holiday and had to fetch water at the well, I would meet boys there. When the boys would be talking their points - you know, they wanted to talk about sexual matters - my ears were blocked. In my mind, I would be seeing the swamp, and I'd say to myself, 'No way. Not that swamp.' Every time I went to school, and every time I came home, I would pass the swamp. So when those interesting, good-looking boys from Mbarara High School or Ntare School came to visit our school and wanted to befriend me, I would be thinking about the swamp. 'Not me,' I'd think and keep my distance. So, that thing sustained me. It kept me from messing up my life. Whenever boys approached me, I had the swamp on my mind.

Whenever I have the opportunity to talk to groups of young girls, I tell them about the hardships of my childhood in hopes that they will be encouraged to persevere. For example, when I was in primary school, all I had was my one school uniform. I never had an extra dress. Everywhere my mother sent me, I would have to wear that dress. On Christmas Day, I would go to church in that same school uniform. In fact, I remember what I used to do in that case. When it was time for church, I would make a point of reaching the church after the service had started and then I would sit near the door. When it was announced that they were singing the last hymn, I would get up and run back home which was just nearby. I did not want my fellow students to know that I did not have any other dress.

The first time that I ever put on shoes was when I went to Bweranyangi Girls' Secondary School, and then later, thanks to the bursary, not only did I have an extra dress but extra shoes as well.

In spite of the generous bursary awarded to me, I had very little pocket money, only a small amount for transportation home. At that time, there were not many secondary schools for girls in Uganda, and because Bweranyangi was a good school, girls from Kampala, Busoga and all over the country were sent there, some of them from wealthy families. At school there was a canteen where students could buy snacks, if they had any money. During our daily break from classes, students could go back to their rooms and take quenchers (sweet, fruit-flavoured drinks like soda), and eat some groundnuts, biscuits or a piece of cake. As you can guess, I had no money for snacks. Good enough, some of the girls from well-to-do families couldn't bear to queue up to buy something at the canteen. Therefore they would send me to buy things for them while they rested on their beds. When I brought them their treats, they would give me a small cake. The next day when girls were enjoying their quencher at breaktime, I would get some water and drink it with my cake. Rather than making me angry or hurt, this kind of experience actually strengthened me. I thought that since I came from a poor family, I must work very hard and achieve what I could, so that my children would never be in that kind of need.

Our father would tell us that he was paying school fees for his children because it was education that mattered, but we all had to work very hard at home for the family to survive. When I was only six or seven years old, I used to wake up very early every day, by 6.00 a.m., to dig in the garden (*shamba*). Our father would measure the piece each of us must dig before we could go to school. At times there would be no water for washing our feet so we would use the dew to clean them on the way to school. I remember one time when I cut a toe badly while I was digging, and that day there was no water on hand to clean it before I had to rush to school. If we reached school late, we could expect a beating.

During lunchtime we would rush home and find our mother just peeling matooke to prepare lunch for us. She would tell me to rush to the well and bring water. I would run to get the water and my brother would hurry to collect some firewood. Many days, before the food was ready to eat, we would hear the school bell ringing, calling us back to our classes. Then mother would take a spoon and turn the matooke cooking in the saucepan upside down to find the pieces which were almost ready so that we could eat them as we raced back to school. In the evening, when I arrived home, I would be expected to fetch water again, prepare matooke for supper or grind millet. Our parents emphasised that education would lead to a better life. Not only did I like to learn but I also saw a better life in the future if I did well in school.

Some time back I went to a certain girls' school to talk to the girls about the importance of education in their lives. Someone tape-recorded my talk describing my life and how poor I was, and the one uniform, and so on. Afterwards, this tape was played again and again on Radio Uganda, the national radio station. Many parents were happy about my story being broadcast, and rang me to thank me for encouraging their girls. They wanted the tape to be played a lot so that the girls would think seriously about these issues. Parents who have daughters seem to be constantly worried about their girls and the obstacles they face.

I must say that memories of my hard life growing up in the village still bring me pain. The pain remains vivid. It has not faded much. When people talk about the hardships of rural life in Africa, I recall that there is little that I did not experience myself. Although today I have education and advantages like any other Ugandan elite, the attractions of an elite life don't impress me much. My frequent trips to my home district keep me connected to rural people. During those visits I am in touch with the daily problems of people at the grassroots. It gives me some level of satisfaction to be able to help these people with their daily problems, especially the women. Of course, there is a larger picture. The solutions to local problems are often not found at the local level. Government policies, programmes and laws impact on rural life. This is the area where I have devoted my efforts, guided by my dream of better things for women and the vulnerable.

It was certainly a special day in my life when in 1973 I arrived at Makerere to begin my studies in the Faculty of Law. The world seemed open to me. Before long my father attempted to assert his authority over me in a new way. This next battle of wills seemed to be a continuation of the power struggle always going on between us. Was this a kind of game we played? Who knows? When I was home from campus for a holiday, my father would begin to talk about the time I would marry and about, as he put it, the person he would allow me to marry. He would describe certain limits he had arbitrarily set about who I could marry. He would say something like, 'I don't want a Northerner here, because I don't speak their language and we cannot have the same culture.'

Not finding anything to argue about - after all, I wasn't thinking about getting married any time soon - I said, 'OK, sir.'

The next time I returned home for holidays, he brought up the same subject. 'Don't bring here a Munyoro,' he said. (A Munyoro is from the Banyoro tribe in the western part of Uganda.)

Playing the part that seemed to be assigned to me, I said, 'Even a Munyoro, why?'

He said, 'Oh, oh, those people are very greedy.' This particular impression was based on a visit he had made to see my brother who was in secondary school in Kampala at the time. The boy was living with a Munyoro, and for some reason father thought that he was greedy. Therefore, all Banyoro were greedy. How strange our stereotypes of others are!

As I say, at that time it was not a problem for me to be agreeable on this issue since marriage was the last thing I had in mind. 'Okay, sir,' I said again.

During my next holidays he had a new restriction. 'Oh, my daughter, when you come to marry, don't marry a Mukiga'. (from south-western Uganda).

I wondered what reason he would give this time. I asked, 'What has happened with the Bakiga?'

'Oh,' he said, 'those people eat too much. I knew a certain family of Bakiga, and Bakiga really eat too much food.'

Again, I followed his lead in this little drama. 'Why don't you want them to eat?' I asked.

He said, 'Ah, they just eat too much. That is not our culture.'

Every time, he was reducing the potential candidates to a very narrow field. This kind of talk presented no real problem to me until my second year at Makerere when I met the man who would become my husband, Mr Matembe. What followed was interesting. Mr Matembe comes from Bushenyi. I come from Mbarara. We are both Banyankore. I felt that I had complied with my father's demands and I took this Munyankore home. I was not prepared for my father's reaction. 'Oh, oh, oh, you can't do this,' he said.

I was really surprised at his reaction 'And what is this?' I asked. 'He is a Munyankore. We have the same culture.'

The pattern of refusal he had set earlier continued. 'Ah, ah,' he said, 'not that one from Igara. There is no way a *Munyakashari* (a person from Kashari) can marry a *Munyigara* (a person from Igara). Banyigara (plural for Munyigara) eat sheep. That is not our culture. No, no, no, you can't bring him.' Here my father had shifted his argument from people of different tribes to people of the same tribe from different geographical areas.

I said, 'But now what? You refused all those other people. But this man is from your own tribe. What do you want?'

He replied, 'But of all these men around here in this village, couldn't you find one to marry?' He appeared to be very serious.

Now I was getting to the end of my patience. 'You don't want me to marry this man. Then I'm not going to marry at all,' I said. 'That's it. There must be a limit to your dictatorial tendencies.'

At this point he decided it was time to call the clan for support. When on the following day a large group was gathered, he told them, 'You see, this girl is a rebel. I told her I have refused the man she has brought here, and then she says, if I don't accept this man, she'll never marry anyone. She's very impudent. You must help me in this matter.'

When it was my turn to talk, I told my side of the story. 'My father has said, don't bring this tribe and I didn't, and not this tribe either, and I didn't. But he didn't tell me not to bring a Munyankore, so I assumed that any Munyankore would be acceptable, and this is a Munyankore.' I told them, 'Me, I'm not going to bring another man. I'll remain unmarried.'

It didn't take the relatives long to agree with my position. They told my father, 'What do you want her to do?' When they refused to support him, he realised that my being unmarried was really not what he wanted. In our culture, when a woman remains unmarried, she's like a curse in the home, and he knew my determination, he knew I was not joking. He would rather have me married to this Munyigara man than to remain unmarried and therefore be a curse on the family. To him it was a choice between two evils!

It was in my third year at Makerere that I married Mr Matembe. Of course he understood that I must finish my course in law. It was an interesting time to be a woman in the Faculty of Law at Makerere. Of our class of about 60 students, 17 of us were women, all of whom graduated. You have to understand that for a woman to opt to study law in that period, she was already cantankerous. I must say that even in the Faculty of Law I was doing my resistance. I remember up to today one particular troublesome classmate (now deceased). One day we were discussing the law of domestic relations, or family law as we were calling it. This chap said, 'You see, you women, you are just chattels.'

Oh!!! I stood right up and said to him angrily, 'Shut up. You are stupid. Who is chattel?' Think of that ignorance, and in the Faculty of Law. Unbelievable!

Our lecturers were all Ugandans. Mostly they treated the women students fairly. However, there was one professor who used obscene language. These days I suppose some of his actions would be called sexual harassment. There were two of us women who were committed Christians and this man didn't make advances to us as he did to the other female students, but he often used suggestive language that I didn't like. Most of the students just laughed about it. I remember one time he was referring to a case in which the judge's name was Darling. He decided to annoy me. So he asked me, 'Koburunga, do you know Justice Darling? You don't know Darling, do you? You are saved. You are foolish,' all of this with a sexual connotation. As I have said, I was serious about my studies. His jokes made no sense to me. They had no place in the class as far as I was concerned. I didn't take part in such jokes.

Then after graduation in 1976, it was necessary for me to go to the Law Development Centre to complete my post-graduate diploma in legal practice.

During the time at Makerere and later at the Law Development Centre it became increasingly clear to me that the legal system in Uganda was totally inadequate in protecting women. The system that was supposed to protect citizens' rights and to provide even-handed justice for everyone in reality benefited some and discriminated against others, including women. Perhaps I was a bit naive to think that this world of 'the law' which I was entering would actually treat women fairly. After all, from my childhood I had seen that women were abused and mistreated with no one to champion their cause. This increased awareness deepened my determination to get into Parliament so that I could play a role in changing the law.

However, events had intervened to prevent my dream of going to Parliament from being fulfilled at that time. In 1977 when I completed the programme at the Law Development Centre, there was no sitting Parliament since Idi Amin had overthrown the government in 1971 and established military rule. Let me describe my situation at that point as I remember it. By this time I had certainly recognised the many deficiencies in the law but it was clear that I would have to wait for the opportunity to go to Parliament. Another factor controlling my destiny was the restrictive political climate during the Amin period. No one was free to raise his or her voice without great risk. To survive that period, people had learned to keep their complaints and their opinions to themselves.

My first job as a lawyer was in the office of the Director of Public Prosecution (DPP), where I began to see how the legal system really worked, or perhaps I should say, how the legal system worked for some and did not work for others. You know, all along, although my main struggle has been for women, I have also struggled for other under-represented groups, especially the children and the poor. As a lawyer in the DPP's office, I spent a good deal of time in court which gave me a chance to see what really went on in the criminal justice system. I soon discovered that those I considered to be the real criminals, all those corrupt people who had figured out how to steal money from the government or from the banks, would be brought to court and the courts would do nothing to punish them or to prevent further illegal actions, because these people could afford to pay bribes to someone.

On the other hand, there were large numbers of ordinary people who had committed some minor offences. These unfortunate people had no understanding of the legal system and no money to pay to settle matters. Because of this, they often ended up in prison. To give a few examples, a woman who brewed and sold waragi (a local brew), or a man who stole a chicken because he was hungry, or someone who stole some other small thing, these people would go to prison while these big robbers would be released on bail. This seemed to be the worst sort of injustice. After a short time in that office, I decided that I could not work as part of such a system, so I left the DPP's department. This system cried out for change but in those times and under those circumstances, I didn't see myself changing it.

My next job was at the Uganda College of Commerce as it was then called (now Makerere University School of Business Studies) where I taught law for the next five years. In the meantime, I began to look for a forum where I could work actively for women's emancipation. I decided to join the Mothers' Union (Church of Uganda) in Luzira where we lived, so that I would have the opportunity to meet with a group of women. It was my hope that something could be accomplished for women through that organisation. I pictured myself telling them, 'Look, you people, we are unjustly treated. We'd better stand up and demand our rights.' Yes, I thought that I would have something to say to these women.

But I found this organisation was still very traditional, with the leaders instructing the members to be humble, to obey their husbands, to cook good meals, and to behave very properly. I soon began to see that it was unlikely I could fulfil my dream in that organisation. But somehow a group was formed there in the Mothers' Union that was interested in doing more than cooking. Someone suggested that we could put on a play about domestic violence. This idea had possibilities. Presenting a play was one way to enlighten people about a problem that during that period was never ever mentioned in public.

I've always been interested in drama. I used to participate in plays in secondary school, especially Shakespeare's plays. So we composed and performed a play in Luganda called *Lubwana Namakage* (Lubwana and his Family). People liked the play, and it was presented several times around the city in the next few years. It was even declared the Play of the Year in 1987 by the National Theatre. Putting on this play enabled us to bring to the public the issue of domestic violence which was taboo to talk about at that time. In fact, as a consequence of this play, a number of marriages which had broken down were reconciled.

We were able to do more than bring the issue of women's rights to a public forum. This project also raised some money to start a community-based nursery for low-income women who worked in the factories in Luzira. We wanted to build a community centre as well, where meetings, weddings, etc. could be held, and in the process the Mothers' Union could generate income. Although the hall was started, it was never completed. The good news is that the nursery continues to serve the community even today.

When I think about that play today, I am aware of how far I have moved from those first efforts to advocate for women's rights within the organisational confines of the Mothers' Union. I view those efforts as a beginning, the best I could do at that time, under the circumstances of my life and the society I lived in. I was very aware that my dream was not being achieved.

In the next few years, I began to see that I had a great deal to learn on the way to my dream's fulfillment. In fact, the first time I found myself in a place and with people where fulfilling my dream was a present possibility was when I joined ACFODE, a new kind of organisation for women, a subject I take up in Chapter Three.

In the early 1980s, life went on like that. After spending my days teaching at the college, I would return home to care for my husband and children. Our fourth and last son was born in Mulago Hospital in 1986 during NRA's (The National Resistance Army) furious battle to capture Kampala. Did this change of government signal a real change for the better for Ugandans? Would I at last have a chance to fulfil my dream? We would soon find out.

At different times people have asked me how I have maintained my confidence when life has not been easy for me, for one reason or another. Certainly I have survived some difficult times, such as the struggle to get the education I yearned for. Then there was the dangerous and restrictive political climate in the 1970s and early 1980s that cut off everybody's dreams and opportunities, and, later when I entered public life as a woman, there were the blows and insults that were heaped on me. It is time that I describe my personal motto, a sa ing of just a few words, that has helped me time and time again in the very toughest situations.

That motto is, 'Don't worry. Don't panic. You are the best of the lot.' This motto came out of my experience in a peasant family where my father was really very dictatorial, very harsh, even up to today. When I was growing up, when I did something wrong, my father would use that as an opportunity to abuse me verbally. He would tell me that I was ugly, that my lips were too big and that my eyes were too small. I can remember him saying things like, 'Look at her ugliness, the tiny eyes, the huge lips bent like a sickle.' He seemed to have no heart. You know, I would feel bad about it, but soon I developed this motto, don't worry what anyone says; you are the best of the lot.

People say that once children are abused when they are young, they tend to lose confidence. Somehow, I have not been permanently scarred by the attacks, the early ones by my father or the later ones in the public arena. Perhaps this unkind treatment even helped to give me an inner toughness that proved to be an asset in my life in politics. I must say that while I was at home, my mother helped me. She used to say, 'This is my best girl. She is so fast when she works. She is the one who does the best job. When you give her millet to grind, she grinds it fast. When she goes to the well, she returns quickly. She is a better helper than all the others.' Also, of the nine children in our family, I was the best student. During my primary education, either I would be the top student in the class, or I would be third one term and then the next term first in my class.

I remember well the scene when we would bring our school reports home. I always did better than any of my brothers and sisters. At the end of each school term, we were supposed to put our school reports on the table for our father to look at. We were all aware how harsh he was. If our grades were bad, we got a beating with a stick. My sisters and brothers developed a clever strategy. They always put my report on top of theirs so that he would say, 'Oh, Koburunga's report is the first.' After looking at my very good grades, he would not be so annoyed when he looked at the other reports.

Anyway, I think at some point I decided if I was ugly it didn't matter. After all I had my dream as a guiding purpose in life, and I had proved I could achieve and perform well. I somehow learned not to be overcome with panic or worry. Those simple words of my motto got me through some very rough times when I was still at home and later during some hot political battles. I do want to say, although some people might not believe this, that I have never thought of myself as better than others in an egotistical sense. Nor do I think that I have more talents than others. Perhaps it is more a case that when it came to a choice between following either the strict rules set for 'proper' female behaviour or following the dream that lived deep in my heart, that I chose to break many of the rules. I have been guided and sustained by my dream and the conviction that I was doing what was right. If there was a price to pay, I was willing to pay it.

This seems like a good place to reveal that I have a major regret in life concerning my mother. This good woman passed away in September 1992, too early to see many of the achievements of the daughter she loved and praised so much. Although both parents influenced who I was as I grew up and who I became later, I believe I inherited my mother's intellectual ability and regard for other people. I thank God for that.

As I have related earlier, my relationship with my father was not so simple. In many ways, he made my life difficult beyond understanding. On the other hand, his strict upbringing provided me with a firm moral and ethical foundation that has grounded my life, and I am grateful to him for that.

I will close this chapter by discussing one other important point that cannot be overlooked. Some Ugandans, both men and women, argue that women's emancipation is a foreign idea that has been brought here by others. But look at my life experience. At the time I made up my mind to struggle for women, when I was about 12 years old, I had never left my village. I had never seen any white women. The first white women I came to know were teachers and administrators at Bweranyangi Girls' Secondary School. These educators were religious women who encouraged us to read the Bible and to accept all those misinterpretations of the scriptures that hinder women's development, that underrate and undermine them. At that time I had never come in contact with a single person, male or female, who was working for gender equality. I would argue that we all recognise injustice and unfairness when we see it, but that some people choose not to see it for some reason or other. For me, because I hate injustice and unfairness, when I see these things, it is impossible for me to keep quiet – truly I must speak up, I must do something. Is this my destiny? It seems it is.

Notes

1   'Sugar daddy' is the term used to describe an older man with money who uses the power of his money to obtain sexual favours from a young woman who has limited resources. It is shocking to think in the new millennium how many 'decent' men who are generally respected in society continue to set up this kind of arrangement. Although it is the man who corrupts the young woman, somehow society tends not to judge him harshly while the young woman is really condemned for her part in such a relationship. This is another indication of the enduring strength of patriarchal structures and attitudes that support such an evil system.

2   A large population of immigrants from India (called 'Asians' in Uganda) started to arrive in East Africa during the 1890s when the colonial governments built a railroad from Mombasa on the Kenyan coast to Kampala, Uganda. Over time, a large number of Indians came to play a dominant role in the Ugandan economy. In the early 1970s Idi Amin brutally murdered or expelled many of these Indian businessmen and arbitrarily handed out their confiscated properties to his cronies. One major consequence of these actions was that the Ugandan economy was virtually destroyed.

CHAPTER 2

Becoming an Activist in the Struggle for Women's Rights

T he last chapter described my interest from a very early age in working to improve the condition of women's lives. However, I must say that in the mid-1980s I began to realise that a great deal had been going on around the world where women were concerned and I knew little about it. In fact, Ugandan women were cut off from the gains that women were making in many parts of the world because those gains occurred during the 1970s and early 1980s when Uganda was fairly isolated, struggling with its own grave, internal problems.

As I've said, I had been searching all along for a place where I could work for women. I had left a job in the criminal justice system when I found out that the legal system favoured people with money and influence and generally disregarded women and people from the other marginalised groups. I knew that I was not in a position at the time to change that. I had considered entering politics but there seemed to be no place in the Ugandan politics of the day for a person with my ideals, goals and outspoken ways. My association with the Mothers' Union in Luzira had only limited success due to the group's very conservative orientation. However, all the time I was looking around, learning what I could, and waiting for my chance.

In the mid-1980s events took place that opened up interesting opportunities and possibilities. One event that impacted on the lives of large numbers of African women and,

26

in fact, the lives of women from all over the world, took place in July 1985 in Kenya. Approximately 15,000 women from 140 countries attended the Third United Nations International Conference for Women in Nairobi to mark the end of the UN Decade for Women which ran from 1975 to 1985. I was supposed to go to the Nairobi conference. Indeed, the Bank of Uganda where I was working had agreed to sponsor me, but the politics in Uganda at that time were very tricky. Because I did not belong to the 'right' political party, it did not work out for me to go to the Nairobi conference.

As I look back now, I see the period of the mid-1980s as a time of real awakening for me and many other Ugandan women. Until then I had only a limited understanding of the global dimensions of either women's problems or of the growing women's movement. Many people believe that the international women's movement came to maturity during the UN Decade (1975-1985) and that the Nairobi conference provided substantial proof of that maturity. The thousands of women from around the world who congregated in Nairobi reported on a great variety of organisations and programmes operating at all levels of society that were changing women's lives for the better. Just think, that world-changing event was taking place just across the border in Kenya, and yet Ugandan women, with only a few exceptions, pretty much missed the whole thing. But soon we were to learn about the interesting activities that were going on around the world and the bold women leaders who were leading the way.

The second major historical event that had a profound influence on my life was the coming to power of the National Resistance Movement (NRM) government in January 1986. The Nairobi conference in July 1985 and the arrival of the NRM government which started to bring peace and stability to the country signalled that a new day was dawning for Uganda and for Ugandan women.

In this chapter, I describe my entrance into Ugandan politics, an interesting and exciting time for me. In Chapter Three, I recount the founding of ACFODE, Action for Development, an innovative, forward-looking organisation that played a key role in the gains that Ugandan women have made since 1985. Throughout these two chapters, I reflect on my growing interest in and connections to the global women's movement and to a large number of other women activists around the world. I must make it clear that these three developments - becoming a political activist, serving in ACFODE, and becoming an actor in the global women's movement – were all going on at the same time and cannot really be separated from one another. However, it is easy to see that the dream I had held all those years now had a concrete outward expression in the political fight for women's rights, and the work with like-minded women in ACFODE, a women's organisation that took women seriously. All the time, I was expanding and broadening my knowledge base, my experience, and my outlook until these took on an international dimension. In this period, I was being transformed by events at the same time that I was influencing events.

When the National Resistance Movement government took power in January 1986, it came with the women question high on its agenda. As President Museveni later observed at the opening session of the National Resistance Council in Kampala on 13 June 1995,

> The National Resistance Movement, right from its inception was, and is a movement of men and women. All of us must be happy that women are coming to the top in politics, administration, the professions, business and all other spheres of human endeavour. It is not sheer tokenism. Women have made a solid impression in the corridors of power, in boardrooms and cabinets, and we are very proud of the NRM that for the first time in Africa our Vice-President is a woman.

The new government introduced a structure of governance at first called Resistance Councils (RCs). These councils were renamed Local Councils (LCs) in the 1995 Constitution. To avoid confusion I will refer to these bodies as LCs throughout the book. In this structure there were five levels of these local government bodies, from LC1 at village level up to LC5 at district level. But where should I start to get involved? When

I heard that in each LC there was a position called Secretary for Women's Affairs, I thought, this looks like the forum I have longed for, the platform from which to raise the issues about fairness and justice for women. I thought, I must join the LCs.

One day in 1986 when I came home from the office, I was surprised to find a half kilo of sugar, a very scarce commodity at that time. When I asked where the sugar came from, my children told me that the Chairman of LC1 had brought it. But, I wondered, what does this mean? The LCs were supposed to be elected by people in the village. I had been waiting for such an election so that I could run for the Secretary for Women's Affairs position. I soon learned the elections had been held when many people had gone to work. This led me to appeal to the leader of the district at that time, the Special District Administrator (SDA, the equivalent of the current Resident District Commissioner, RDC). I wrote a letter that said, 'Excuse me, sir, there has been an illegal election in our village. It appears that elections were held without people being informed, yet I had intentions to participate in the elections.' So the SDA called a meeting of the whole village, as we were demarcated in villages.

When we arrived at the meeting – it was on a Saturday - we asked, 'Where is the committee?' and some people stood up. We asked them who elected them. I should explain that before the meeting I had mobilised a number of people I knew from around the Port Bell area where we were living to attend the meeting. At the meeting, we made it clear that since we had not been informed about the elections so that we could take part, that this was not democracy. We must be allowed to participate.

After listening to us, the SDA nullified the previous elections and a new election day was set. During the new elections on another Saturday, I was elected LC1 General Secretary. Then we were told that on the following Monday we should go to Luzira Parish to elect the parish committee (LC2). According to the LC system, those people who had been elected members of each LC1 in the parish then constituted the LC2. Since Luzira

Parish had 23 villages, on the next Monday, the LC1 people from those villages gathered to elect the nine officials for LC2.

When we reached there, somebody said, you know, the Secretary for Women is the most important position for women. Up to that time I thought I should run for other offices, but if this one was really the most important for women, it would give me access to women, and that was better than just being a secretary who called people to meetings. So I changed my mind. Some people nominated me for other positions, but I said, 'No, me, I'm waiting for the women's post.' I was then elected LC2 Secretary for Women's Affairs.

Now was the time for action. Within a week, I started visiting the 23 villages in the parish. After working all day at the office, I would use public transport or walk to these villages to spread my message of equality for women. I would tell the village women that we had been denied our rights and that it was time to rise up and challenge the status quo. Now was the right time to speak up and to challenge the unfair and unjust treatment we all faced as women. What I had to say was like an eye opener to those women. I spent about one month moving around in this way in my position as LC2 Secretary for Women. My activities in this period began to make an impact. I could even be heard on Radio Uganda talking about women's rights, through an ACFODE initiative, which I'll describe in Chapter Three. In addition, stories about my addressing LC meetings began to appear in the newspapers. This was the time when the name Matembe started to be known.

The next step on the political ladder was to elect the LC3 in the sub-county, designated as a division. In my case, that was Nakawa Division. At the election meeting at the sub-county level, I found another woman who was as serious about politics as I was. This was Dr Speciosa Wandira Kazibwe, who later became the first woman Vice-President of Uganda, and in fact the first woman vice-president in Africa. A medical doctor by profession, Kazibwe lived in Bugolobi, also in Nakawa Division. Kazibwe and I were acquainted as we had been together at Makerere. When we reached the meeting, the two of us decided that we needed some strategies. No campaigning was allowed, but of course I had already mobilised the villages. At the meeting, Dr Kazibwe stood up and said, 'I'm not going to campaign, but you people must give women more positions. This Secretary for Women is not enough. Please look kindly on the women and give us more positions.' That was a good tactic, very polite. She was appealing to people's idea of fairness.

We started the elections. I was nominated for Chairperson, but I lost. However, people at the meeting had seen me, and when they said Vice-Chairperson, Matembe, I won. So I became the Vice-Chairperson for the whole division of Nakawa which consisted of seventeen parishes. Also Dr Kazibwe was elected the Secretary for Women's Affairs. This was good. Women were getting somewhere.

So now, I again set out going from place to place, this time from parish to parish, not wasting a minute. But moving around as Vice-Chairperson was different. Instead of mobilising just the women, this time I would call people, both men and women, together, and then I would talk about a better life for women. I travelled around the whole division, talking about women's rights and settling family disputes. I was also invited to other divisions to talk about these issues.

Over time the normal expectations for politicians in Uganda has been that wherever they go, they show up grandly and put on a grand show. My political work at this time was of a very different nature. We were getting no salaries, not even allowances, and there were no vehicles for our use. Add to that, personally I had little money. Let me describe a visit I recall making one Saturday to Mbuya II Parish. I had written a letter to say, 'The Vice-Chairperson for Nakawa Division will visit your parish on a certain date at such-and-such time.' I left the office early, around 2.00 p.m., and with my briefcase full of books I boarded a taxi. No taxis went all the way to my destination, so I took a taxi as far as I could, and then started to walk.

Along the way, I found several good women waiting there. I greeted them and they returned the greeting. 'How is life here?' I asked.

And they said, 'Things are fine. We are waiting here for our guest of honour who is coming to address us at the parish.'

I said, 'How long will you wait? Why don't you come and we go to the venue for the meeting? Then when that guest of honour arrives, we can receive her from there.' They agreed.

We walked together, and when we arrived at that place, the leaders stood up and announced, 'The guest of honour has come,' and people started clapping and coming to greet me.

Those women who had walked along with me looked quite surprised and said, 'So, this is the guest we were waiting for.' The reason I am including this story is that these women were waiting for 'a big person' who would arrive in a vehicle and instead, here was this ordinary woman just walking along to the venue carrying her own books.

All the time I was busy with this political work, I was looking forward to entering the highest level of local political office. That meant the elections for LC5 in Kampala District which would be coming up soon. In Kampala District there was no LC4, county level; therefore LC representatives went directly from LC3 to LC5. These elections turned out to be the most amazing I have ever contested. I optimistically set my sights on the office of Deputy Mayor, although at that time the elections were marred by sectarianism on the basis of tribe and religion. To be elected for a Kampala District seat, a person almost had to be a Muganda and most likely a Catholic, but I was neither a Muganda nor a Catholic. Some would say that the outlook offered no chance for me, but I didn't care about such predictions. I went there knowing that I had worked very hard and that many people were aware of the work I was doing. It was through these elections that I came to realise that to some people, hard work is not an important basis for being elected to office.

When the elections started, I didn't contest for the Mayor's seat since I wanted the Deputy Mayor post. I thought if I don't get the deputy position, at least I will get Secretary for Women's Affairs. I felt fairly confident about this as I had mobilised women in the whole Nakawa Division. Among other things, I had organised groups of women to use traditional music, dance and drama to demystify the issue of women's emancipation. One group I worked with had won a cup for a performance at a national festival organised by Janet Mukwaya, when she was still the Director of Women's Affairs in the NRM Secretariat. This performance and the award for it were reported in the press and, because of things I was doing such as this, I was convinced that women, and men, too, from all around Kampala knew me and knew my work. Surely I would be elected. So I went to the elections for Kampala LC5 with great hopes.

The proceedings continued. I ran for Deputy Mayor and 'Wapi!' I lost. As I describe what followed, I will tell you one thing. With all the support I received, I felt like a wealthy person. You should have seen me nominated for each position, except for Mayor and Secretary for Youth (I was past the required age). You should have seen my patience and determination to win one of the posts. Imagine, someone even nominated me for security, and then for finance. When it came to the Secretary for Finance position, I wanted to decline, but Mrs Nsubuga, the wife of the late Bishop Nsubuga, said, 'Miria, you can't let us down. We want you on the committee.' I pleaded with her that I had no training as an accountant, and so I could not hold that post. She refused my plea and said, 'Just take up the post. We shall help you count the money once you are in that position.'

As the elections went along, someone else won each time. When they had finished electing the first four of the nine positions, I realised that things were not going well. Then the Secretary for Women post went to a woman who had not even been in the LCs before. It was time to revise my strategy. I must begin real active politicking. Let me describe the scene that day in more detail.

The elections were being held in the City Council chambers. The presiding officer, the SDA, sat at a table in the front while the councillors sat facing him. We were 63 elected LC3 councillors, nine from each of the seven divisions in the district. We were the ones who would elect the LC5 committee that day. We knew each other well as we had met together and worked together at different times.

During these elections, we were using a secret ballot. A position would be announced, nominations made and seconded, and then we marked our ballots. Then each councillor walked to the front corner where the ballot box was located and dropped in his or her ballot paper.

During the voting for the first four positions, people didn't talk as they moved to the front and returned to their seats. I also didn't talk. Really, I was feeling very confident that I would win one of these seats. But now after I lost the Secretary for Women's Affairs, the fifth position, I could sense that things were serious. Was it possible that these people were going to leave me out? My instincts told me, 'Be honest. Be direct. Tell them what you're thinking. Since they're leaving you out because of sectarianism, bring it out into the open.' Yes, when I thought that I might lose, I decided to talk candidly to people.

Now whenever I would go to the ballot box to deposit my vote for the next candidate, I would meet others who were putting in their ballots, and would tell them as we passed each other, 'You people in Buganda are very bad. You mean you can't elect a non-Muganda?'

They would look surprised and say, 'But Matembe, why are you saying that?'

I said, 'You see, these are five positions and you are all Baganda, and you are leaving me out, because I am not a Muganda. Otherwise,' I said good-naturedly, 'why aren't you voting for me? You know how very well I work.' When it was time for the seventh position, I found another different group, and I said similar words to them. When I went for the eighth position, I found another group and said more along the same line. Of course my words were making them feel guilty, as I intended. It seems this strategy really worked, because when they came to the last position out of nine, Secretary for Mass Mobilisation and Education, I won easily. As I look back, it seemed that those voting didn't think that this last position meant much.

Before moving on, I want to describe one small incident that took place at the LC5 elections that makes me smile to this day. Just as they were counting the votes for the ninth position which I won, the then Vice-President of Uganda, the late Dr Samson Kisseka, walked into the chambers. He was coming to officiate at the swearing in of the newly elected officials. Just as he walked in, the presiding officer was counting votes. He was saying, 'So and so, so many votes, so and so, so many votes, and Matembe,' and I had the most votes. When he announced that, everyone applauded. This was even heard on the radio since Radio Uganda was covering this important election. Imagine I was able to hear the broadcast on the radio as I was going home. When the presiding officer declared me the winner, people cheered and shouted, mostly in sympathy for what I had gone through. In the vehicle I laughed so much about the whole thing. I had really struggled as I contested for seven of the nine offices, not giving up since I was determined to win one of these positions. But the Vice-President thought they were cheering because I was popular. I remember him saying, *'Mwana muwala ono* (this young lady), I knew she would win because she is hardworking and popular.'

The reader can see how determined I was. I had gone to these elections confident that I would win a position easily. After I lost three of the first four contests, my confidence slipped. Then when I lost the Secretary for Women's Affairs, which I was sure was 'my' position based on the work I had been doing for women all over the country, my hopes vanished. I could see that the politics of that election – sectarian politics – were so strong against me that I was about to lose out entirely. This was not acceptable. I had to change my battle plan. No more being quiet. It was time to tell the truth about what was going on. This new strategy led to my victory. Let me add that at the moment of victory I hardly knew what a victory it was. I will explain.

Sometimes it turns out that the plan we make is not the best one after all. I really wanted to be Deputy Mayor or Secretary for Women, but the position I got turned out to be the best one in the long run. Think of it. I was being given a mandate to mobilise and educate. Actually that is exactly what I had been doing since joining the LCs, mobilising and educating. Also I had begun to realise that if you call meetings about women, then only women come. Yet, I wanted both men and women to listen to my message. After all, it is men who hold most of the power, and unless they agree to release some of it, women will not enjoy their rights. I wanted both women and men to attend these public meetings so that change would occur. Later I learned that this kind of mobilisation is called gender sensitisation. I was learning to use the language of gender sensitisation. That is exactly what I was doing. Now I would continue to mobilise and educate as my new job title mandated.

As I look back, I recall how I joined the LCs heart and soul because I had found the forum I had dreamed of. I had found space to realise my dream. I had no time to waste. I just embraced this space, with interest, vigour, conviction and commitment. I should add that I also visualised the LC route as the way of getting to Parliament, my ultimate dream. It appears that my hard work while working as the Secretary for Mass Mobilisation and Education for Kampala District (LC5) popularised my name so much that by the time I contested one of the seats in the NRC, the equivalent of Parliament, in 1989, the election was just like a walk-over. When I tendered my candidature to the people of Mbarara, they asked, 'Isn't this the Matembe we hear on the radio talking about women's rights? Isn't this the Matembe we read about in the press? Then why waste time considering other candidates? She must be the right person.'

So, let me tell you, in my new position as Secretary for Mass Mobilisation and Education in Kampala District I really went to work, although none of us were being paid anything or even given any money for transportation. By this time my name was commonly identified with the issue of women's rights, but my work doing mobilisation and education was not limited to women's issues. Let me explain.

When the NRM government came to power, it presented a manifesto called the *Ten Point Programme*. I was aware that although I had suffered badly, as most Ugandans did during our dark period, I had not suffered as much as those who fought in the bush war. The people who had suffered the most were those who had fought in the bush between 1980 and 1985 to liberate Uganda from the tyranny of the murderous and dictatorial regimes of the past leaders. I felt a great debt to those brave liberators, men and women, who had rescued us from what I would call the worst sort of 'hell'.

By the time of our liberation the majority of us had lost hope in ever having a life worth living. The uncertainty under which we lived was a terror of its own. When you left home in the morning to go to work, you didn't know whether you would return. When you went to bed at night, you doubted whether you would see the next day. You didn't really expect any peace or security because of what was called *panda gari* (Swahili: climb the vehicle) which could find you in your bed or on the road. At any time, in any place, army personnel could come along rounding up everybody they came across, in the streets or at home.

If you were lucky enough to escape the round-ups on the streets, you could be picked up at your home, packed onto lorries, naked or half-naked, and carried to some unknown place. At these secret locations, the people rounded up would be paraded before the captured NRA soldiers who were pressured to identify other people, innocent or not, as collaborators. If you were lucky, you might survive the identification parade and be allowed to return home. However, many didn't survive this terrifying exercise. Perhaps the best payment I could give to those brave freedom fighters was to support their programme. That is, if I could in conscience support it.

I quickly obtained a copy of that Ten Point Programme and I read it through and through. Following several pages of background information, the ten points were listed and discussed in some detail:

- Establishment of popular democracy
- Restoration of security
- Consolidation of national unity
- Defending national independence
- Building the national economy
- Restoration and rehabilitation of social services

- Elimination of corruption and misuse of power
- Resettlement of displaced people
- Regional co-operation and human rights
- Following a strategy of a mixed economy

This manifesto was called by some 'the original constitution of the NRM.'

I wanted to really grasp this programme. As I read, I found virtually nothing to disagree with. I decided not only to put the ten points into practice personally but also to preach the message of reconciliation and unity to all the people I was in contact with. Where the programme said 'unity', I made a point to unite with everybody and love them irrespective of region, tribe or religion. Unity and non-sectarianism were also important objectives of ACFODE in its formative years, even up to today. In early 1986 I joined and started to serve this pioneer organisation. The emphasis on unity in the NRM Ten Point Programme and ACFODE's organisational vision supported each other as I dedicated time to both these bodies and their programmes.

At that time, in 1986, Ugandans were so badly divided on sectarian grounds that if one was from the North and another from the West, or if one was Catholic and another Muslim or Protestant, it was taken for granted that you were natural enemies. I have to admit that until I read the Ten Point Programme and thought seriously about it, I used to believe that all Northerners were bad and that they, and no one else, were responsible for all the killings and atrocities. We had been living on politics of division and hatred, with nothing to unite us. By the time NRM took over the government, Uganda was at what I would call the highest level of balkanisation. I was so blinded by the divisions and hatreds that infected Ugandan life that I could not see those Banyankore (my tribe) in Obote's second regime who were openly torturing and killing people. Let me give one instance.

During that time, if someone from Ankole found a Munyankore manning a roadblock, he or she could expect trouble. There are certain features that distinguish someone who is a Munyankore, the main one being a pointed nose. So, if this soldier from your own tribe recognised you, you would be tortured and abused, possibly even more than a Northerner would be. And yet we somehow still believed that the Northerners were the bad ones while they also believed we were the bad ones.

The Ten Point Programme opened my eyes to see that a bad person is bad irrespective of his or her tribe or religion, and a good person is good irrespective of his or her origin or belief. I was able to understand that there is no tribe or religion which has a monopoly of good or bad people. Studying the NRM's small booklet actually made me look around in a new way. It was like taking a cloud from my eyes.

For example, we had good friends in our neighbourhood who were of the Langi tribe from the North. In fact, these people were more than good friends. We were like brothers and sisters. My husband and I were godparents to their children. I wonder now how it was possible that I was hating and condemning 'people from the North' and, at the same time, loving these good people (from the North) who shared our lives. How could I be so blind to this contradiction? In fact, we were all running away from the oppression of the Obote II government, being harassed together and running away together.

More evidence of the contradiction that I hadn't seen occurred at my workplace. Two of my colleagues were Langi (from the North). One was a former Prime Minister, the late George Adyebo. In fact, he was a very good man. He was also resisting the oppression and the suffering of the Obote II period. The second one, the Principal at the Institute where I taught, created serious difficulties for me. Because Museveni and I were from the same tribe, the Principal, my boss, chose to associate me with the war. He would really torment me. He would say angrily to me, 'You, go to your brothers in the bush.' He said similar things to students from Ankole. Working with him was extremely difficult, to say the least.

As I think further about this issue, I have to mention one of my closest friends, Mary Maitum, who is from Soroti in the East, and is married to a Langi. I worked with Mary on the

Uganda Constitutional Commission for several years. In truth, Mary from the East and Matembe from the West are more sisters than friends. It should be admitted that many Ugandans have not yet given up these old hatreds and divisions based on the stereotyping of and competing against people from other tribes, regions and religions. If we are going to progress as a country, we must find a way to unite as Ugandans. We really don't have a choice.

In any case, I was truly inspired by studying the Ten Point Programme and attending the seminars and workshops organised by NRM cadres. I even began to have hope that within a short time Uganda could be a totally different country, a country of peace and stability where people would be blessed instead of being cursed. It was an easy assignment to take this message of unity and reconciliation to the people in my district.

Of course, I combined all these aspects of the Ten Point Programme with the message of women's liberation. Taking my dream and the NRM manifesto to the people gave me such joy, satisfaction and a sense of purpose that I never bothered about whether there was payment or not, or how much of my own money I used. As far as I was concerned, I was paid by the blood of those who died for the struggle, by those who were maimed, and also by having been given a platform on which to promote the cause of women's liberation.

Leaving the lecture room at work, I didn't go home. Rather, I would go straight to address the people in my constituency. My LC5 territory consisted of five divisions: Nakawa, Makindye, Lubaga, Central, and Kawempe, and Makerere University and Kyambogo College, the last two treated as independent units within the district. So I went everywhere, mostly on foot, talking about the message of NRM and gender equality.

On Saturdays and Sundays there was no rest for me. Instead, I travelled around the district, explaining both the Ten Point Programme and the cause of women's liberation to a variety of audiences, large or small. I often reached home at about 9.00 p.m. The peace and freedom brought in by the NRM government enabled me to move without fear even at night, a small miracle in itself. Here was the opportunity I had waited for a long time. I was eager to do my part. However, at one point, my husband said, 'Eh, woman. This will not work. Are you married to the NRM or to me?'

I said, 'But, my dear Nicky, you know where the NRM found us. At that time, when someone would knock at the door, men would be the ones to hide under the beds while women would be the brave ones, to stand at the door and say, "My husband is not at home. *Taliimu*" (Luganda: He's not home). Have you forgotten where we had reached? Don't you think it is important to really move forward so that the past doesn't come back? And don't you think it's important that we people who remained here during the war join in the struggle now since we were handed this peace and freedom on a silver plate? And to pay back, shouldn't we also make a contribution to the cause of the NRM and the cause of women? As for me, I have chosen to serve the NRM with all my heart because it has brought hope into my otherwise hopeless life and has given me a platform from which to talk about women.' When he saw my determination and conviction, he simply left me alone to do this important work.

My husband was not the only one who questioned me about the work I was doing. I remember one time the LC5 Chairman, the Mayor, called a meeting and said, 'We have to understand our roles. I hear Matembe is in Mubende (a town north-west of Kampala). I hear Matembe is in Masaka (a town south of Kampala)! I am the one who is the LC5 Chairman. Why is she going to all these places?'

I said, 'Mr Chairman, I am Secretary for Mass Mobilisation and Education in this district. Therefore I am free to go anywhere I am invited in Uganda to articulate these important issues.' Perhaps the Chairman was feeling threatened that I was becoming more known than he was. Perhaps he wanted to curtail my movements. But I refused to stop. I went ahead to mobilise and educate the people in any part of the country where I was invited. Because my activities were being reported in the media, leaders from other districts started inviting me to mobilise the people in their areas. This gave me the opportunity to take my message of gender equality and national unity beyond my constituency to other parts of Uganda.

Just about this time, near the end of 1988, ACFODE chose me as its representative to attend a seminar held in Zimbabwe for Eastern and Southern Africa on the subject 'Women and Politics'. I was chosen because I was the most prominent woman politician in ACFODE, and I was the only Ugandan woman at that time who had been elected on a portfolio other than Secretary for Women on the District Council (LC5) in the whole country. My work as Secretary for Mass Mobilisation and Education in Kampala District was widely known. In addition, I was serving ACFODE as the Chairperson of the Legal and Political Committee. By Ugandan women's standards, I was a big politician! Going to Harare gave me my first chance to attend a meeting on women's issues outside my homeland. I could hardly believe that my dream was taking me to another country. I had longed for a platform in Uganda from which to talk about women's rights, but here I was going outside the country to meet other African women and to learn what they were doing. What a wonderful opportunity!

I was asked to address a seminar of about 40 participants. At this time, I was not yet talking from an informed point of view, but I was just beginning to learn the specific language being used in such women's meetings. However, the audience was moved by my enthusiasm, my convictions and my commitment to the women's cause. I described the kind of things I was doing, and the participants clapped and cheered. Some of the women concluded that here was an important politician. When someone asked me if I was a Member of Parliament, I said, 'No. I am only standing with one foot in the air, ready to step into Parliament.' I assured them that by the time we met again, I would be in Parliament. True to my word, in February 1989 I entered Parliament, called the National Resistance Council (NRC) at that time.

It was in 1988 that a law was passed expanding the NRC. This law included an affirmative action component that would bring more representatives of unrepresented or under-represented groups into this parliamentary body. Women actually gained a great deal under this initiative, as the position of District Woman Representative was created which guaranteed that in the next election at least 34 women, one from each district, would enter Parliament the NRC.

From independence in 1962 to the 1989 elections, women were hardly represented in Parliament. At independence there were two women in Parliament compared to 88 men. In 1980 there were 143 parliamentarians, with only one being a woman. But change was on the way. Other groups that were granted special seats in the NRC were the youth, the workers, and the military. When I heard the news about the coming elections, I thought, now is the time for me to enter Parliament.

Soon, however, while I was still rejoicing about this new development, I realised that I faced a dilemma. In what district should I stand for election? In fact, people in Mbarara, the district in which I was born, were calling me to go and run there. As part of my effort to mobilise and educate people in the country, I had gone to Mbarara and addressed a large meeting of leaders from all sectors of the district - religious leaders, government officials, educators, etc. This meeting was organised by the Mbarara Special District Administrator (SDA), the equivalent of the current Resident District Commissioner (RDC). At the meeting I talked about women's rights, which most of those attending were hearing about for the first time. After listening to me (many of them had also heard my radio programmes), they said, 'You are one of us. Why do you stay in Kampala when we have nobody here to teach us about these things?' Little did anyone know on that day that soon the NRC would be enlarged and that the new seats would include women district representatives.

The first news I heard about the expansion of the NRC was at a three-day conference organised for all the LC5 councillors in the whole country held at Kyambogo, a major educational training centre in Kampala. At the end of the conference, President Museveni announced the intention to expand the NRC and then he listed the new designations, including the seats for women. That was something to think about. As I left the meeting, the Vice-Chairperson of Mbarara District Council

(LC5) called me to his vehicle and told me that people in Mbarara wanted me to engage in politics there. About two weeks later the SDA Mbarara rang my Uncle Kazoora, asking him to tell me that people wanted me for their district's woman representative. These people turned out to be the ones who very soon helped me organise my activities in the district leading up to the elections.

However, going to Mbarara to contest presented certain problems. A powerful inner voice was saying that surely I should stay in Kampala. What about my marriage? What about my family? How can I possibly go to Mbarara? How can I tell my husband that I want to enter politics in Mbarara, over 300 kilometres from our home in Kampala city? Another strong argument for contesting in Kampala rather than in Mbarara was that I was already an established political player in Kampala. People in Kampala recognised me and were acquainted with my work. Wouldn't it give me an advantage if I ran in Kampala? As I was thinking about these things, I was more and more convinced that I should run for the Kampala District seat.

One person on whom I always relied for good advice, my uncle, John Kazoora[1], reminded me of the struggle I had faced running for the string of LC5 seats in Kampala before finally getting the ninth, the last possible position. 'And this time,' he said, 'there is only one position. Do you think you are not at risk? Why don't you go to Mbarara? After all, people from Mbarara are calling you to contest there, and they will look for votes for you.'

As I was thinking how I could possibly leave my family, the issue was unexpectedly resolved by others. One day when my husband was conversing with Uncle Kazoora, my husband said, 'You people advising Miria, why don't you tell her to go to Bushenyi (my husband's district)? Does she think she will win in Kampala District? Such a race will be very difficult since she is not a Muganda. She might not win here.'

When Kazoora told me that my husband was asking, why doesn't she go to Bushenyi, I realised that it was okay with him if I engaged in politics outside Kampala. So I told him, 'You know the people of Mbarara are calling me.' He told me that he was actually worried about the outcome if I ran in Kampala. It was now clear to me that he didn't mind me contesting the parliamentary seat and that he didn't mind my going up country. This helped me relax and begin to make plans for the upcoming elections.

Since entering public life, I have found one thing very interesting. Many people categorise me as a rebel, and they are convinced that my husband must be suffering. What they aren't aware of is that what I struggle for is what I live in practice. You see for me, I can't tell women what I don't do. My husband and I accept each other as partners in our marriage, and as human beings. We know our roles and rights. Each of us recognises that this is the role of the husband and this is a right, and this is the right of the wife and this is her role. Of course, at the beginning, when I am not sure of what he is thinking about something, I might have fears, but, while I am thinking about a situation, he is also thinking about it. Sometimes we don't talk much about these things, but one thing is certain. He is very supportive.

One incident during this next election showed me how supportive my husband really was. We had started consultations.[2] Then on the day before we were scheduled to go to the polls, the Electoral Commission announced on the radio that the candidates were required to present their educational certificates on the polling day. Now, what could I do? My papers were in Kampala. I was busy in Mbarara. Travelling to Kampala, a four-hour drive each way, would be a real hardship for me. However, I had pretty much concluded that I would have to go to Kampala the next day, and I must say I was really dreading that trip. To my surprise, when I arrived from the consultations that evening, I found that my husband had sent the driver with three files of my documents, hoping that I would find what I needed in one of them. When I saw the driver and the files, I said, 'Wow!' The required certificate was now in my hands. 'Wow!' What a supportive husband I have!

I entered the race in Mbarara with my usual enthusiasm and energy. As we began, there were five candidates. I learned later that at some point the four other women got together and decided that this Matembe woman who, according to them, was not well known in the district, should drop out of the race. They decided to call me to a meeting and advise me to quit. When we met and they gave me their advice, I told them I was not quitting the race, whether I was known in the area or not. Actually, I had done a number of consultations already, and I felt sure I would win. When they saw my determination and commitment to win, three of the women dropped out of the race, leaving only two of us. My one remaining opponent was actually very impressive. She was older than me but less educated. I thought that the last point, the educational difference, gave me an advantage, although it was clear that she was better known in the district, at least as the consultations got under way.

Of course the main reason I was hesitant to go to Mbarara to run for the NRC was that I feared losing the political base I had established in the LCs in Kampala District. I had waited a long time to enter politics, and by working hard, I had accomplished a good bit since my first election in LC1. Now, what if I ran for Parliament in Mbarara and lost? What would that mean? What would I do if that happened? Because I had never lived there since I married in 1975, I felt a bit like a stranger in Mbarara. So, on one hand, this election seemed like a very high risk. On the other hand, I had dreamed a long time about going to Parliament, and a number of people I respected and trusted were advising this course of action. Since I had started in politics, I had always looked for different settings, and as many settings as possible, in which to talk about the two causes I was advocating, the NRM Ten Point Programme and the emancipation of women. Was this choice going to lead to a new platform for my advocacy, or would I soon be back in Kampala working in local government? Only God knew.

What Others Say *(Jolly Mugisha)*

In July 2000 Nancy Dorsey interviewed Jolly Mugisha, District Gender Officer, about the work she and Miria do in Mbarara District. Jolly has been District Gender Officer since 1992.

For some time, I have wished that I had the facilities to write a book about Honourable Miria Matembe. She and I were talking about this just recently. When she told me that someone was working with her to produce her life story, I said, Wow, that is good. It will be good to have a book about Miria. I have known her for a long time now, and I must say that people like her are very few, very few indeed.

The first time I saw Miria Matembe was in 1986. She came to Mbarara with a group of women from Kampala looking for prominent women, women who were holding positions in government, in the social sector, or in business. The women in Kampala who had started ACFODE wanted to inspire and train such women. Because I was working as a culture officer for Mbarara District, I was invited to that meeting. And there was Miria. These ladies really talked. They talked about women's rights. They talked about how women have been trampled on. They talked about how women have been left behind. They talked about all sorts of things about women and how it was now time for women to come up. They were saying, 'This is a new era! Get up, you women out there!'

But I was newly married at that time. I had one baby, I had a happy marriage, I had a job. So, you know, I was looking around at these women and thinking, What are they talking about? Surely, is my husband mistreating me? Am I left back? I was a university graduate. I'd just left Makerere when I got married. At that time I didn't get the message, and I'm sure many other women in Mbarara didn't either. From my viewpoint at that time, I didn't have problems, and I certainly didn't want to associate myself with big-mouthed people. I'm sure many women are like that until they get a problem. That's when they say, 'Eh, by the way, I think what Matembe is saying is true.'

In 1989 Miria returned to Mbarara. There were national elections for the NRC and she was running for the women's seat. There she was again. I remember people were saying, 'That is the woman! That is the woman!' Somehow I still didn't understand much about 'women's issues' or what Miria was trying to accomplish. At that time she got overwhelming support from people who were active in district politics and in the social sector. She later told me that she got that support because she had been involved in local councils in Kampala. The Special District Administrator was very active in politics, and he knew what the country needed. He said, 'This is the woman,' and he convinced people in Mbarara to support her, and they put her in the NRC.

As a Member of Parliament, Miria has been doing a variety of things in the district. The work that she does focuses on three issues, first, sensitisation, and training in skills and leadership; second, economic empowerment for women; and third, counselling and mediation, that is, solving people's personal domestic problems. The last includes legal education.

In 1989 Miria started an NGO called Mbarara District Women's Development Association (MDWDA), and through that organisation, she has been able to do a lot, especially in terms of providing training workshops for development. You know, if you can train women in business skills, they can survive on their own. They can take leadership positions right from LC3 (sub-county) level.

Whenever new leadership comes in, Miria says, 'now we must train these women, because if we don't, they will go to their councils and just sit, and then women will not be heard. Also they will not be budgeted for. They won't be planned for.' So she sees that they get five days of training, training in advocacy, the art of lobbying, the art of talking in public, etc. When these women go back to their councils, in fact they are all sharp, and they will even tell you, 'I'm very sharp'. If you come to an LC5 meeting in Mbarara, you'll see that every woman is able to stand up and talk strongly on issues. You cannot believe it. They are trained, and it is Miria who is mainly responsible for that.

I remember when she had just joined the NRC, she asked ACFODE to come and train the women of Mbarara in leadership skills. The theme was Peace and Development, or something like that. Now Miria was there again with a very big workshop. They called virtually all the women who were well dressed, if I may say that, (*laughs*) women who could be leaders, women who could be identified as future leaders. So they trained us, about 50 women, just women: heads of departments in the district, nurses, opinion leaders, elderly women, and some inspired young girls.

It was from that time that women started picking more interest. They said, 'This one (Miria) must be a sharp one.'

Then, of course she has embraced economic empowerment. In 1998 through MDWDA she started a loan credit scheme to give poor women some start-up capital. Some time back Global Fund for Women donated $8000 for this purpose. Now we are running a very big credit scheme for women. The credit given to women is like a starting point. We give loans of small amounts up to 300,000 Uganda shillings ($180) to a group or an individual. This credit has changed the lives of many women.

Miria was also able to obtain funds from Mbarara District Council (LC5). You know, in most districts, there is no money in the budget for women's activities. I remember one day she came to the Council and almost shed tears. She was saying, 'How can we develop if you are thinking about roads, if you are thinking about water. Of course we need those things as well, but women have special needs which are overlooked.' So Mbarara District Council put aside 17 million shillings. I remember the year, 1992. It is a women's fund, a district revolving credit scheme being run by the district, but specifically for women. Every year the district government puts in 20 million. Different women and women's groups access different amounts for their income generating projects. I do believe that without Miria, we would not have had this scheme and the yearly budget allocation in the district.

She has also focused on the legal aspect, bearing in mind that women's rights have been trampled on in this part of the world, because society is male dominated. She has really emphasised legal education, teaching women their rights through massive legal education. Also, there has been training for paralegals who then can give women some advice about their problems. This also reduces the influx of people going to courts for these minor cases which can be handled out of court.

The work she has done in these three areas, leadership training, legal education, and credit will be remembered for a long time. Now you will hear a woman say, 'My life was a mess before. I was unable to contribute even a little money for my children's school fees nor even buy food but now I can. My life has changed because of this kind of arrangement,' you know, the credit scheme, or the training, or just ordinary sensitisation.

Another one of Miria's initiatives has been to promote the democratisation process taking place in the country. In 1994 she carried out massive voter education in the district. It was really massive. She went from sub-county to sub-county. Mbarara is quite big compared to other districts in Uganda. It has 47 sub-counties and many cells, the smallest administrative units in Uganda. She went from place to place, especially talking to the women, saying 'Now you women, come and make a decision, a decision that is going to affect your lives forever, and the lives of your daughters and your grand-daughters.'

These days, in Mbarara District we have large numbers of women in politics, not just because of their 'third' (all government bodies are required to have one third membership of women), but because women in Mbarara are empowered. The women of Mbarara cannot be compared with the women elsewhere in this country. We may have a woman Vice-President from Busoga, but I don't think the grassroots women of Busoga are as sharp as the ones we have in our part of the country. And we attribute all that to the noise Hon. Matembe has been making. She'll say, 'You women, get up! Get up! Get up and come and join me if you want something to be done for you.'

The second kind of work that Miria does for women in the district has a very far reaching effect. When I first started working with her, I wasn't really enthusiastic about doing this kind of work, specifically for women, visiting women where they are, down there, at the grassroots, where Miria has always gone. But later, my attitude changed. In 1992 I lost my husband. When Miria came to the district, people told her my problem, 'You know what? That lady (we were not friends yet) has lost her husband.' She said, 'Oh my, this poor girl! At her age!' It was from that time that Miria took an interest in me, and whatever she has done for women in the district since that time, we have done together.

We have gone down even to the lowest administrative unit at LC1, working to settle domestic problems, returning children to their mothers, or dividing up properties fairly. At times we have even taken the law into our hands, dividing up cows or banana plantations, where we felt that justice should be done. When women have problems, they seek her out, telling her, 'I have been beaten,' or 'My children have been abandoned by their father,' or 'I'm a widow and all my property has been taken.' The arrival of many women coming for her help is like a daily routine. In fact, I remember her husband, Mr Matembe, at times takes up this work himself. He even started taking the women who came to their house in Mbarara down the street to the Administrator General's office, to seek redress. I could say that helping women in this way is like a contagious disease. If you come to my house now, you would find women are there, because they think that where I am, then Matembe is there, or that I will take them to her, and she will help them.

Something interesting here is that, although she is an MP from Mbarara District, women come to see her from all over the country. If you go to her house, you'll find women from Kitgum, (Kitgum is far north) and Kabale and Kasese (in south-western Uganda) who have come for her help. Many of the women of Uganda look at her as, shall I call her, a saviour, because she's there to listen to their problems. With Miria they have a shoulder to lean on and cry. There is a listening ear.

In 1993 Miria went to America where she made some friends at the McKnight Foundation. When she told people at the Foundation about the problems of women in Mbarara, some of them agreed to come and see for themselves. Miria and I took them around the district. In a very remote place that had no health facility, there was a group of rural women, grassroots women, women who walked barefoot. The McKnight Foundation provided $20,000 to put up a maternity clinic complete with its own water tank. For another village very far off, this Foundation gave money for an income generating activity. The women there used that money to buy beehives, and now they have a project producing honey.

As I've said, these days the women in Mbarara are very sharp. If you go around to the villages and ask anybody, they will tell you that all the women who are strong, all the women who are inspired, all the women who are hard-working, all the women who can stand up and talk, are referred to as 'Matembe.' Somebody will stand up in a meeting and say, 'For me, I'm the Matembe of this cell (LC1),' which means that she's seen as a model for women, women who demand their rights, women who have achieved things, women who won't keep their mouths shut, women who are truthful, women who are trustworthy, women everybody depends on.

Not only in Mbarara but in Uganda, women are saying, 'Now we can sleep.' When women were asked during elections, 'What does Matembe give you,' they said, 'Ah, she doesn't have to come and dig my garden. She doesn't have to come and give me money, but I sleep! At least I know when she's there, I can sleep. Nobody can touch me because she's there. People who might make trouble for me know that I'm going to report to her. So I can sleep comfortably in my bed, and that's all I ask for.'

You can go to almost any village in the district and find that when women stand up to talk in public, they say, 'You know, I'm so-and-so, the Lady Councillor. I'm the Matembe of this village.' That is the introduction everywhere, and wherever we have been, women want to have their photographs taken with Honorable Matembe because those photographs provide them security in their homes. They put the photos in very nice frames and hang them in their houses. Now when the husband or son begins to make trouble for the woman, he'll stop and say, 'She's there. I'll go, I'll go.' And the wife says, 'Not only do I know her, but we are personally connected. You beat me, I'll run there and you are in trouble.' That's what they are doing.

In schools, wherever we have been to visit, all the girls, you know the clever ones (of course there are some who may be a little indifferent, who don't want to be associated with this controversial woman), you see the clever ones approach her, 'Honourable, I want to take a photograph with you,' and they go boasting with the photograph, 'I'm going to grow up and be like her.' They are doing this in all the schools.

One statement she uses when she's making her concluding remarks at schools is that, especially where there is some resistance, she tells the girls, 'You girls, I want to tell you that the women's movement has started. Whether you accept it or not, we have started the journey, and we are not going back.' In connection with that, when she talks to men, she tells them, 'The best thing for you men to do is to keep on releasing some of your power, relinquishing some of your authority, so that we can be at par.' This seed is now implanted in the young ones, and it can't be turned back.

If you went to visit primary schools, or any women's function in a village, there would be a song greeting the guests, and that song would be about 'Matembe'. In many cases I've watched other people who are guests of honour being embarrassed. Some person is a guest of honour, but every group sings, 'I'm a woman, Matembe.' It is hard for the guest of honour not to be a bit uncomfortable. This is true even when Miria's not at the meeting. Every song, every women's group, all the girls' schools.

Miria visits many girls' schools, carrying out role modelling and career guidance, telling the young ones, 'Here I am. You can see me. I never had twenty pairs of shoes like you want. I never had a mobile phone. I had no shoes. But here I am. I can now buy a hundred pairs. If you are patient, if you read hard...' She has been going around to schools, even to boys' schools.

There is a general criticism that educated women are not interested in women at the grassroots. Let me describe one case that shows what Miria does for such women. We had a neighbour who had a housemaid whose mother was being chased. Her father had married a new wife, and was chasing the mother from the home. Immediately Miria jumped into a vehicle, even when she was tired, even when her back was aching. She said, 'We must go and help this woman.' So we went to her home. People there were insulting that poor woman, but Miria intervened, and she settled the problem. The old woman was brought back into her house and they even divided the banana plantation and the cows. You know, an agreement was reached.

One thing I want to say is that people out there in the villages respect Honorable Matembe's decisions. Once she has become involved with a problem, they know that certainly that problem is a problem settled. They respect her decisions. They accept the kind of justice she gives.

Of course Miria has faced a lot of problems. When she was first elected as Woman Representative, there were a number of negative forces at work in the district. For instance, the person who was working as Secretary for Women's Affairs in the district at that time did not have the same vision Miria had. It was not easy for Miria to work with this woman since they were not moving in the same direction or at the same pace. So Miria decided to go to a sub-county and start working with the women there. In 1994 the CA (Constituent Assembly) elections were held. Before the elections, Miria came to the district many times. She wanted the women in her district, and especially the women leaders, to understand what it meant to write a new constitution. She went from village to village, calling together grassroots women, asking them how they wanted to be governed in this male-dominated society, and she held several seminars.

By then I was beginning to understand more about what was involved in women's struggle, but I have to admit I recall being passive during a large three-day workshop that Miria organised at the Nganwa Hostel in Mbarara. I'd just come and sit there like most other women. At that workshop she took us, chapter by chapter, through the draft constitution. She would ask the participants, 'What do you want us to put into this constitution for women?' She challenged us to think about issues such as women and property rights, things most of us had never thought of before. From Mbarara she went to Ibanda, and another sub-district in Mbarara called Kikagate to carry out similar workshops. Basically, she was getting women's views in terms of constitutional legal provisions.

The elections were a little bit tough. There were two other women running, who were even in our camp, women Miria had helped to sensitise and motivate. These women now came to her and said, 'But you are the one who was telling us that women are behind. Now we have come up. You had better step aside so that we can now go there.'

In response she said, 'But look here. There are things for women that I must make sure are in the constitution. If I don't go there, women will lose.' I remember that she used to say, 'If I don't go to the Constituent Assembly, I'd rather die.' Competition was hot but she went through. Then she was involved in the constitution-making process, up to, I think, 1995.

Now the presidential elections were held in 1996. Miria campaigned for the President with vigour. After the President went through, she said, 'For me, if the President did not go through, I don't think I would be a good contestant for Parliament. Because of the NRM government I have had a platform from which to talk about women and their problems, to say what I have been created to say.' She always says, 'I came into this world to talk about women.' She says she felt it right from her childhood, maybe because of the environment she grew up in, seeing women suffering around her home. After the presidential elections, Miria started her own campaign for the parliamentary elections.

You know, one remark that Miria made continues to follow her wherever she goes, and this remark and misunderstandings about what she said were used against her in the elections in 1996. In 1994, during a public demonstration in Kampala against men who rape and defile, she said that such men should lose their dangerous instruments. The implication was that such men should be castrated.

I remember when we were campaigning for her in 1996, some woman would say, 'Ah, ah, we should not give our vote to Matembe. I don't want her to castrate my husband.' Others supported her statement, pointing to the many cases of rape and defilement being reported in the press. These crimes are rampant in Mbarara, and in Uganda in general. You can't open a newspaper for a week without seeing that a 3-year-old has been defiled, a 16-year-old has been defiled. So, on one side she's seen as somebody who is inspiring women to work hard and to be independent, most of all to be independent, and to refuse to be mistreated. On the other side, she's bashed because she challenges the oppression and exploitation of women. And she is bashed by both men and women.

It may seem surprising but many elite women do not support Miria. In general, these women tend to have ideas and approaches different from Miria's. I attribute that kind of lack of support to gender, the problems of gender. We have a saying in our language: *Kwoza kugaya abakazi obanza nyoko*, meaning that when you are going to ridicule or belittle women, you start with your own mother

Many women, because they have grown up in this male-dominated system, they look at men as superiors, and at themselves and other women in general as inferiors, as people who are incapable of doing much of anything. I've worked with many women like this. I know how they are. I feel they contest elections just for the sake of competing, not because they want to change anything for women. This kind of woman doesn't want to accept that, perhaps she is capable of doing so much, and that another woman may be more capable than she is. It seems that as women we don't understand this. I don't know for men, but women, we don't get it. So some educated women work against Matembe. Perhaps, they need a lot of sensitisation about what Miria has accomplished for women, and to understand that most women could not do what she has done. For now, they say, 'Who is she after all? Who is she? Why should she be better than me? Isn't she a woman like me? After all, is she better than me? Can't I also do what she does?'

And secondly, you know the politics of Uganda is not seen by some as a service to the people. Instead it is seen as a source of getting money. One day you are very poor, but when you join politics, the next day you are a millionaire, even a billionaire, if there is such a thing in Uganda. So these educated women see politics as a source of income. They think, 'Why should somebody keep on earning all that money when actually I too could go there and earn the same money, earn the same respect?' And they don't see the service she does. That is, until they get domestic problems themselves and then they start running around looking for her. But of course the village women, who know their vulnerable position, who know what she has done for them, are the ones who are grateful. Honourable Matembe is seen by some as breaking the social order. Now think about it. If women are supposed to be quiet, if women are not expected to take an active part in politics, if women don't generally talk loudly, if women are supposed to be soft and feminine, then what would people think of this woman who breaks many of those old rules?

I remember when she was campaigning for the CA, people were saying, 'Ah, but this woman, can't she also talk like a woman?' No, she doesn't talk like a woman, and she'd tell them, 'You know, it's because of these traditions. Look at the way we dress in Ankole. When you are married, you have a dress, and you get something like a sheet, and to wear it you have got to fold your arms, permanently. How can you get up and talk to people so they understand if your arms are folded on your chest?' So these people see her as someone who is breaking the social order, who is changing from what is considered normal, and they are resisting. Of course change is always resisted, since it's not comfortable for those who don't understand. However, when you take time to explain, they say, 'Yes, I think it's necessary that we do this, I think it's necessary that we change direction.'

But of course there are the die-hards, those ones who don't want change. They say, 'But what about culture?' Then Miria says, 'What about women? Surely women are human beings who should be favoured by culture. Culture should not keep on treating women as if they are not human beings.' However, attitudes about her are changing now. A newspaper in the village, our local newspaper, was conducting research about support for the current politicians. Miria got 98 per cent because a lot of people now understand.

You know, when you talk about rights for women in our community, men tend to look at their wives. You know Banyankore men don't value their wives, although they like their sisters, and they love their daughters. Let me give an example. When Miria was advocating women's rights to land, you know, men don't want to give their wives land. Basically, the argument is that if a man dies, the widow will get married again. The men say, 'Ah, but somebody will get my land and will bring another man, a man of another clan.' But supposing that it is a man's daughter who is suffering. You say to a man, 'Wouldn't you want your daughter, if she lost her husband at a tender age, at a young age, wouldn't you want her to have land?' They say, 'Ah, for my daughter it's okay.' And what about the sister? 'For my sister it's okay.' 'But,' you ask, 'what if you died? What about your wife?' Then they say, 'No, no, no, let her stay married to the clan. My brother is there. She can keep on looking after our land.'

What I'm saying is that many men don't have those very big feelings for their wives, because to them a wife in our society is bought with bride price. You buy a wife with your cows, and she's part of the property you own. Actually men are really possessive. They don't want this wife - say for example if the man is dead - they don't want this wife touched by another man. This is because they don't consider that wives are human beings in their own right. Wives are treated as part of the property, and when somebody owns a property, a property she remains. So men don't have that respect for their feelings. That's why you find many widows floating in this country, and I think this is common in Uganda, not only in Ankole but in Africa. The majority of the widows don't remarry. If you remarry it means your former husband's family takes the property. They even take the children. We are hoping that this wave of change which Honourable Matembe has spearheaded will continue, not only in Ankole, not only in Uganda, but in the whole world.

Traditionally women were not money-makers in their communities, but now that we have tasted some bit of money, we want to make more and more, and joining politics is seen as a way of making money, as I said before. Most of these women who enter politics, if you don't give them an allowance, they are not willing to work. They are not inspired by their own convictions. They are not devoted to that kind of work. They come there to make money, and when there is no money, they pull out. In other words, they don't have a genuine interest in serving their constituents.

Although Miria is very controversial, she is also very friendly. This quality has helped her succeed in politics. Because she is friendly, people are ready to listen to her. It is something to attend one of her talks. Even if she has talked for five hours, for example at a funeral, everybody's very attentive and everyone's laughing. They even clap their hands, which is a taboo at funerals. Sometimes she says to me, 'Jolly, do you think these people have understood what I am saying, or are they just amused?'

I say, 'I don't know, but I think they are getting the point.' But she really captures them when she is talking, and I think they take the points, because the results are seen. You know, after she has talked, people go out and change in the way she has been urging them to change. The communities out there are not all that ready to change. They're not all that enlightened. New ideas may be resisted. Miria is patient and tolerant, but determined. Those attributes I can say have helped her in successfully advocating women's rights.

I should describe International Women's Day activities in our district. Since about 1992 Uganda has been celebrating Women's Day in March as a national holiday. We never miss it because it is a very important day when women of all walks of life come together. They discuss women's issues, programmes and activities. They evaluate what they have done, and they look forward to the future.

So we have taken it upon ourselves to have celebrations at the district level. But this year we decentralised it because we felt that now the women who live in remote areas have problems with transportation, you know, going to one common place. So we agreed to have these celebrations at the sub-county level, so that the women who live far away can walk in from their villages to the sub-county. Then we get guests of honour to preside over the celebration. We put it on a competitive basis, like we find a programme where women are successful producers. They grow agricultural produce, they make crafts, they excel at home management and cleanliness, you know, that kind of programme. Then we give awards to these women. You know, all the songs on that day will be '*Matembe*'. You send a guest and the guest will sit there, and all the songs will be '*Matembe*'. That shows what these women think of Honourable Matembe. Let me describe my work with Miria. I don't work for Miria. I work with her. I am a District Gender Officer so we are doing similar work. We are both interested in uplifting the status of women in Mbarara, and our work is focused on the very poor rural women of the district.

Whenever she generates an activity for women in the district, she gets in touch with me, and I do the organisation for that through MDWDA.

For example, recently there was a women's group in Bubare Sub-county which didn't want a loan in terms of cash. They wanted goats. They said, 'Our nutrition is very poor. Our area is very dry. We cannot keep cows, but we can keep goats.' Miria asked me to work on this project. I went to Makerere University looking for Biana goats, from South Africa. Then I went back to the village and bought local goats to breed with the imported ones. I organised the project actually. So that is the kind of working relationship we have. Sometimes the district doesn't have funds for a project, and Miria helps find what is needed. Apart from working together, now I can say we are friends, very great friends.

I want to say that I am what I am because of Miria, Miria as a person, Miria as a politician, Miria as my mentor, Miria as somebody who has inspired me to keep on living. She came into my life when there was a very big gap and she filled it. If you ask all the widows in Mbarara - these days there are many young widows - she has helped them, and they know that whatever happens, she's there for them. If you asked the old women, elderly women - we have a pastoral group, where people keep cows and women's sons sometimes mistreat them. If you ask the elderly women, they will tell you 'We are here (alive, safe) because of Miria.'

In fact, I walk with my head high, because nobody can tamper with my life now. I was somebody who was very quiet, but now I know what I want, and I know how to get it. And the same is true of many other women in this country. I have three children. I also have an orphan who I look after, my brother's child, but recently I picked another one on the street, a street child. So I have five dependants. In our culture here, it's not easy, especially when you have children, but I live as I am.

When I was writing my research paper for my post-graduate degree in Development Studies at Mbarara University, I dedicated it to Honourable Matembe in these words, 'To you, my friend, my mentor, and my benefactor'. It's not that she gives me money, but I can call her my social benefactor because she has raised my status. Of course, I can't deny that working with Miria gives me special status. She has been my social benefactor. She has been my mentor. She has inspired me, just as she has inspired many other women in the district. Now, as I've said, I've come to know Miria very well. If someone writes a book about her, I would want them to describe her work for women and some of the things she has accomplished in that area. She is absolutely dedicated to this work, and her work has brought major changes. She is so busy with the work that she really has very little time for herself. I know her at that level. At the same time, I know a different side of Miria and I would want people to know Miria as a special human being.

You know, people fear her. They think she is a very tough woman, and in many ways that is true. At times she has had to be tough to accomplish her goals. But for me and my children, and for many other women who have come to see her at home, in Kampala and Mbarara or Bushenyi, we know her as a very friendly, very loving person. For example, sometimes my children and I stay with Miria. When we stay with her, she will get up in the morning and ask us, 'What do you want for breakfast?' One of the special items she likes making for us is scrambled eggs which we call the 'Miria Special'. You will find her there doing the cooking herself and persuading the children to eat their eggs.

She will make a bed for you, or prepare coffee, or even cook a meal for a whole group of people. When I considered writing Miria's story, I thought I would call it, 'Miria, the Human Being'. I've known her in times of joy, when she was very happy, and then all of a sudden she thinks about something else we should be doing for women, and the joy disappears in the face of the realities of women's lives. She can change like the wind from one direction to another. Or maybe after a busy day that left her exhausted, she sleeps a little and then wakes up in the middle of the night and starts making plans for new programmes and projects.

I would want the book to show some of the contradictions in Miria's life. I wonder how many people know that Miria loves to dance. Yes, Miria likes very much to dance when she has a chance. These days she says, 'I think now, Jolly, I'm old, because we can't even go for a dance!' But whenever there is an opportunity, she will dance all the records from number one to the end, and she really enjoys it. When she starts to dance, everybody on the dancing floor will surround her and start clapping. So we go for dances. When there is time and she's not very tired, we go to the club.

Recently she was given an award as one of the 100 heroines in the entire world, given to women who have done a lot to change women's lives the world over. Think of that! I know her as somebody at that level. And yet she spends a good deal of time at the grassroots, making herself available, speaking to and listening to the humblest of women, urging all women to get up and fight for their rights.

Perhaps one incident will make this point clear. I remember one time we went to a very remote part of the district to address women, and our car broke down so that we had to walk. It was very far to our destination and the road was very steep. This kind of thing is why her back bothers her, I think. Then we had to spend the night somewhere. Now imagine! She had just come back from attending the UN Environmental Summit in Rio de Janeiro, Brazil. From one extreme at the international level to another at the local level since we could not reach home that night.

The LC Chairman took us to a home where they kept us overnight. We were sure that the goats were sleeping in the house, or that at least they had been sleeping there. There were holes in the ceiling and in the walls, and it smelled very bad. Luckily we had our luggage, so we sprayed around. Miria said, 'You know what? Sometimes I don't understand my life. Yesterday I was like in 'heaven', in a luxurious hotel in Rio, and here I am now sleeping in a hut like this one. Even a snake could come in this hole.' 'We didn't sleep the whole night. Instead we stayed awake while she told stories about Rio, about what she had seen there and how she had talked and the whole world had listened to her. And yet some village men were whispering things like, 'We don't want her here. She wants to castrate us.'

During the 1996 race for Parliament, Miria and I knew the race was very close. Many candidates were buying votes with money, a rather common practice. I was scared that we would lose. Early on election day Miria left us and went to a certain place where she stayed relaxing from the stress of campaigning. People had been coming and demanding money, but she never gave money. She would tell people, 'You know for me, I'm an honest person. I cannot tell you a lie that I'm going to bring heaven and bridges and whatever, like these other politicians. Me, I give you my words, and my words will change you.'

I had to say to her, 'But surely, why don't we look for money and give it to them?' She replied, 'You, Jolly, you know me. I'm an honest person. I don't bribe people. For me, I cannot bribe.' But every morning people would come with their demands, 'We are thirsty. We want to drink' (we want money). So Miria would read the Bible for comfort. You see the contradiction. One time she is very confident. The next day she's there on her knees saying, 'God, I know you can do it.' Yes, I know her as a believer in God. Each morning she would say, 'Jolly, let's pray.' Someone might say, 'Even Miria,' even this strong woman who has moved the world over believes in God. But I can assure you her God is so strong and faithful. He answers her prayers all the time.

I am beginning to be convinced that He really answers her prayers because when the situation is complicated, especially during elections, she will say, 'My votes come from God,' and indeed God brings them because she has so far won elections four times.

I know that Honourable Miria Matembe is a very great woman. History will confirm that. A book about Miria should describe her achievements personally but should focus on what she has done to change things for women, not only in Uganda, but in Africa as a whole. It is a great honour to know her and to be her friend.

Ruth Sabiiti, the Chairperson of Women Council III, Kakiika Sub-county, is known as 'Matembe' in her community. Jolly Mugisha asked Ruth to explain what that means.

When you are performing duties in women's affairs, people tend to associate you with Matembe. They refer to you as a 'Matembe' of that area. In my sub-county in Kakiika, whenever I am insisting on fairness for women, people refer to me as the 'Matembe of Kakiika', This happens mainly when men think they can dispense with their wives will, without any compensation or any care of their children and their wives. They just discard them and say, 'Go back home.' If I insist that there must be an agreement on what follows next, how to look after the lady and the children, these men will say, 'You are another Matembe in this area. You want to force us to be humble and good to our wives.'

Or when the LCs are choosing a committee and you remind them to be gender sensitive, they say that now Matembe is at work. Whatever committee they are forming, such as a school committee, the men want to have more men than women, or even no woman at all. Then I insist that the committee has to be gender balanced. That's when I am referred to as Matembe. In any case, where they tend to favour men, and I challenge them, I am called Matembe. Another group that calls me 'Matembe' are the women themselves, when they are happy with what is done for them. Whenever we are associated with that name, you know you have fulfilled your duty to stand in for women. You feel proud because you know that what you are doing is actually right and according to the law of Uganda.

Miria Matembe has really done a lot for women. When there is a rape case or a defilement case, and you take it to police, they tend not to care, but the moment you call in Miria, she comes and then something happens. Actually every woman who sits on the council is referred to as Matembe. The main thing this shows is that this woman cares for her fellow women, and she is a fighter.

Notes

1   John Kazoora was the Special District Administrator for Kampala District when I contested for the LC5 seat there. Currently he is MP from Kashari County.
2   During these elections, campaigning was not allowed. Candidates were expected to make 'consultations' with the people who were going to cast the votes. In that sense the elections were indirect. For instance, I was elected by an electoral college of 89 district councillors, two from each sub-county, and a Chairperson. Eight of the 89 were women.

Miria with her brother, Sam, and the family dog Kacuukuzi in 1967

Miria with her best friends Joy Karaara Emuron and Edith Mirembe (centre) at Bweranyangi Girls Secondary School in 1969

Miria and her childhood
friend, Joy Kafura-Kabatsi,
taking part in a play *"The
Merchant of Venice"* at
Bweranyangi in *1968*

Miria with one of her favourite
teachers, Miss Ashton, at
Bweranyangi Girls Secondary
School in 1970

Miria with her elder sister, Kamagwabe, and her brother, Sam, at home in Rutooma 1972

Miria with her friend and room-mate, Monica Mirembe Kyobe, at Mary Stuart Hall, Makerere University in 1975. Miria is wearing the shirt and trousers that Nekemia had worn on the first day they met.

Miria marries Nekemia on 12 July 1975 at St James Cathedral Ruharo, Mbarara

Miria and Nekemia with their first baby, Godwin Miyaabe, at their home in Port-Bell in 1976

Miria and Nekemia with their sons, Godwin Miyaabe (right) and Gideon Magembe, at their 5th wedding anniversary on 12 July 1980

Miria and Nekemia with their four sons. To the right of Nekemia are Gideon and Godwin and to the left of Miria are Grace and Gilbert at their Silver Jubilee Wedding Anniversary in July 2000

Miria and Nekemia at their Silver Jubilee Wedding Anniversary in July 2000 at their home in Port Bell, Luzira

Miria as Guest-of-Honour at an 'Oldies' Dance, at Viper Room, Hotel Equatoria, opens the dance with Nekemia in 2001. They both love dancing very much. Remember they first met at a dance!

CHAPTER 3

Action for Development (ACFODE)

I t is naive to think that Ugandan women in the past just accepted oppressive situations without resistance or complaint. It is also naive to imagine that some kind of inaction prevailed across society until the women in the last 16 years took up the struggle for gender equality and justice. It is more accurate to recognise that from long ago women in Uganda have always looked for ways to challenge unjust and inequitable conditions in their lives. However, we can see that something new and revolutionary has happened for women in Uganda starting in the mid-1980s.

The two events mentioned in Chapter Two, the UN International Conference for Women in Nairobi in 1985 and the coming to power of the pro-women NRM government early in 1986, brought positive change for women. One aspect of that change is the more favourable climate for women. I am happy that I have lived in this period and that I have played a part in what happened. Today, a strong women's movement in Uganda is a reality. This includes women at all levels of society who are resisting oppression in large and small ways and demanding an equal place in society for themselves and other women.

Broad-based social movements like the women's movement are dispersed, consisting of diverse elements and even containing contradictory and opposing forces. Many women

64

who are clearly resisting gender oppression would even deny they are part of something called the women's movement. In my view, there is presently a climate in Uganda that is conducive to women's efforts to reach their full potential. Because people these days know much more than previous generations about gender issues and about women's rights, women are in a position to move forward. Of course, the barriers in their way are large and many. In spite of the barriers, women, and many men, are challenging the gender inequalities and women are refusing to be second-class citizens.

One organisation that has played a leading role in the positive things that have happened for women in Uganda during this period is Action for Development (ACFODE). The founding of ACFODE was a direct result of the Nairobi conference. The story of the founding of ACFODE is not only interesting, but it is important for people, especially women, to understand why and how this organisation was created, the particular goals set by its founders, and the contributions it has made to women's emancipation in this country.

Up to the changing times of the mid-1980s, the general view of women in Uganda was very traditional and limiting. Women were thought to be first and foremost wives and mothers. Domestic space was women's domain and their main responsibilities were family related. Generally women were not perceived to be public actors or public decision-makers. The government delegation to the Nairobi conference in 1985 reflected this mind-set. This delegation was led by Mrs Miria Obote, the President's wife. She was accompanied by women who fit into one of two categories. The first group consisted of 'wives of big men' either in government, or in religious bodies, etc. The second were executives in national or international women's organisations who learned about the conference through their global linkages, for example, YWCA, University Women's Association, National Council of Women, Mothers' Union, Catholic Guild, Association of Muslim Women, Girl Guides, etc.

The official delegation numbered about 30, while an additional 30 or so went to participate in the informal side of the conference known as the NGO (Non-governmental organisation) Forum. A good percentage of the Ugandan women participating in the NGO Forum were members of a music, dance and drama group from Makerere University. This group also reflected traditional views of women held at the time. That is, these women went to the conference in their role as public entertainers who performed cultural songs and dances at important events.

In addition to the official delegation and those participating in the NGO Forum, other women from Uganda went to Nairobi on their own, but the total number didn't reach 100. Dr Maxine Ankrah, who at the time was a senior lecturer in the Department of Social Work and Social Administration (SWSA) at Makerere, remembers that she started hearing news about the upcoming conference 'right across the border' in early 1984. She decided that she could not miss 'this monumental event,' the closing conference of the UN Decade for Women, in July 1985.

While the conference was taking place in Nairobi, we in Uganda were getting some interesting reports about what was happening there. What we were reading in the press were negative statements such as (as I recall), 'the streets of Nairobi were infested with the ugly faces of women from all over the world!' According to these reports, the women at the conference were demanding equality. In my naive manner, I was saying, what equality are they demanding? At the time I could not understand this at all. Of course, a man cannot be equal to a woman. These women should be demanding equal rights. The press reports were saying that women were demanding equality, and I was condemning them. How can they demand equality, I wondered. A man is a man and a woman is a woman. The two cannot be the same. They are biologically different and in any case, why should women want to be men? Besides, I was proud to be a woman.

You know, I was talking like that because I had not yet learned what women around the world were saying and demanding in this period. I truly did not understand what was going on. It was not clear to me what the subject of the conference was anyway. Mark you, by that time, I had neither attended any meeting discussing issues of equality, rights or opportunities for women, nor had I yet known about or attended any conference at all. So, uninformed as I was, I was influenced and confused by the press reports.

When Maxine Ankrah returned from Nairobi, she started to discuss the conference with other women and to try to assess the significance of the conference for Ugandan women. Soon five or six women who worked at Makerere were holding weekly discussions in Maxine's office.

Maxine had noticed two factors that distinguished most of the other women at the conference from Ugandan women. First, the women from various countries appeared to be united in their goals and objectives. For example, the very large number of women from the host country - more than 4,000 - were seen to be Kenyan whether they were urban or rural-based. Others, like the American women, overall spoke with one voice, as did the women of many other delegations. In addition, the women from different countries were communicating easily with each other. Notices announcing country meetings - for example, all the delegates from South Korea - were posted, even on trees, and women were rushing to attend. No one who knew the situation prevailing in Uganda would suggest that Ugandan women were united in any way. In fact, the divisive political situation in Uganda at that time appeared to have followed the women to Nairobi. Some women who went on their own said they felt that they had to hide from the government delegation to avoid being asked, 'What are you doing here? How did you come?'

The women in the post-Nairobi discussion group at Makerere asked themselves, how is it that women in Uganda don't work together? Surely all of us have similar problems and concerns.

The second factor Maxine observed at Nairobi was that while the National Council of Women (NCW) and other women's groups in Uganda were concerned with social affairs and welfare issues, the women in Nairobi were discussing issues of equality, peace and rights, and talking in terms of women and development. For instance, the Ghanaian women brought displays of the latest appropriate technology for women. Issues of development were clearly foreign to the Ugandan idea of women's affairs.

So, these women meeting at Makerere said, what do we need to do? How can we bring this spirit of unity to women's affairs here? What would be required to have women talk with one voice on a common platform? What must we do to begin to understand women and development issues and to get away from the social welfare approach to women's problems?

As these women met weekly from August through mid-November to see how they could bring the Nairobi spirit of unity and the orientation towards women and development to Uganda, their numbers grew. They soon decided to formalise their meetings by forming an organisation. These women had some rather revolutionary ideas about what they wanted to accomplish and the ways and means they would use to accomplish their goals. They concluded that there was no existing group which could accommodate what they were setting out to do. Neither the Mothers' Union nor the Catholic Guild was likely to be interested in these revolutionary ideas. FIDA, the Association of Women Lawyers, had not yet taken up its role of active advocacy for women. Although FIDA was a professional group of lawyers and I'm a lawyer, my only regular contact with that organisation up to that time occurred when the Chairperson approached me once a year asking me to purchase tickets to FIDA's annual dinner.

Another factor was that at that time women were prevented from forming an organisation without the approval of the National Council of Women. The National Council of Women was established in 1978 as a response to a United Nations resolution, an initiative of the UN Decade for Women, which required UN member nations to set up national machineries for the advancement of women. When the NCW was formed under Amin's rule, it was established by a decree that placed it under the Ministry of Community Development. NCW was not an independent body in any way. It was set up to be an umbrella for women's organisations, and yet the decree which created it was used by those in government to limit the formation of women's NGOs. For instance, if a group tried to register as an NGO, NCW had to clear that organisation in accordance with the decree. So, in a way, although NCW was established with the stated intent of promoting the integration of women in development, in Uganda this body was really used to control existing women's groups and the formation of new ones. In addition, both the Amin (1971-1979)and the Obote II (1980-1985) regimes distrusted organisational life. These dictators certainly did not want Ugandans to go outside the country where they would be in a position to report about the terrible things that were happening here. The group of women meeting at Makerere in 1985 considered it highly unlikely that NCW would approve the new kind of organisation they visualised.

In addition, there was a second important issue involved in applying for NCW approval. These women wanted a totally autonomous organisation, answerable to no one but its members, an organisation not under the oversight of either the government nor of men. This is the point at which I entered the picture. As the group searched for an organisational structure that would accommodate this vision, Joy Kwesiga, one of the original members of the Makerere group, suggested that they contact this woman lawyer she knew, Miria Matembe. They found me at the Chartered Institute of Bankers, Kampala, and invited me to one of their meetings. Joy and I knew each other through our husbands, and Joy's sister and I had been together at secondary school in the 1970s.

I remember sitting at my first meeting with them and listening as the women described their plans. They proposed to create an organisation having a new spirit, a spirit of unity, an organisation which would focus on development issues that concerned women. This organisation would be quite different from the usual ones which operated separately and were mainly interested in social and family matters. I told them that no one should evade the law, that evading the law was wrong. However, I added, sometimes it was possible to work around the law in a particular way.

After giving it some thought, I suggested to them that they could avoid Amin's decree by forming the organisation as a company, a company limited by guarantee. A company is a different kind of entity, separate from the members that form it. If they did this, people would not look at it as a women's organisation, but as a company limited by guarantee. Ahaa! They were very excited. They agreed on this approach. Another lawyer, Audrey Weguro, and I were asked to draw up a constitution for this kind of company, and it wasn't long, towards the end of 1985, that Action for Development (ACFODE) was launched.

When I think about it, I believe I started to feel part of this ACFODE group from the beginning, although in a way, we were not even talking the same language. Let me explain that last statement. When Audrey and I submitted the constitution to ACFODE, we used the universal 'he' to mean everyone, the standard practice in Uganda at that time. Now these ACFODE women were arguing against the use of 'he', telling us that since ACFODE's members were women the proper pronoun to be used would be she'. I remember that Sebina Nalwanga, a member of the founding group at Makerere, was especially adamant on this point. I had never heard this strange idea before and I was surprised at the 'level of ignorance' of these women. Couldn't they understand my explanation that legally the word 'he' included 'she' which was obvious.

Little did I know at the time that, in fact, I was the one who was ignorant, to be more specific, gender ignorant, although all the time I was struggling for gender equality. I didn't yet understand that words have a huge effect on the matter being discussed or described. Imagine, ten years later I was one of two women, Hope Mwesigye being the other, who vehemently argued for the use of gender-neutral language in the writing of the Uganda Constitution during proceedings of the Constituent Assembly.

By the time the new constitution was being written in the late 1980s and early 1990s, I had come to recognise that such gender neutral language was absolutely essential if discrimination against women was to be eliminated. If only the pronoun 'he' is used in public discourse, we are all influenced by this discourse to think that men ('he') are the main public actors doing something important. Meanwhile, what about the women? Is the perception that the women are at home cooking and cleaning, doing something that's not very important? This kind of traditional, sexist discourse is part of patriarchal structures that position women in dependent relationships to men.

Anyway, working with ACFODE members in 1985 I demanded what I thought at that time to be the proper wording. I argued against the use of the word 'she' in the constitution and told the members that they either accepted my legal advice or they could leave it. Since they needed my services, they went along with me.

Let me expand on this point a little more. At that time, in late 1985, the perceptions that guided my life and my work were based on my inner convictions about the oppression of women and my long-time dream of creating something better. I had really been fighting against the injustices and unfair treatment which women were subjected to, but until this time I had had little contact with people who spoke about women from an informed viewpoint and used gender-sensitive language. Terms like gender sensitisation, gender conscientisation, gender-neutral language, even the word gender itself, were foreign to my vocabulary. Whenever I came to attend these women's meetings at Makerere, the participants used such words all the time. I remember that Hilda Tadria, the first Chairperson of ACFODE, would talk about 'gender, gender, gender,' and I would wonder, what is gender? Sebina Nalwanga would talk about gender conscientisation and, truthfully, I had trouble understanding what any of these women were talking about. Yet, for the most part, these women didn't bother to explain.

At that time, I didn't care much about learning new words. All I desired was a platform from which I could articulate about the discrimination women were facing. I simply wanted to get a public forum and speak forcefully about this problem. I hoped that my efforts would convince women that they should take action. I also hoped to convince men that they should be decent and fair. As a lawyer, I knew about human rights, and it was clear in my mind that women were being denied their rights. A burning desire in my heart was driving me to talk, act and do what I could.

Now for the first time I began to recognise that there were things I needed to learn. It was obvious that some women had moved beyond where I was positioned on this matter. They had learned from experience and from interactions with others that certain strategies and actions were needed if women were going to be liberated. My ignorance notwithstanding, when I listened to these women discuss the Nairobi conference, I thought that this group was the right place for me. I felt at home with them, and I believed I would soon catch up with their language.

As ACFODE was launched, its major goal was to uplift the status and standards of women to enable them to participate more meaningfully in development. The name ACFODE, Action for Development, set the tone. The founding members structuring this organisation were not content to just talk. They wanted action! They wanted forward movement for women. A motto was carefully worked out to include the organisational goals. To this day, the sentiments in this motto are there to inspire us: 'Breaking through, Building up, and Binding.' When we looked at women's place in society and the conditions of their lives, some things needed to be broken, broken down, and women needed to break through all the constraints on them. Then we needed to build women up, to inspire and empower, to build confidence and love for ourselves and for each other.

As I have mentioned, the binding part had a parallel in the NRM's Ten Point Programme. Ugandans needed to unite if we were going to build and develop our country. Women were in a particularly fragmented situation, divided not only by tribe, region and religion, but also divided by patriarchal structures that demanded that women be loyal first to family and religion, often at great cost to themselves and other women. Patriarchal society encouraged unity among women only in loyalty to social structures led by men that discriminated against women. For example, in the Mothers' Union, members were supposed to serve a male-led religious body. In this organisation, women were the servants and the leadership was exclusively male. The major decisions in the church were made by men, while women cooked meals for guests and sewed religious pieces for the altar.

In ACFODE, committees were formed. I was elected in absentia to be the organisation's first legal adviser and Chairperson of the Legal and Political Committee. In that role I was very soon asked to write about the rights of women so that ACFODE could distribute this information to women and women's organisations. The exact conversation that led to this initiative may be interesting to the reader. As I recall it, Chairperson Maxine Ankrah remarked one day that women didn't know their rights. I said, 'I know them.' Quickly recognising the opportunity, she asked me to write about this subject for publication. I first wrote a poem called 'Women, Know Your Rights' and then a booklet that provided an overview of women's rights in Uganda.

The booklet, *Know Your Rights,* covered such topics as laws of marriage and divorce and inheritance, and so forth. The booklet was used for several years thereafter to teach women their rights. Soon after this publication was issued, the decision was made to broadcast this important information on radio. In a short time I was on air on Radio Uganda every Wednesday evening talking about women's rights. The programmes which were broadcast in Runyankore, Rukiga and English (the three languages I could converse in) to reach a wide audience, were recorded ahead of time and then played on Wednesday night. This programme was one way that people started to know my name and to associate me with the struggle for women's emancipation.

It was an exciting time in ACFODE in spite of the fact that we had no office, not even a room of our own, not a single typewriter nor a phone. We laughed about working out of our handbags. But we were starting to take action. The organisation had exceptional leaders and a growing number of committed members ready to work. Dr Maxine Ankrah, the Chairperson, was an organisational specialist. Maxine combined the ability to lead with her vision from Nairobi about how women should work together in unity.

I should add that Maxine was a driver. She drove us to take action. It seemed like sometimes there was a mile between Maxine and those following her. It was very clear that she had ideas, and on many occasions others could see that she was moving in the right direction, and they would rally around her. One challenge I had working with Maxine was that at times I didn't understand her because she talked so fast and I had trouble picking up her American accent (Maxine is an American married to a Ghanaian). Another challenge I had working with Maxine was that at times she wanted us to follow before I myself was ready. In general no one drives me along unless I fully understand what is happening. Maxine was sensitive to this. Sometimes I would ask her for more information about something that I didn't really understand. When that happened, she would come to my office and carefully explain the matter under consideration. We would then discuss the issue at length until the two of us had agreement on what was at stake and what action to take. It soon became obvious that Maxine's vision and my questions about how the vision could be translated to the local setting were a good combination.

As the organisation was taking shape, Maude Mugisha, one of Maxine's students at Makerere, was chosen to be ACFODE's first executive secretary. Maude brought a rare talent as an administrator to the organisation. She had the ability to take ideas and desires and implement them, turning them into *action*, which after all was what everyone wanted. Maude's outstanding work behind the scenes kept the organisation on track for the nine years she was there.

Perhaps the best way to describe that early period in ACFODE is to say that we were learning on the job. I recall the day that Maxine brought me a book on how to write proposals and asked me to write a proposal for funds for legal education. I sat right down with paper and pen and the book on my lap and wrote the first proposal I had ever written. With some input from others, the proposal took shape and was soon approved by OXFAM. One thing I learned early about ACFODE is that once a woman joined ACFODE, she would never be the same again. She became truly empowered. That is precisely what happened to me. I became empowered in a special new way and then went out determined to help other women empower themselves.

As 1985 drew to a close, things in Uganda were at their darkest. Violence was out of control. The country was not under one central rule. The Western region was controlled by Museveni's National Resistance Movement, while the rest of the country, including Kampala, was under the military rule of the late Okello Lutwa who had overthrown the Obote government through a coup d'etat in July 1985, in fact just a few days before the Nairobi conference concluded (some delegates to the Nairobi conference didn't return to Uganda but went directly into exile). One consequence was that there was hardly any rule of law to talk about. The violence against women by the military was unbelievable, as numbers of girls and women were raped and killed. This violence took some very ugly forms. To give just one example, some pregnant women were being cut open with bayonets, supposedly in search for bullets. Life was actually impossible.

ACFODE had been founded with a burning desire to work for the betterment of women, and we had promised ourselves that we would take *action*. The members decided we must now actively protest the violence against women. At one meeting we agreed that we would go to the City Square (currently called Constitutional Square) to demonstrate against rape. In this way we would denounce violence against women as our first public act. Somehow those in authority learned about our plans, and, as we were soon informed, the army quickly made plans to send soldiers to City Square to rape the women demonstrators. Lucky enough for us, Agnes Mujaju, an ACFODE member who worked at Radio Uganda, heard about the army's intentions and informed Dr Hilda Tadria, ACFODE's first chairperson.[1]   So, in the night, word about the army's intentions was spread among the ACFODE members. The result was that we did not demonstrate against rape at the City Square, and we really felt bad. We felt defeated.

We were however not prepared to accept defeat, so we hatched another plan. We decided to write to the army commander seeking an appointment with him to discuss the rape and other forms of violence unleashed by army soldiers against women. When it was time for the meeting, the army commander sent Uganda's First Lady, Mrs Lutwa, to meet us in his place. What an insult, to send this wife of the President, who had little education and not one bit of power or authority herself, to talk to us! Talk to us about what? Womanly things? We intended to talk about this critical issue, the rape of our women by soldiers, and they sent us this lady!

When I was informed, I refused to go. Some members of ACFODE decided to go and meet this lady. But what could one expect from such a meeting? I heard it was a disaster. Incidents like this prepared the way for us to be very grateful when the NRM government took over power in January 1986. The important point here is that with all our convictions and commitment, with all our vigour, the atmosphere in 1985 and before was simply not conducive to women's active participation in public life. In spite of our burning desire to work for the advancement of women, under these repressive dictatorships, we were helpless.

However, the New Year brought a change. When the NRM government arrived toward the end of January 1986, we at ACFODE said, this looks like our chance. One of our early successes concerned International Women's Day, March 8. 1986 was not the first year that Women's Day was commemorated in Uganda. Previously a small number of women close to the government were the ones who were invited through the National Council of Women to Women's Day programmes at the State House.

In 1986 Women's Day was celebrated more meaningfully because for the first time women participated in organising it, with ACFODE playing a leading role. President Museveni was our guest of honour in Kampala that year. This was his first meeting with women in the International Conference Centre. Over 500 women were present at this event which closed a week of activity. This was the beginning of more visibility for Women's Day. I was not able to participate in the first real celebration of Women's Day in March 1986, because by that time I had delivered my last child. I had a rather difficult childbirth and had to remain in Mulago Hospital with complications for a whole month.

Later, in 1989, the NRC, spearheaded by Hon. Rubega Byekwaso, at that time Minister of Gender, voted to make International Women's Day a national public holiday in Uganda to honour all the women in the country. This created an entirely new atmosphere on that day, with countrywide celebrations. Since that time, each year one district is chosen, on a rotating basis, to hold the national celebration for the day. However, every district takes charge of its own Women's Day celebration with large numbers of women and girls taking part - women's groups of all kinds, girl guides, primary school girls, and so many others. There is singing, dancing, drama, and poetry reading. Oh, it's a glorious way to celebrate being a woman, and to thank women for their contribution to the country, to take stock of women's advancement for the past year and to lay new strategies and plans for the next year.

One of ACFODE's next projects was to conduct a national conference, funded by UNIFEM, in Mukono in December 1986 to inform the women of Uganda about what had taken place at the Nairobi conference. It was our intention to bring to these women the spirit of Nairobi which had so inspired us. Not only were four women from each district invited to participate, but a general call went out for all interested women to come. We invited a Kenyan woman to be the keynote speaker for the conference. Dr Eda Gacukia was our first choice. She was unable to attend, but she sent another Kenyan woman, Njoka Wainaina, to come in her place.

I was asked to present a paper on the weaknesses of the National Council of Women and the need for a national machinery to integrate Ugandan women in development. After carefully studying the decree establishing the Council, I presented a critique of the NCW, showing its many contradictions. For example, the NCW was a government body supposed to be an umbrella for women's non-governmental organisations, and yet it was used to ban them. The NCW was supposedly set up to serve women and yet it was actually suffocating women's initiatives to create their own organisations.

Presenting that paper was not the most important thing for me at that conference. What was important was the keynote address by Njoka Wainaina. That address really caught my attention. This Kenyan woman stood on the platform and talked to a large gathering of people who were strangers to her. She talked confidently from an informed position on 'gender' and 'development.' Because of the way she presented the ideas, it seemed that every woman there understood what she was talking about, even though some of the terminology and the ideas were new to us. Her presentation on African women and development made sense to the women listening. After all, she was talking to us about our own circumstances. Additionally, her talk made us think in new ways.

In comparison to that woman speaker, at that time I didn't even know for sure how to use the word gender, and I certainly did not know how to talk from an informed perspective about development. The woman was self-assured and very impressive. As I watched her and listened to the message she brought to that group of more than 200 Ugandan women, I wondered if I would ever be able to stand before an audience like that with assurance and something of value to say. This was 1986. As described in Chapter Two, in 1987 I attended a small group seminar on Women and Politics in Zimbabwe. Additionally, I went to a conference in Moscow but did not speak. It was in 1989 that I had my first chance to address a very large, prestigious audience, and to receive a warm response to my words.

This time I went as the official representative of the Government of Uganda. The conference held in Abuja, the capital of Nigeria, was organised by UNECA (United Nations

Economic Commission for Africa) to evaluate the Arusha strategies on integrating women into development and to share the national experience of development efforts. Mr Kasirye, the Permanent Secretary in the Ministry of Gender, called me in to tell me that I had been chosen to represent Uganda at the conference. He told me something that makes me laugh even today. He said, 'You see, we don't have much money to send a big delegation but when we send Matembe, it is equal to sending four women.' When I learned that I would be going to this conference, I immediately thought of my long-time dream that I had cherished for so many years.

You know, the Abuja conference in October 1989 was not like a national conference in Uganda or even a sub-regional· gathering. It was for the entire African region. Not only were there country delegates from across the continent, but also there were donors and representatives from international women's organisations. A representative from each country was given between five and ten minutes to talk. I had carefully prepared my paper, gathering statistics and other information from many sources. However, when I stood on the conference platform, I didn't need to look at the paper. In fact, I am aware that if I try to read from notes or read from a paper when I am giving a presentation, it goes flat. Instead I spoke from the heart about the NRM government's pro-women programmes - affirmative action was a special point - as well as what women activists and women's organisations were doing. I know how to blow the trumpet, and it was easy to blow the trumpet for the NRM government. Within five minutes, towards the end of my short report, I got a standing ovation. I couldn't believe it. When I finished, people stood a second time, clapping enthusiastically.

Afterwards, many people came to shake my hand and thank me for my report. Immediately after my presentation, to my surprise, I was called to address a press conference organised by a reporter working at the UN. At the press conference, members of the press asked me about what was happening in Uganda. I found myself answering their questions confidently. After all, they were asking me about the work I was doing as a Member of Parliament, as Chairperson of ACFODE (since 1989), and as a member of the Constitutional Commission. I was not talking from the books I read, but about the work I was immersed in and the progressive movement I was part of. As the reader will know by now, it has never been hard for me to talk in any place, to any audience about my favourite subject, the emancipation of women. Another point is that I think I was saying what people wanted to hear. I was telling a story of moving forward, of action, of success for women and for the country of Uganda, indeed for Africa.

When I got back to my hotel room, I thought about that day in 1986 at ACFODE's conference in Mukono when I had heard the Kenyan woman speak, and I had wondered if I could ever do such a thing. And now here I was. I remember thinking that my mother would be proud of me. But this day had another surprise waiting for me. Later, between sessions, a representative from the UN Economic Commission for Africa, the sponsors of the conference, told me that he had heard my presentation. He said, 'You are the right one to go to Arusha and talk on popular participation in the economic recovery of Africa.' 'But,' I asked him, 'What is popular participation?' I truly did not know.

You see how uninformed I was at that time. But I was beginning to figure many things out. It wasn't hard to see the difference between my presentation in Abuja and the presentations of other women representing their countries. My report on Uganda described a country that had gone through a major fundamental change that included a new outlook on women, and I was proclaiming our successes. Other delegates used more traditional approaches. One would say that in her country the law says this, or, you see, the law of succession says this. But, the real questions were, were these laws being implemented, how were they being implemented and what did those laws actually mean for women?

I was reporting that in Uganda many women had entered politics at every level, that by then we had nine women ministers and 41 women MPs. I described the revolutionary LC system that had a Secretary for Women's Affairs at each of the five levels of local government. Additionally, we had both a Directorate for Women's Affairs in the NRM Secretariat and the Ministry of Women and Development.

If the integration of women in development was the subject of this conference, well, that is exactly what we in Uganda had been doing, with good results. Then there was the Uganda Constitutional Commission which in that same year (1989) had been given the task of writing a new constitution based on how people said they wanted to be governed. As a Member of Parliament, a member of the Constitutional Commission, and Chairperson of ACFODE, I was speaking with authority, but backed by all those structures. While we in Uganda were addressing the integration of women in development, we were dealing with the real issues, looking at how to implement the law, and we were taking action. It seemed that others were just talking and perhaps in the process deceiving themselves that they were doing something.

It is interesting that for me, one thing led to another at these women's conferences. Here I was in Abuja, talking about the many exciting things that were happening for women in Uganda, and, because of my input, I was being asked to participate in the next conference on 'popular participation.' It appeared that, after a late start due to political insecurity, Uganda was playing a leading role in Africa on women and development. My story of women's successes in Uganda appeared to inspire other women who were just getting started in their countries, who needed viable ideas and the courage to take action. One might say that Uganda was serving as a role model on women and development in Africa. You know, when you are declaring what is real, telling it to the world is no problem. You find no difficulty in telling it.

When I arrived home from Abuja, I received an official invitation to the conference on popular participation to be held in Arusha, Tanzania in 1990. Of course, I attended, and in the process learned about another subject being discussed in development circles at that time. This was the first international conference for Africans to discuss popular participation in the economic recovery of Africa. On the first day of the conference, there was a general discussion about the conference goals.

Since I had little idea of the meaning of 'popular participation', I listened carefully to what different presenters were saying on the subject. What I got from that discussion was that popular participation meant that *everybody* should participate. In any programme to promote Africa's recovery, stability and sustained development, everyone had to be included as an active participant.

Then, in that very large, international gathering of men and women representing government and civil society, I put up my hand to speak. The Secretary General for UNECA, Adedeji Adebayo, who was acting as Chair, called on me. Earlier he had said that there had been popular participation in Africa since before colonial times. I had to disagree. I said, 'If popular participation means allowing everybody to participate in important discussions that concern their own affairs, then you people are not speaking the truth. There has never been popular participation in Africa. There hasn't been popular participation even in the home.' I said, 'The decisions of the elderly men are the decisions that bind the home, forgetting the voices of the women, the children and the youth.' I said, 'Even you people here. In your offices how many of you allow your secretaries to come in and discuss the matters that concern the management of the offices you run?' I said, 'There is no popular participation at all if that's the meaning that I'm getting.' When I said that, many people stamped their feet and clapped and clapped.

Then, in the evening, the Secretary General called the women delegates together, and told us that the next day when President Mwinyi of Tanzania officially opened the conference, they wanted to have a statement given on behalf of African women. Immediately all those women looked at me and said, 'Let Matembe give that statement.' I couldn't believe that I was being chosen to address that large gathering, speaking for all African women.

You know what I did? I used the popular participation method. I asked women to come to my hotel because I needed their help to write the statement. At the meeting in the hotel lobby that evening, I asked them what they wanted me to say at the conference 'on behalf of African women', and they gave me their ideas. For me, in my head and in my heart, I knew this was the time for me to talk about African women and their suffering. Since the time I had become an activist for women, I had tried to understand the position of women in African society. Think about it. Women bear and raise the children. They care for the sick, the elderly and the handicapped. In Africa, women grow most of the food, and then process and store it for family use. They prepare the meals, which also means collecting water and firewood. And what do women get in return for all they do? They have no rights to land. Throughout their lives they have only temporary homes from which they may be chased at any time. They get little respect or praise. They have almost no voice in decision making at home or in public affairs. And, if they speak up about the injustices of their lives, they get themselves in trouble. Yes, I had a lot to say.

When I gave my statement the next day, I spoke from my heart for all the women living on the African continent. I have a poem called, 'Women of Uganda, What shall I call you?' At that time I had not yet written that poem, but I had thought about these things so much that I had the right words ready when it came time to speak for my sisters across the continent. I started by saying that women in Africa are the factories that produce the children, children they neither have rights to nor control. Women are the 'water pipes' that transport water from the streams and wells to the households, carrying that water on their heads. Women are the donkeys, the most common beasts of burden, who carry all kinds of heavy loads on their backs and heads, even when they are pregnant. Women are the tractors that break the soil, working the land which they neither own nor control.

When I finished, I got a standing ovation again. President Mwinyi asked, 'Who is this person?' and he called me over to shake his hand. When someone told him I was from Uganda, he said, 'Oh, this is one of President Museveni's women.'

When I was making my statement that day there was a cartoonist in the audience. The next day a cartoon he created was pinned on the notice board, a cartoon reflective of my speech. He called it 'The Credentials of the African woman.' The cartoon shows a woman who looks a bit like me. She is walking 'on all fours,' like a donkey.[2] She is wearing eye glasses and women's shoes on her feet, the way I was dressed that day, but she also has a tail. In one hand this woman is holding a section of water pipe with water coming out of it. A sleeping baby rests on her back. A large, heavy-looking bag draped around her neck hangs in front. The woman is harnessed to a small plough that is being guided by a man who has a whip in one hand and is saying, 'Haraka', Swahilis 'quick forward'. Four statements are listed about the woman: 1) Most efficient beast of burden; 2) Plougher of most of the land which she does not own; 3) Manufacturer of children she doesn't own; 4) Most effective replacement for water pipe.

Everyone who saw the cartoon on the board said that they must have a copy. So copies were ordered for everybody. Later on, the cartoon was reproduced in various magazines. Of course, I wasn't credited but that didn't matter. The cartoon has been circulated throughout Uganda. Even these days, I will see a copy of it on some office bulletin board, no doubt put there by some woman worker who agrees with the sentiments expressed.

One year before the Beijing conference which was to take place in 1995, there was an Africa regional meeting held in Dakar, Senegal, with the goal of preparing the Africa Platform of Action for Beijing. You should have seen the delegation from Uganda! What a contrast to the Nairobi conference in 1985. In 1994 in Dakar the Ugandan delegation was large, made up of representatives from the government and the NGOs. We had prepared well, and we were united in purpose and spirit. Although at that time I was a Member of Parliament and a member of the Constituent Assembly, I went to Dakar as an NGO representative for ACFODE. The delegation from Uganda went to Dakar with high expectations. We were ready to do our part in making sure that African women were fully prepared for the Beijing conference.

As I arrived in Dakar on the evening before the opening of the conference, I was in for a major surprise. The Ugandans there were informed that the Hon. Specioza Kazibwe, Gender Minister at that time, the government appointed spokesperson, would not arrive at the conference in time to present the country paper as scheduled the next day. An emergency meeting was called. The government delegates who had arrived that same day sat together with the NGO representatives and decided that Matembe should be the one to speak for Uganda. I was told that in Kazibwe's absence I would be delivering the paper. 'But,' I said, 'I don't have the paper? Where is it?'

The answer came. 'With Kazibwe,' I was told. 'But,' they added, 'we know that you'll be able to deliver the paper, even if you have not seen it.'

'Fine,' I said. So the next day I went onto the platform to speak for Uganda. However, my words that day were not quite as usual. In fact, I almost caused a riot. From the beginning of the conference everyone could see that it was being badly managed. First of all, the site was a disaster. In Kampala, meetings of this size and importance would have been held at the International Conference Centre which is specifically designed for such meetings. In Dakar the conference was being held in a business centre which was just not able to provide the necessary support services for such a large, prestigious group. Imagine, the first day's events had to be postponed because there was no electricity in the building. It's true. The meetings started a day late. While the organisers were trying to get the problems corrected, we were just hanging around the conference site. Things were bad. Because of the problems with the lights, the women felt very insecure, especially when going to the washrooms.

When I was thinking about what I was going to say when I went to the platform on the second day, I decided that this was not the time to be polite and pretend that everything was all right. Instead I decided to speak the truth on behalf of African women. Standing on the platform I boldly stated some of the things that the women delegates had been saying among themselves.

I started, 'I am so happy that the African woman has mobilised herself to this level of magnitude.' It was noticeable that at this conference African women filled the hall. At earlier conferences there had been a large number of European and American women who sometimes spoke on behalf of African women. This conference was different.

I continued, 'I'm so glad that we are here to talk about what concerns us. But,' I said, 'can you imagine the African women gathering to this extent, and I don't see the President of this country here to welcome us and open this conference. What is he doing? As if that is not enough, how can he bring us here to meet in this business centre? I want to ask, if this was the Organisation of African Unity, full of male delegates, would they be put here in this business centre where the electricity disappears and we are subject to insecurity? Where is the conference centre in this country? Why aren't we in the conference centre? How dare you treat African women this way?' Everybody was standing and clapping and shouting.

'How can we gather here and show the magnitude of our power and muscle in this continent, and we are marginalised to this extent? How dare you?' I said again. 'If we can be marginalised on this continent, on the soil of Africa, how shall we be treated far away, there in Beijing?' And I said, 'You women of Africa, rise up and resist all these things.' When I finished this angry accusation, the women in the hall were clapping and cheering.

The man in charge of the conference arrangements, the Executive Secretary for UNECA, decided that I had said enough. He said to me, 'Your time is over'.

I said, 'No. You are telling me that my time is over because yesterday our meetings were spoiled since you arranged badly. So let me talk.' As on other occasions, when I was speaking up in public for women, I got a standing ovation. People were saying, 'Ahah that's very good.'

From that time, for the rest of the conference, that UNECA Executive Secretary, whenever there was a question and I put up my hand, he would come and say, 'You know, madam...' I'm smiling now as I think about this poor man. He'had to befriend me, to be very friendly so that I didn't raise more hell for him. In fact, this UNECA Executive Secretary who was responsible for the conference arrangements was sacked before the Beijing conference was held.

After I had cleared the air about the bad situation at the conference, I made a statement describing Uganda's impressive record on women. As I had done on so many occasions I blew the Ugandan trumpet about our achievements on women being integrated into development. In the evening we heard the news that the Hon. Speciosa Kazibwe had been appointed Vice-President of Uganda. Several women came up to me saying, 'You must be the one.'

I said, 'No, I'm not the one.'

They said, 'You mean there is another woman in Uganda as forceful as you?'

I told them, 'In Uganda we are so many.'

The next year, 1995, a delegation from Uganda of more than 200 went to Beijing. This time, four Ugandan women were invited to address plenary sessions. Hon. Winnie Byanyima talked on women and globalisation. My subject was strategies to increase the participation of women in politics. Hon. Byanyima and I both got standing ovations after our talks in the NGO Forum. By the time the VP arrived, the name of Uganda was being passed all over the place. The Vice-President and the First Lady, Mrs Janet Museveni, also addressed plenary sessions of the official government conference.

Another highlight was that the members of the Ugandan delegation were hosted by the Ugandan Ambassador to China in Uganda House in Beijing. For the first time, the VP, the First Lady, parliamentarians, representatives from the NGOs, all of us were there, singing and eating together. So didn't ACFODE reach its objectives? Women united and speaking with one voice!

At this point I want to return to my participation in ACFODE, where I was getting a proper education. Working for that pioneer organisation, I was learning how to analyse situations, how to talk proper gender talk, how to write proposals and convince donors that they should fund our activities, and so

many more things that later proved useful. Working with
ACFODE was really satisfying. Imagine, planning strategies
and working with a large number of dedicated women activists
who believed in 'action'. We ACFODE women looked for
creative ways to use our talents to forward women's cause. We
were conducting seminars, workshops and training of different
kinds, but when I was Chairperson, I felt that perhaps we could
communicate more effectively to the public by presenting a
play. Yes, Matembe, the dramatist again, Matembe, the actor.

A proposal I wrote for $5000 from the Global Fund to do a
public relations campaign about gender equality was approved.
I decided to work with the Ndere Troupe, a group of young,
very talented, local performers who featured African dance,
music and drama. At that time I served as a member of the
Board of Trustees for the troupe, a position I still hold. I told
the Ndere performers that we had money for posters but asked
them if we couldn't make both posters and do a play. They
agreed.

Actually, I spent a lot of time with them discussing what I
wanted to achieve. The message I wanted to get out to the
public had several factors: what is meant by gender equality;
what is it that women want; what leads to discrimination
against women and undermines their status; and what can be
done to change the situation.

This play depicted a family in which a husband was
mistreating his wife. The woman went to several places to try
to get help. She went to the clan elders and was told that a
woman should be beaten. She went to the police and was told
that this was a family matter. She went to the neighbours and
they refused to get involved. Finally, she went to FIDA, the
Association of Women Lawyers, which took her case to court
where the woman won the case.

At the end of the play, all the men were lined up on one side
of the stage, and the women on the other side, for dramatic
effect, and they were all shouting at each other. At that point,
I walked to the centre of the stage to discuss what this ugly
scene was all about. Now this wasn't a lecture. It was drama,
and I made it fun. I asked the players, what exactly was causing

the problem? And the women said – the men, and the men said – the women. That's when I discussed the factors involved: poverty, discrimination in customary law, religious misinterpretation, and so on. There were about five factors. In the end, we said, 'so now, who is causing the problem?' The answer was not who, but these factors. And women ended up learning that men are also prisoners of the system; they are also victims in this unfair system.

The players named the play 'Time Bomb', because women in Uganda were obviously moving forward, and if men were not willing to give women space and fair treatment, the bomb would blow. The play included role switching and a lot of humour. This very entertaining show was presented at the National Theatre and attracted a lot of attention. It was called back twice.

The impact of the play was noticeable. Remember, the subject of domestic violence was really taboo in Uganda at that time. People just did not talk about wife beating. The poor women had to suffer in silence with no help in sight. Now here was this play breaking the rule of silence. The play gave people a beginning for talking about this problem. I should describe a funny incident.

One woman, whose husband beat her all the time, mobilised her fellow women to come to see the play. The man came, too. This man was actually very mad because he thought he was the one being played on the stage. Later he beat his wife, yelling at her, 'How can you go and tell the whole world to come and see me up on the stage?' Of course, the extra beating wasn't good, but he got the message, as did many people who attended.

As I've said, when you worked for ACFODE, you found yourself empowered without looking for empowerment. The poem I wrote called 'ACFODE, My Second Mother' reproduced on page 115 is about how ACFODE empowered me. But as ACFODE empowered me, I realise that I also empowered the organisation, as reflected in my poem, 'ACFODE, My First Daughter'.

One thing that we in ACFODE had learned from Maxine Ankrah was never to say 'if.' This tough woman with a vision taught us to remove 'if' from our vocabulary and replace it with 'when'. In her view, there was no chance for failure. ACFODE's move to Spear Motors illustrated this approach (see page 109).

When Maxine was ready to step down as Chair, she urged me to run for that position. She even came to our home and lobbied my husband to convince me. I was very reluctant to take up this leadership role in part because I didn't see how I could do it, measuring myself next to her as I was doing. But Maxine has always been good at identifying talent. As I look back, I can see that right from the start, she recognised my commitment, my outspokenness and my honesty, and she saw these qualities as assets to the organisation.

When I was elected Chair in 1989, I played a different kind of role from the one Maxine had played. What did I do there in that position? I was the 'big mouth.' I was good at initiating ideas. Maude (Mugisha) is an expert at translating those into fundable proposals. And then, with my big mouth, I would talk loudly asking for funding on the basis of those proposals. Once we had funding, the extraordinary women of ACFODE turned those plans and programmes into action. Under the leadership of Maxine, ACFODE built its strong foundation. When I was elected Chair, that foundation was complete, ready for the rest of ACFODE to be constructed. It was then my privilege to lead this organisation during the period of its greatest growth and success.

When I left my position as Chair and handed over that office to somebody else, I wrote the poem, 'ACFODE, My First Daughter.' Remember I have four sons, no daughters. So through this very special organisation, I was being empowered and at the same time helping other women to empower themselves. When I think about my experience in ACFODE, it was like I was in a *shamba*, where all the fruits were ripe and I was really picking those fruits.

Women of Uganda

Women of Uganda!
What shall I call you?
I am desirous of giving you a name
But which one

Please advise me
Which name should I give you?

Shall I call you tractors?
For you till the land
Which you do not own?
Yes, you till the land all day long!
But what is your pay?
What payment does a tractor receive
for tilling the land?
Please help me to answer

Women of Uganda!
What shall I call you?
I am desirous of giving you a name
Women of Uganda
You deserve yet another name
But which one?
Please advise me
Which name shall I give you?

Shall I call you factories
For you produce children,
Whom you neither own nor control
Yes, you are factories for you have no
control over your uteruses
Yes, you are factories when you
produce sons
But rejected factories when you
produce girls
But what is your pay?
What payment does a factory receive
for production?
Please help me to answer

Women of Uganda
You deserve yet another name
But which one?
Please advise me
Which name shall I give you?
Yes, you are donkeys

For you are ever heavy laden
With heavy luggage both on the
head and at the back
Today it's a water pot on the head
And the baby on the back
Tomorrow it's a load of firewood on
the head
And a seven months pregnancy
But what is your pay?
What payment does a donkey
receive for carrying a load?
Please help me to answer.

But women of Uganda
Donkeys are treasured by their
owners and users
Tractors are also valued by their
owners and users
Factories are great assets to their
owners and users
But what about you?
Who knows your worth?
Beasts of burden they call you
Chattels is your name
For they buy you with bride price

Women of Uganda
I mourn for you
You are at the centre of Production
But at the periphery of benefit
You hold half the sky on your head,
and humankind in your hands
But have no home, you only own
one, at the will of men
You have no children

Women of Uganda
For how long will this be
For how long will you be silent
Time has come that you must talk
Yes, you must shout, that the world
may hear
That society will understand
And your cry for your rights will be
heard
And Ah! A better name you shall get.

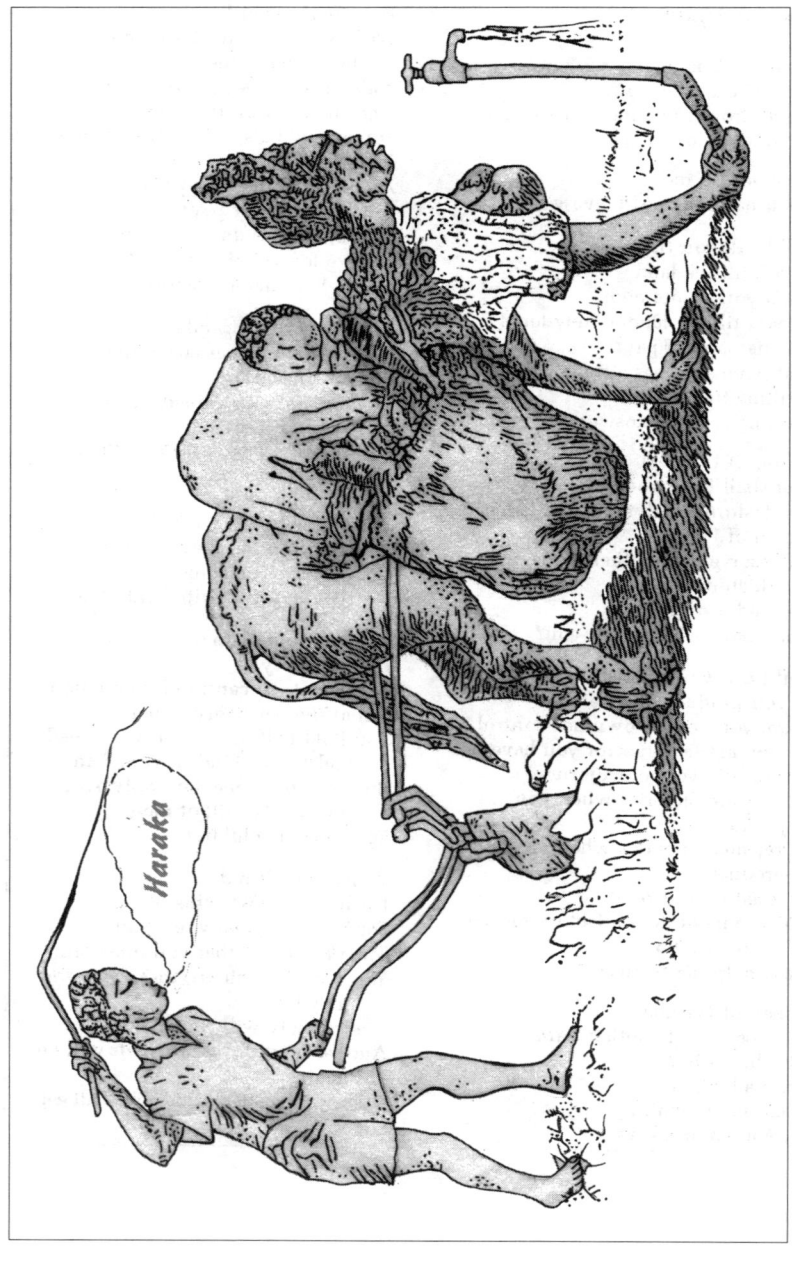

What Others Say *(Maxine Ankrah and Maude Mugisha)* Their dialogue with the author on the founding of ACFODE

The women's organisation, ACFODE, was founded in the wake of the Nairobi conference. In June 2000, Hon. Miria Matembe, Dr E. Maxine Ankrah and Maude Mugisha had a dialogue about the founding of ACFODE. Nancy Dorsey acted as facilitator.

Dorsey: We're here together so that the three of you can recall those first days of ACFODE. What was it like? What made ACFODE special? Why was it different? All those things.

Ankrah: I think that what was special was what Maude was saying yesterday when we met. She said we were pacesetters. Pacesetters are people who will take risks, people who are not afraid to venture out, to be different. Now, you must have heard how we came to call the organisation Action for Development, and what we perceived as women together talking with each other.

Many of the organisations for women in Uganda at that time had a lot of talk, but not much action. And a lot of the talk was about tomato planting, Bible verse learning, being good wives if you were married and 'bad women' if you were not - that was one of the bases of the sectarianism. Such organisations did little to reach women beyond their little cliques and clubs. And so there was an awareness that if we were going to really be different then we had to do and not simply talk about action. People had to see us make a difference, and this difference had to contribute to the development of Uganda. It couldn't just enrich 'me.' Some of us might become professors and executive officers and government ministers, but our organisation had to be beyond ourselves. And it was that vision. What could we do to really contribute to the development of Uganda? What could we show as action of women? How could we really, really be ourselves? That drove us. It was energising.

It was then as we sat together in some little cubby hole of a room, most often at Makerere, that we came up with the motto. 'Breaking through, Building up, and Binding'. First we were to realise that we had to break down all those barriers that limited women, even among ourselves. But also we had to build up ourselves and other women. And then we had to bind ourselves together for real strength. Right now as I'm talking about it, I can feel the excitement again of that time in 1985.

Matembe: Yes, there are two things that must come out clearly. The name and the motto. They were not just for the sake of having a name and a motto. The name: 'Action for Development.' From the time the women started getting together, I think there was no rest in their minds. Every time the meetings broke up, they were thinking, now, what are we going to do? It was in that perspective of thinking about what we're going to do to bring the spirit of Nairobi to the women of Uganda, that this name came to Joy Kwesiga in a dream. She dreamed that the organisation should be called Action for Development, ACFODE, because we wanted to be women of action. That name, you can see, is reflective of what the vision was.

Number two, we wanted to have action for development, but in which way? We wanted to break down the barriers that keep women in bondage and slavery, and in disunity. So, break these things down so that women can be free. Then, we wanted to build up the things that women need, such as confidence, skills, knowledge, commitment, hard work, so that women can fulfil their full potential for the development of the country. And then we wanted to bind ourselves in solidarity and love for one another. So 'breaking down, building up and binding', these ideas were very crucial. They kept giving us the direction in which to move.

Mugisha: Maybe I can talk about my experience of being attracted to ACFODE. I remember that Maxine was our lecturer. When she returned from Nairobi, she was so excited about the conference, and talked about it in class. To me, this was something. She said that a few women had been meeting in her office. After the lecture, I asked her if we were allowed to come to the meetings, and she told me I could go. So one time I went to the office and there were six or seven women there. I was a student and was expecting a baby, but I listened. I soon realised that these people were talking about something I'd never heard before, but things I had thought about.

I was a member of Mothers' Union, a very keen worker, but I felt there was something I was missing there. At Mothers' Union I thought, but this is not my stuff. There was a longing for something else, but I couldn't have said what. But when I heard these women talk, I just felt something. I couldn't touch it, but I thought, this is something different. So, from that time, whenever

I would pass Maxine's office and see those women there, I would just leave what I was doing and join them.

Dorsey: Which took some nerve since you were a student.

Ankrah: But she was a mature student.

Mugisha: I was 29 at that time. So I just kept on listening in, listening in, and I started following up the meetings. When they talked, I realised they were talking about injustices against women and women rising up. It was something that I had always wanted to hear. Even when I was young, I was always wondering why, as a woman, you know, you don't talk, you don't challenge men and such things. My father would tell me, you know, no man will marry you. But when I heard these women, I said, this is where I belong. I'll find out how I can take part. And that's how I came to ACFODE. And then I was eventually asked to work with ACFODE. I had met Miria before in school. She was older and I know why she couldn't remember me, because if I saw her I would hide *(laughter)*. I would literally hide because Miria was so outspoken and, should I say, just different, non-conformist. I would enjoy when she was acting, like in *the Merchant of Venice*. I avoided her. I was afraid of her.

As I said, Maxine was my lecturer. When they talked, I saw that these women had something to offer. I thought we needed to get involved in this. When I came to work with ACFODE, I didn't mind what happened. I just felt, this is where my heart is, and this is what I want to do. I remember my husband asked me how much they were going to pay me, and I said, I didn't care, I hadn't even asked what the salary would be, because this is what I really want to do and to me, ACFODE was like a fulfillment of myself. That's when I got self-fulfilled. After I joined ACFODE, I was never the same. It turned my life around. Before, there were things I aspired to but I didn't know how to achieve. What I know is that what I'm describing is what ACFODE has done in many people's lives. ACFODE has built each one of us.

Matembe: The making of women.

Mugisha: The making. It has made us. And people will tell you, since I came to ACFODE, I have been able to discover myself.

Dorsey: Good, I think that has covered very well the goals and the vision. Now someone take up either activities or... You know, when I think about ACFODE, I think about how very different it was. Imagine, lobbying on women's issues, women really lobbying in Uganda at that time. Or doing things like finding out that there were government positions open and calling around until you found women with competencies and turning their CVs in so there would be more women considered. Wasn't that very new in Uganda?

Mugisha: Those things were very new and I think it was not understood. Recently, I was with someone who was in a certain position back then and she felt threatened by ACFODE. She said, 'Do you know these ACFODE women? Do you remember when they started struggling for jobs, when NRM had come and they wanted jobs. And they started turning in their CVs.' And I thought, my God, people didn't understand. Some people misunderstood, they thought ACFODE members were looking for jobs.

Matembe: Yes, we were badly misunderstood. You remember when we had just started in '85, then the NRM government came in '86. And it came in with some women who had been fighting in the bush war. And for us, we looked at NRM as the saviour. When they arrived, we were intending to lobby for the appointment of more women in decision-making positions. In the meantime, NRM arrived, and there were women there already.

Ankrah: Yes, but to understand this, we must remember, these were commanders. For the first time in Uganda, women were commanding men. Women also were soldiers, and they were fighters. But the most important thing wasn't that women were fighting, but that women were commanding. Mrs Njuba had the authority to shoot men who did not obey her orders. Mrs Zzizinga, a woman with little formal education, was one of the others. Mrs Mukwaya, at that time was not a university graduate. This was something absolutely unheard of in Uganda, that a woman would be in the army in the first place, and in the second place would be in a command position over men.

Matembe: So, for us, we actually looked at NRM as like our home, because they had women at these high levels, and we felt that this opened up the way for us to participate as well. So we would submit a list but, unfortunately, some of these women in NRM looked at us as if we wanted to take their positions. They were women who had come up, who were fighting, who were involved. Now, they said, who are these women who have been enjoying life at home, who went to school and got degrees, and are now coming to take our jobs. Who are they? So that's how they perceived us.

Ankrah: And the other part of that is who they thought we were. We were graduates, at the beginning, at Makerere, and so the perception that we would take the jobs was tied into the difference between the university graduates and the ordinary women, most of who were rural. They could not believe that we had no such motive. The women who came out of the bush were not university women. And that largely is why they didn't understand at the beginning.

Matembe: Then there were the existing NGOs which were already in position, mainly the National Council of Women which had been accepted as the main voice for the women. Because it was dealing with the government, the leaders really saw us as a threat. And what they did, they went to the government, some of them, to report us as traitors. I mean, as CIA agents. This American woman here (*Ankrah*).....

Ankrah: American-born.

Matembe: They went and told these fighters who had been in the bush, beware of these women called ACFODE because they are CIA agents. They are here to destroy you. And Maxine was really suffering. In the meantime, I had joined the RCs. When the National Political Commissar (NPC) called Maxine to go and defend the charge that she was CIA, she told me about it. So I went to the NPC. The NPC said, you are CIA since you have this American woman. So I said, but don't you know that I'm RC Secretary in Nakawa Division? I was a big woman there in the RCs. How can I be a CIA agent when I'm your supporter? Then I said, what about this message that the NRM came with. You told us about unity, that a good person is good irrespective of where they come from, and a bad one is bad irrespective of where they come from. Therefore, this American woman falls in the category of the good one. I told him, look, you have this Mr Pike, William Pike, at *The New Vision*, editing your government paper. Isn't he a white man? But you found him good just as we find Maxine good. So we won the case. Because I was a big woman in the RCs, there was no way I could have been dealing with CIA agents. But they really tried. But the women's NGOs.....

Ankrah: In a way they were our greatest enemies, other women. But there was another part of it, where the enemy was within. In November 1985 - this was just before we called on Miria to help write the constitution - when we contacted NGO women to see if they would just allow us to report back what happened in Nairobi.

Literally, that was our only request. We weren't yet looking to start a new organisation, but we wanted to discuss the conference and its significance for Ugandan women, to discuss this with Ugandan women. We asked, can we share ideas with you? And we were unable to get a single organisation in Uganda to respond. And so by November we said, let us start a new organisation, and that's when we found Miria to help us with drafting a constitution.

There was a problem here because I was not a Ugandan. However, I was the only one in the group who had been to Nairobi, and I was bringing people together to talk about the possibilities we had all been missing. When the first elections were held in ACFODE, Dr Hilda Tadria, a Ugandan, was chosen as leader, and it didn't matter to me. What we had in mind was bigger than my being the Chairperson. On the 19th of November 1985 ACFODE came into being. Then came the Christmas holidays, followed by Museveni's army taking over Kampala. When we met again, Hilda had taken a position out of the country, and we had to think about who would now occupy that position.

People kept saying that we must have a Ugandan, but nothing was decided. Finally, on the 26th of March, I gave an ultimatum. And it was Miria who understood what was being said: 'Have we not matured?', Miria asked. 'If this woman has the leadership qualities needed, and in fact if this woman is a woman, and we're going to be non-sectarian.' And that's when it came out, and I said to the Ugandans, 'Either you put me in this post or you take it.' Because, I thought, if you don't, you have not grown. You're not ready for me to lead you. And somehow that experience to make a decision for 'a woman' set a foundation that ACFODE has never abandoned. And that was the catalyst for many women to move away from the secretarian position that she's Muganda; she's Catholic; she's not a university woman; she's not married.

Mugisha: And I think that I found that very important. During the time we were in ACFODE, it never became an issue to know where somebody came from or what religion they followed. We just worked together.

Ankrah: Months and months later, we would say: 'You mean you're from there? I didn't know that.'

Matembe: Let me tell you the situation about tribes. When we organised the Mukono conference in December 1986, then we needed some interpreters. So we'd say, now there is this woman from Ankole. Who will interpret for her? What about the ones from Acholi? Someone would speak up, 'Oh, me, I speak Luo.' 'Oh,' we'd say, 'that's where you come from.' We really didn't know.

Ankrah: And that was a year after ACFODE had been inaugurated.

Matembe: As I think about what it was that made ACFODE an organisation with a difference, I think it came at a time when people had certain gaps in their lives, and it filled the gaps. Because if you join the organisation and you are fulfilled, now where is the time to ask about the tribe or the religious affiliation?

Ankrah: It was totally irrelevant, the tribe. And I think for the first time, as you said, women could begin to be themselves in a new way. If my tribe doesn't matter, then my sex matters much less, and my status, and what you think of me. As Maude said, then women really began to unfold. When we decided to be different, we thought, 'How can we be different in structuring our organisation?' And we looked around and said; One of the reasons is that in some NGOs women get to be the big bosses, and capture an NGO. Then, the NGOs don't change. An example of this is the tradition of an annual general meeting. That is, once a year the membership comes together, but all the rest of the year, the five women lord it over everybody else. Let us do it differently. Let us bring the membership together every month around whatever the subject, issue, or what have you, and so first 10, and then 20, and then 30 women began to attend the monthly meetings.

Mugisha: And then 80, and 150, so this has continued until the present time.

Matembe: And then in addition to that, we said, no opening of branches.

Ankrah: In fact, we said, if indeed we have branches like Mothers' Union, then everything will be flowing from the centre and people will look to the centre. But, do you remember this? We said, let's give the African spirit. Let's give other groups our agenda and then let them make their own agenda of whatever they want it to be.

Matembe: So we decided we would go to them, because, when you open a branch the executive officers are in Kampala. The other ones are isolated and they just stay there. And only once a year you call them together after which they go away. So, for us, we said 'No.' Anyone who wants to, should come and learn from ACFODE for their own agenda. When we go to the districts, we mobilise and educate them. If they want to learn about the organisation from us, okay. Then they can form their own groups with the ACFODE spirit, but not necessarily be a part of the ACFODE organisation.

Mugisha: Actually, that was very important, because you find that when you go to the rural areas, there are different groups. There's UWESO, TASO, NCW, many different groups. But that outreach, networking strategy we used would connect with the different groups of women. And we thought, if you form an ACFODE branch, then there would be another small pocket of women determining their own directions.

Ankrah: Do you know something that has just come to my mind? In '85, '86, or '87, neither Maude nor I thought in terms of 'networking.'

Mugisha: The word. (*laughter*)

Ankrah: We did it but we weren't conscious of what we were doing. And even now, it is just occurring to me what we were doing.

Mugisha: And that strategy of networking, we would make ourselves available for all the women's groups that wanted to take advantage of what we were doing, but especially working with us. So that any women who found what we were talking about interesting, who needed our expertise, who wanted to link with each other, could do so. And really we wanted women to do their thing. We didn't want to impose our wishes on them, but we could help to strengthen their own initiatives, to build on what they have. That is exactly what the networking strategy has achieved.

Ankrah: And guess what else. Even today, those women adopted from us what they wanted, but what they didn't need, they felt no constraint to do. However, across the whole of Uganda, ACFODE's agenda got taken up, adapted and imbibed. Suddenly, in addition to Mothers' Union and the National Council of Women, you had this women's NGO coming up, that NGO coming up. In the context of agriculture, law, education, what have you, and we energised and gave to women the model that became the women's rights agenda which was nowhere in the psyche of Uganda and in none of the organisations that were 5-10, 20, 30, 40 years of age. Therefore, by not putting our label on other women, we achieved far more than we even dreamed of. We had no idea what we were doing in that regard.

Mugisha: Actually, yesterday we were talking and we were remembering what ACFODE has packed off. It has packed it off. It went ahead, and we didn't even mind whether we were mentioned or not. I remember that conference in Mukono (December 1986). In fact, FIDA, as it was to become, was born at that conference, if I can say that. At that time FIDA was not involved in advocacy as yet.

Matembe: You know, when we started ACFODE, you (*Ankrah*) had this idea of writing about the rights of women. Remember, you assigned me to write a pamphlet on women's rights. You know, I had never been a member of FIDA. But when ACFODE took up the issue of women's rights, I told them at ACFODE, you know, here is FIDA, an organisation of women lawyers. Let us go and ask them to join us on the issue of rights for women. I went to FIDA and took out a membership. And there was Rebecca Kadaga who had also come in as a young woman with revolutionary ideas. She also wanted to move FIDA away from dinners and such things into real action. So when I joined, I told them that in ACFODE we are doing this. Why don't we work together? So we formed a committee to begin the discussion and then to reach out to the rural woman. We had served as volunteers. I remember Jennifer Bitalabeho was one of the group. We were talking about legal rights.

Mugisha: What I was also saying is that at the Mukono conference, there were other areas explored. There was also the issue of credit.

Ankrah: Everything, even the girl child, even prostitution, education, property rights. I don't remember specifically if land was mentioned, but every major area in the lives of women was touched upon. We met December 8-13, 1986 from Monday to Saturday morning.

Matembe: I think this was the first conference of its kind that brought rural women into such discussions. Not in a particular organisation. They just came as individuals to this first national conference for women in Uganda.

Ankrah: And guess what? Just as we were unable to get any single organisation to hold meetings about what happened in Nairobi, from the time of the conference in July 1985 to March 1986 when we organised ACFODE, until September when we started planning for the December 1986 conference in Mukono, no other group of women in Uganda had planned to bring women together to tell them about what had taken place in Nairobi. So we stepped into that gap, and that's why we said, 'Call, call, call everybody! Let's just tell people to come.' There were four representatives from each district, women from NGOs and individual women who came. We met right down here at the Theological College. It was nothing plush.

Mugisha: There were over 200 participants.

Ankrah: I remember walking into the dining room the first night. I lived on the college compound. It was unbelievable the numbers who came, and most were ordinary women. So this was truly a first in Uganda. No labels. Just women.

Mugisha: At that time, having more than 200 women together in a place like that in Uganda was unprecedented. Maxine mentioned the issue of credit, and it was the Mukono conference that stimulated the Uganda Women's Finance and Credit Trust. After they attended that conference, the women who founded UWFCT decided that they must do something tangible. They must form themselves and start giving service to the rural women. That's how they started.

Matembe: So the conference was an important catalyst.

Mugisha: It was a catalyst that led to different initiatives.

Ankrah: All across the whole spectrum of women's lives. And what we've not talked about is the perception and the opposition that remained. On the one hand, there were those who were saying, we must do something, As soon as she got involved, especially for Miria Matembe, because straightaway she started shouting.

Dorsey: That's what the book's about. Her shouting.

Ankrah: You should call it that. Big Mouth. I really mean it. Call it Big Mouth.

Matembe: Yeah. I don't mind.

Ankrah: Miria Matembe. Big Mouth. So, what we have here in me is a technocrat. I am a task oriented person. I get jobs done. We needed this political person, Miria, who could get the message across. And then we needed a very efficient person (referring to Mugisha) who, as you can see, was totally understanding and was caught up to move this thing day by day, year after year. It is only God alone that brought the three of us together for the women of Uganda.

Dorsey: (to *Mugisha*) How many years were you at ACFODE?

Mugisha: Nine years.

Ankrah: So what happened was, Maude had been my student. I taught, among other things, the theory and management of organisations, and the profession of social work. But I changed social work into a very devout, mental oriented profession, that you don't go and just read. You change things. And she caught almost everything that I was giving. And so I had two options, another woman, and guess what determined it. We offered her 25,000 a month....

Matembe: She was earning five thousand shillings!

Mugisha: It was 5,000!

Ankrah: At the beginning?

Matembe: Yes. I remember it very well. It was 5,000. Her salary was 5,000.

Ankrah: Of course, I never had a shilling from ACFODE, over all those years. What happened was that the husband of the other woman refused to let her take the job, because she had another job offer at a bank. Maybe that's where the 25,000 came in. Maybe her other offer was for 25,000. So Maude could take this job as executive secretary, because she could see what it was all about. The other candidate thought about salary.

Dorsey: All right. Let's talk about this issue a minute. You know I was in Women's Studies at Makerere with Joy Kwesiga for four years, and I was fascinated by Joy's stories talking about the organisation. ACFODE calls you at 10.00 at night, - you go! When the Indian woman was killed by her husband, the way women mobilised around that case![3] But Joy and her niece, who is a medical doctor living in Entebbe, went to the second autopsy, the official one, on Sunday morning at 8.00 a.m. Others were called to come, but these two busy women went. You could say that they didn't have time to do it, that no one could ask them to give up their Sunday with their families, but they went. That was the ACFODE spirit. So that sacrifice was made. Talk about that a little bit. Why did people give their time and effort and resources to ACFODE, and they gained.

Ankrah: Who talks about sacrifice? (*laughter*)

Mugisha: But what encouraged me in ACFODE was that ACFODE would never let you down. For me, as somebody who was working there, you call the members anytime, they would be there. All the time I was there, I never saw an executive meeting of ACFODE flop. I never saw any activity flop because members didn't turn up. And actually somebody, one of our drivers, described ACFODE very well. He said, 'ACFODE is like a church. People come in and go without anyone paying them. People come and take up activities without payment, without anyone compelling them to do anything.' What amazed me, even the first months at Makerere, when they were meeting in different offices, people would find stencils to do the work. They would use their own resources to come to the office. Because we didn't have anything when we started. We didn't have a typewriter. It was the members who would go and type the minutes and bring them ready.

Ankrah: And you sat over there on that side of my office, and I sat over here and taught over here (referring to her desk.)

Mugisha: There was just one desk. I would sit at one side and she sat at the other.

Matembe: And some meetings would be in my office.

Ankrah: Or wherever there was a free room. For the next year and a half, we were organising and moving with our handbags, either with the minutes or the notes. Now, for me, there was never an issue of sacrifice. It never entered my mind. It was 'to be done.' And there was a reason, a compelling reason, to do it. Sacrifice is a notion that you lose something. We never felt a loss. So, the term sacrifice is not appropriate.

Mugisha: When I had just started working at ACFODE, I remember Christine Lubwama, the treasurer saying, 'We need to be very careful and watch Maxine, because Maxine keeps putting in her money. She doesn't even notice it.' (*laughter*) This made accounting procedures very difficult, since the accounts could not balance, and no one could know where the extra money came from, because we paid for this and we paid for that, but we didn't know where the money came from.

Matembe: The other thing which I want to say is that ACFODE was a puller. Just like we were pulled there, the husbands of many of the members were also pulled. You would just go, like Maxine's home here, when she was Chairperson - that was our permanent home. No question about it. Also other husbands, even the husbands of the employees. You know that man who became a Deputy Governor of Bank of Uganda. His wife worked for us. That man, when we meet, he never fails to thank me. 'Yeah! Our ACFODE', he says. The men thought it belonged to them too, and they really loved it. They were ready to put in a shilling or two, a little something, or they would offer their offices or their transport.

Ankrah: One thing that slipped my mind a short while ago... While there were some husbands who used to say, Miria is splitting the homes, and say our women are being spoiled, at the same time, we began to see very supportive men, already very sensitive men. And it began to give us a different view of relationships between men and women. It doesn't have to be this male dominance or competition between men and women. This woman's (*referring to Matembe*) husband is a great man because they said he didn't have any 'balls'. 'Any man who would stay with this woman doesn't wear the pants in the house, and on and on.' But they didn't realise there are different kinds of men. Not all of them come in and beat up the wives. So, even as we gained status within ourselves, there began to be - and that is an area where ACFODE now is moving in terms of gender - there is need for more of the same kind of a thing. To let families know that there's a different kind of relationship that is possible. And it's not women under the feet of men.

One other thing that should go on the record: she (referring to Matembe) came out and said something that '...à man who does this should be castrated'. That was the news for the next two or three years!

Matembe: Up to now.

Ankrah: Up to now. How can a woman say a thing like that? Women don't say things like that. And how can she say things like that to men? Women don't do that. They kneel.

Matembe: The President said to me, 'You, Matembe, why do you say these things? How did you come to say that about castrating men? You tell me what you said.'

I told him, 'You know, I said that all those rapists and defilers, those people who in one way or another commit sexual offences.' I said, 'They are in possession of potentially dangerous instruments!' Even in '94 when he was going for votes, when I would come to be introduced, he would say, 'This one, remember she's the one who said ...!' And then one time when he went to Luweero, he said, 'In fact, Matembe should have said it earlier'.

Dorsey: I think that should go in the book, that the President agrees.

Mugisha: Even in the papers over the years, many people said Matembe was right.

Matembe: Don't you know they were looking for me when this three- month-old child was defiled. They were looking for me. They came to my office. They said, 'You have to go and talk on the radio. People are looking for you.' I said, 'But why should they look for me? When I was there, they were cursing me.' They were looking for me until one day I accepted. One radio station said, 'You have to go there because everybody is saying, why is Matembe quiet?' So I went there. It was a call-in programme. So they said, 'Ma-temmmm-be, it is good we have heard you are there. Oh, Matembe, I want to support you.'

Ankrah: But back then, she was ridiculed because such pronouncements are too profound for society, generally. It requires of society a maturing, and the kind of receptive male leadership in Africa that Uganda has. Let me just mention AIDS here. If Uganda hadn't had a leader with foresight, who understood that the time had come for women, we would have been struck down. We went to Nairobi in 1985. Kenya organised the UN Women's Decade conference. Almost immediately, Kenyan women were victimised. In the year 2000 the women of Kenya are nowhere. Even the women who organised the conference are nowhere, because Moi has kept the lid on for 15 years.

Mugisha: The social/political environment in Kenya has not been friendly to women.

Ankrah: Since 1986, we have had men in the state and in our households that understood. That's something that's almost unheard of. There were enough of us who had men who could appreciate what we were doing. I don't know anyone who divorced because of ACFODE.

Matembe: Let me tell you what I learned about ACFODE. ACFODE's members were very interesting. You know we were being accused of being desperate women who don't have husbands, or they don't want to marry. They are just there. They are cantankerous and elite.

Mugisha: They are B*anyakyeyombekyeire.*

Matembe: *Banyakyeyombekyeire.*

Ankrah: What does that mean?

Mugisha: Women who build for themselves.

Matembe: You know what I found out. First of all, most of the women who came to ACFODE, including the rural ones, and the ones in suburban areas, were married. And you remember that the husbands of those rural women who didn't even know English at all, their husbands also were with us. And what I realised afterwards, which proved that what they were saying was really wrong with ACFODE women, the minute you call ACFODE women, they come and do their work. And after they do their work, they go straight home. When I was the Chairperson, and I was now a Member of Parliament, I had some small funds to give them a drink. Whenever we would discuss serious matters and we'd be tired, I'd say, 'You people, why don't we go for a drink, maybe at Nile Hotel?' One would say, 'Excuse me, me, oh....., the child is at school.' Another would say, 'Oh no,..... I must go home now. You know my housekeeper is not there.' You know I never gave anybody any drink during that period.

Ankrah: I don't know a single scandal...

Mugisha: ...that was because of ACFODE.

Ankrah: And one other thing that will show you the values upon which we stood. In April 1987...

A discussion followed about one officer of ACFODE who attempted to use her position in ACFODE for her own personal financial gain. When the facts were learned, action was taken quickly. The officer was suspended for a year. A very important precedent was set that members were expected to serve ACFODE. They were not free to exploit the organisation for their own gain.

Matembe: Afterwards she tried to kill ACFODE. But we were not killable, I'm telling you. We would have died first.

Dorsey: You've said that this incident will only be mentioned in passing to show what it meant to ACFODE. Let's move on to a new subject. I want to know how you got to Spear Motors.

Ankrah: What happened was, we decided, after going up and down looking for a room in which to meet, for more than a year and organising from our various pocketbooks, that if we were going to be taken seriously, we would not be an appendage of Mothers' Union or any other group. If we were going to be independent of these other groups, we had to have an office. We had to have our own home. So we started looking. Spear Motors was opening. We became the first tenants, without the money, but... (*laughter*)

Dorsey: Without the money? (*laughter*)

Matembe: We said we didn't want to be in a small corner somewhere.

Ankrah: Now Evelyn Nyakoojo and I had the responsibility to find a place. We were eyeing this nice new building that was on the main road. We weren't going to hide in a corner. We walked in to the Spear Motors building on a Saturday. They allowed us to see the place. We liked it. We told them, we'll take it for seven months. On the third floor. Brand new building. A lot of money per month. But we've always had a sympathetic ear in the Ford Foundation. Ford knew where we were going and literally helped us to begin to conceptualise a number of things, including Women Studies. So Ford then was willing to allow us to take money that might have been for programming in order to pay that first rent. That is how it came about. We had the idea to be on our own, and to be visible.

In the part of the conversation that follows, there was a lot of laughter about the fact that ACFODE had no money in hand to pay this considerable amount for rent when the decision was made to take the space.

Matembe: She *(Ankrah)* would come and talk about Spear House, and I didn't know where the money was coming from. She told us how they negotiated. So, she's the one really who got us that place.

Ankrah: It wasn't getting the building. It was having the courage, the capacity to take risks, and to see our way ahead, that this move would give us credibility like nothing else. So we became the first women's organisation to go into a place like that. We were not a branch with guaranteed money coming from the mother organisation. That was what really set us apart as an indigenous organisation.

Matembe: When we sat there - we got our mats...

Ankrah: Before we had any chairs. Literally we went in without furniture.

Matembe: We went there.... I remember that first day. This lady you see, Ankrah, had the ideas. For me, my role was to talk. The moment I understood what she was talking about, it was action!

Ankrah: And then it was this one *(referring to Mugisha)* to implement it.

Matembe: We got the mats. So Maxine brings people, Ford, Oxfam. I even had to read a book she gave me in order to write the first proposal. I didn't even know what the word proposal meant. But she gave me the book and I wrote a proposal which went to Oxfam and we got money. I wrote the proposal as I was reading the book on how to write a proposal. So for me, these people came in and sat. Then they started asking, 'But what about this, and what about that?' I said, 'Look, you know, this is what we want.' And I'd articulate it in such a way so that whoever is listening knows that this is a real organisation and that they must fund it.

Mugisha: You know sometimes I think that in that Oxfam meeting that the man was just too intimidated to say no. He just had to give the money.

Ankrah: So that is it. We stayed there from '87 September 1...

Matembe: ...until we went to our own home.

Ankrah: But the other thing that happened was that we decided we didn't want to keep paying rent. So we decided that we ought to have our own building. And that was another jump. Our treasurer, Christine Lubwama, was another great asset to the organisation. What she did, when the shilling was being devalued against the dollar, she'd say, 'Eh, we'd gain 100 shillings by virtue of the exchange rate — Put that money aside. Eh, duetschmark...' And the first thing we knew, when we got ready to buy, our excellent treasurer could tell us where the money was, how to get it, without anything being illegal. Her expertise was in banking.

Matembe: And it's interesting, she was not a speaker. You know people had their talents. Each one had a talent which was used.

Ankrah: And the other thing is this. She (*Matembe*) said I was an ideas person, but do you know what? Somehow I don't come across as being anything different from that brilliant woman who you would never see, except for ACFODE. And somehow we don't intimidate each other. ACFODE didn't intimidate, even the Hajat or the rural woman. All of us could do our individual thing. So that was a gift to the organisation. Each woman had a time when she could really shine. Returning to the subject, Spear Motors became ACFODE's house. And we were the very first to buy our own house.

Matembe: And everybody has followed. ACFODE was the first, but now others have their own houses: FIDA, Akina Mama, UWONET, ISIS-WICCE.

Ankrah: For some years we were the only one.

Matembe: And they came where we went.

Ankrah: You know, ACFODE is way over there. People thought we were crazy. I remember saying to you (*Matembe*), 'If we have something to offer, they'll find us.'

Mugisha: They will come. And they have never stopped coming.

Ankrah: And now, men as well as women. It was that kind of thing we did that was so far-sighted, far ahead of the others.

Mugisha: I just wanted to say something about the men. I remember one time we used to have these parties and men would come. One time Mr Matembe said, 'I think we need to form an association of husbands of ACFODE women.' One other man said, 'What do we call it?' And another one said, 'Do we call it ACFODE widowers or what?' (*laughter*) 'When these women are working for ACFODE, we have to assist.' And they were always with us, even in our small corners. When we had our parties and we didn't have money, they would be with us.

Dorsey: So, they got caught up in the spirit of what was happening.

Matembe: And let me tell you, we used to have an end-of-the-year party and it would cost us almost nothing because I would write to Uganda Breweries, 'ACFODE is a women's organisation which is doing this kind for work on women and development. We have husbands who have been so supportive of our organisation, and our children... We would like to give them a party at Christmas. We have also been promoting you. And I want four crates of beer paid out of your advert account.' They would bring them. Then Pepsi, then Nile would be delivered or they would bring them.

Ankrah: In those days such things as sodas were hardly available without a chit. Now we can just ask for 500 crates and they're there. But in those days it was difficult. Even the soft drinks were hard to get.

Matembe: Then the retreat. Maxine, you better talk about the retreat. I think we were the first organisation that ever had a retreat.

Ankrah: Yes, this was a strategy. We began to realise that we had many faces among ourselves, but we didn't often unmask ourselves. I don't remember the origin of the insight. But we thought, okay, we see each other every month, but there are things we won't say in the meeting. We need a time together where we don't have an agenda. We may have something to discuss but that's not the issue. Sometime there we must just let down our hair. So we began what we called the 'retreat', first, just to get away for a long enough period to let down our hair, because if the hair's pinned up, you don't just suddenly let it drop. And that led to our first meeting from Friday afternoon to Sunday afternoon, year in and year out, once a year.

The 'encounter' session part came after supper on the first day. 'Shall we start an *Arise Magazine*? Shall we do this? Or that?' At the end of the day, we would have a place where we could sit. And we would say to someone, 'You know, so-and-so, we really don't like the way you are doing things.' And then, when there was anger or words, we would apologise. So the retreat had the encounter built into it to ensure that a real dialogue took place.

Mugisha: We'd sit on the floor, literally.

Matembe: And come nine, everyone's looking forward to the encounter. We'd sit for hours with the intense discussion going on between our members.

Ankrah: The encounter would go on until one o'clock, until we had untangled ourselves as an organisation. People would tell me I was too hard. They would tell me, 'You know, you're a steamroller.' And I'd have to say I was sorry. And then on Sunday, we would come back and review with each other what we had heard, what we had learned. It was a combination both of strategising in a very technical and practical way, at the same time it was an opportunity for bonding, truly bonding.

Dorsey: And really getting rid of the garbage before the binding...

Ankrah: Yes, so that next time we are really relating in a practical way as an organisation. The garbage or baggage is gone.

Matembe: And that's how we built each other up. Because if they came and said, 'You know, Matembe, you're really driving us, you're breaking us down,' and another would say, 'Yes, it's true,' I had to change.

Ankrah: So what happened was that a yearly retreat became a tradition. It started very early with ACFODE.

Mugisha: I think it was in 1987.

Ankrah: And last year in December it was here at this conference centre before it had officially opened.

Matembe: You had this retreat and you don't call me.

Mugisha: No, they don't call you. They didn't call me either.

Ankrah: You see, the thing about Miria, and this should be recorded here. The problem is this: Miria called me recently and in the course of our talk, she said, 'Where have you been? I need you,' and so on.' So all I could say to her was, 'I'm always there for you, Miria.' Under no circumstance will I ever not be there for Miria. But Miria's a big lady now. How do you call a minister and say, 'Look, I want to just come and talk.' Now when she's no longer the Minister, she'll still be Miria. So when they were having their retreat, they don't expect Miria to have the time.

Matembe: I would come.

Ankrah: You might, but we think we might be imposing. Look at the term I'm using. And nothing has changed between us. It is the perception...

Mugisha: Our perception of her. It's the office.

Matembe: I'm actually deserted. I want to tell you what I feel. Nancy, this is good for the book. I want to say what I feel. When I got this job, for me I knew the women will be with me, will go along with me, will help me to do this job. I knew they would come. Then we would work out even the agenda. Then they will suggest how I might move so that we succeed like we succeeded in ACFODE. And that's what I had thought. So I went there in this job. I tried actually organising the first meeting to work out my action plan. I called ACFODE, FIDA, even you (Maxine), and specifically, even Nyakojo, the - whatever. Some people, I called them individually. And a few came there, very few. Then we worked out this programme. Then recently I called another meeting, I called you (*Ankrah*) again...

Ankrah: Yes, you did.

Matembe: The first meeting Ankrah came. So now I wait. I asked these people to come here and give me ideas about this job. And Hope Mwesigye actually had told me, when they give you a job, you accept. I was saying, 'But what if they give me this Ethics and Integrity position; what shall I do?' She said, 'We shall come there and structure it.' I tell you, Hope has never been to my office. So now, I find myself alone in that office. I don't see the women's support that I need. I'm just there.

Dorsey: You need a brain trust.

Ankrah: However, the brain trust she needs can never be formal. It can't be the government calling us to a meeting.

Mugisha: Yes, that's right.

Matembe: So why don't you, or any of you people organise that one and then call me.

Ankrah: Let's look at this situation. Every day she's in the newspaper. She's been called all over the country in every kind of fora. In fact, will you ever think that Miria will have time to come?

Matembe: Nancy, I think you had better get that point for the book, how lonely women in these positions can be. And without that support, let me tell you. When I'm bashed and abused in this press, and at times I'm bleeding internally, and I can tell you, if it was not for God, I wouldn't survive.

Ankrah: Nobody will believe that Miria is bashed and bleeding and what have you. People believe that everybody is being bashed and crushed by Miria. You see what I'm saying. If I, her good friend, can see it that way, Miria, how much more some of the rank and file of ACFODE see it. You see what I'm saying. Now it is for you to say, come over. I need you.

Matembe: Maxine, when you go, and think about it, you should realise that you should be the one to say, 'Hey, Miria.'

A discussion about this point

Ankrah: I can assure you, that right now if we would call the staff from the kitchen, guess what the news of the day would be-Mama, Matembe, she's here. You mean she's here? Let me tell you something you may not believe. This morning, some of the men attending this workshop were coming into breakfast. One said, 'Oh, Miria Matembe, oh, she has a lot of power.' 'Oh, no, one disagreed.' 'Oh, yes.' Back and forth. Here in the hallway these men were talking about Miria Matembe. Now, here's the difference. The men going to breakfast and we here, we don't know that Miria is bleeding. We don't know how we can support her. We have this exalted, literally exalted, position in our mind. Now we've transformed ourselves from being colleagues and friends and sisters, and suddenly we're part of the public. And we see this unusual, exalted woman with a public perception. Miria is a symbol, and how do you approach a symbol?

Dorsey: We're writing a manuscript together. You think it's not hard for me to figure out what my relationship is with her? You know, do we use her exact words? Do we change this? And do I call her and tell her I need her time?

Ankrah: Precisely. That is what I mean. Miria must always say, 'Maxine, come over.' And I will be there tomorrow. I will drop everything because you (*referring to Matembe*) are so precious to me.

Mugisha: What I would say, especially as ACFODE, is that we have sort of taken as tradition that when a woman is exalted that they are there and you don't have anything to do with them. Maybe that is sometimes the attitude that the women have.

Matembe: But what about the woman?

Mugisha: So now, that's what I'm saying, that we have also let Miria down because we had thought that if Miria becomes a minister, we shall support her. But we have, you know, let her down.

Ankrah: Of course, if Miria had become the Minister of Gender, this discussion would not be taking place. But they have moved her completely out of the Miria context that we knew and put her in Ethics and Integrity. Now she's talking about corruption, and she's saying 'the police' and 'the judges,' etc.

Mugisha: And we failed you. It's true, if she had gone to Gender, we would have continued to work with her.

Ankrah: We have let you down, Miria.

Matembe: Let me tell you about one time that I was being bashed right and left, and Evelyn and Mugisha and somebody, they wrote a letter to the paper and said, 'Leave Miria alone!' That was wonderful! That helped so much! So when they wrote to the press 'Leave Miria alone,' and they signed their names, that day was the best day! Afterwards they sent me a copy.

The recorder was turned off, and these long-time friends visited together for a long time.

In Praise of ACFODE[4]

Acfode, My Second Mother

Oh ACFODE
I mean,
You,
My second mother
I am thinking of you.

You,
The great organisation of
Women of vision
And commitment
My mother on whose lap
I have stood since
I was too old to sit
How I love thee.

You
Whose great name has proved
complicated to pronounce,
Some call you
"OXFORD"
Others say you are
ACTFORD
And others call you
ACTFED
Never mind,
For what you mean
To those who care,
Understand.

My mother
How sweet your name
sounds in my ears!
And how sweet,
it should sound to those
that love and are committed
to development.
How I wish
I could have
a thousand tongues
to sing about you.

My love
How I cherish and honour
your existence.
How I love to praise you
for shaping me into

a character that I am.
Your six years
of existence have
moulded me
and shaped my sense
of direction.

As I walk through
the hardships of my work,
I fear nothing
For you are by my side
The sound of your name
fills me with awe and joy
Oh, how I like to think of thee
I am thinking of you.

The qualities
that make you unique,
Your membership,
great motto,
and methods of operation,
Are for the organisation
of your calibre and zeal.

Your motto,
with triple Bs
Makes me feel great,
Innovative and unique.
Breaking through
Building up, and
Binding.
How many people know and
understand your motto?
To sing your great
motto to the world
I cherish telling its meaning.

Breaking through
Barriers that keep
women in bondage and slavery
Barriers of ignorance,
customs and cultural practices,
poverty and
religion.
Oh, how I wish you success
In breaking through
the barriers that deny women

their freedom to live as
full human beings in their
own right.

ACFODE
How I love to see you
Building up knowledge,
Building up information,
honesty and integrity
courage
commitment
and,
building up confidence
with which to shake
the barriers down.

You
my second mother,
Your commitment to bind
together your members in
love and solidarity for the
advancement of humankind
gives me great courage and hope.

In times of despair
My love,
I feel proud to be
identified and with thee.

You
my second mother,
How I admire
and appreciate your
unique methods of work
Your Executive committee,
the policy making organ
Your standing committees
have made work easy
and manageable
Oh, how I treasure
and long for
your unique feature
The annual retreat
that always refreshes
and enriches me
releases my tension
and prepares me
for a fresh beginning
of another year of hard work.

Every time I think about
your achievements
my heart is filled
with pride and joy
I get overwhelmed.
You my second mother,
I shall live to love you
To treasure your existence
to honour and trust in you.
Oh ACFODE,
How I love
to think about you
How I pray
for your success and prosperity
I shall continue
to stand on your lap
And I shall dwell
in your shelter
For the rest of my life.

*   *   *

Acfode, My First Daughter

ACFODE, my first daughter
or should I say our daughter
For you are a unique child
Mothered by more than one woman.
Your first kick sent sparks
Into the eyes of some unloving women
who were envious and jealous
Of those who resented and resisted
Your noble birth.

To the authorities
Your mothers pleaded
As the accusations of being a CIA spy
Were being labelled on you
And to the rest of the Ugandans
Your mothers employed
in attempt to convince society
About the importance of your timely
birth
to the women of Uganda.

ACFODE my daughter
Through persistence and resistance
of your loving mothers
You managed to break through
And grew
into a lovely beautiful girl that you are.

ACFODE my Dear,
Now that you have grown up
I wish to remember
And share with you
The agony and sleepless nights
Your mothers went through
As they looked for your food
And the desparations and despairs
They experienced in search of your
clothing.
Do not be mistaken my dear girl
It has not been easy.

As I deliver you
into the loving hands
of one of your mothers
I implore you never to forget your roots
I urge you to continue to behave
yourself,
So that to greater heights you will
grow.

Good bye ACFODE
My dearest daughter
The love of my heart
You are always welcome home.

Notes

1 Dr Tadria, who was elected the first Chairperson of ACFODE, had hardly taken office when she resigned to take a position to lecture at ESAMI (Eastern and Southern Africa Management Institute) in Arusha, Tanzania.

2 See poem and cartoon, pages 92 and 93

3 Joshi Renu an Asian woman was murdered by her husband Kooky in 1997. This act enraged the leading women activists in Uganda who vowed to ensure that justice was done. As a result, Kooky who would otherwise have escaped was sentenced to death since then this conviction has been upheld by the Supreme Court.

4 Miria Matembe using poetry in her struggle for gender equality.

Miria addressing an LC meeting when she was the Vice Chairperson
Nakawa Division in 1988

Miria with women colleagues at her first seminar outside Uganda in
front of Monamotapa Hotel in Zimbabwe. She was representing
ACFODE at a seminar on the role of women in politics

Miria with the core members of ACFODE at one of their retreats at Lweza in 1989. Standing on her immediate right is Maxine Ankrah, the second Chairperson and big brain behind ACFODE

Miria poses for a group photograph with the First Lady, Mrs Janet Museveni, and participants at the official opening of a seminar on women and health, organised by ACFODE with the Centre for Family Life Education in 1990

Miria awarding certificates to ACFODE trainees of a secretarial development course in 1990. Standing on her left is the first Executive Secretary, Maude Mugisha

Miria and some members of the ACFODE Executive Committee celebrating the acquisition of ACFODE House in 1991. To her left is Dr Hilda Tadria, first Chairperson of ACFODE

Miria Matembe

Miria with women colleagues in Bonn, Germany, where she represented
ACFODE in May 1993 at the invitation of Fredriech Ebert Foundation

Miria and the late Zerida Rwabusyagara representing ACFODE on a
networking programme with KULU Women and Development in
Denmark in 1993

Miria facilitating at a skills development workshop of the district women councillors organised by ACFODE in 1996 in Mbarara

Miria with fellow women participants at a seminar on children in conflict situations in Addis Ababa in 1994

Miria received an award as heroine when she was selected among 100 women heroines of the world in 1998 by the Women Heroine Project in New York. This is the certificate award

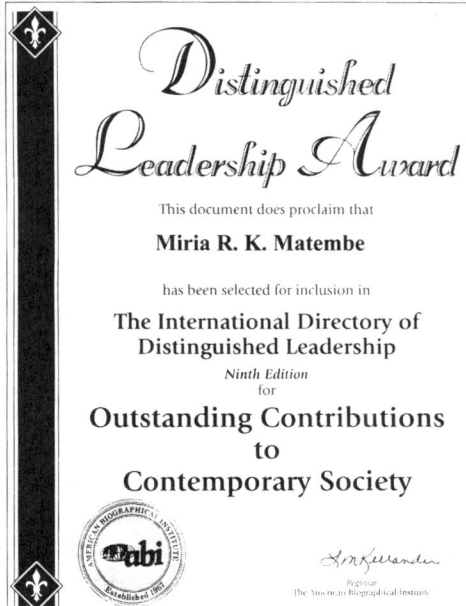

Miria was recognised for her leadership by the American Biographical Institute

CHAPTER 4

Constitution Making: The Uganda Constitutional Commission

When parliamentary elections were held in early February 1989, I was voted into the National Resistance Council. Of the women elected to the NRC, there were only two of us who had been actively involved in the LCs, Hon. Gertrude Lubega Byekwaso being the other. Finally, I was in Parliament and therefore no longer just Miria Matembe, a woman burning with a dream. I was now officially Honourable Miria Matembe, Member of the Ugandan Parliament. I was 35 years old. This position gave me not only a national platform from which to talk about women's rights, but it presented the opportunity to translate the talk into real laws for the promotion and protection of women's rights. I cannot describe what I was feeling at that moment, but God knows. It was hard to believe that a dream that had appeared out of reach for so many years had actually been realised.

Up to that time, not much had been done in Mbarara District by way of mobilising the people either around the NRM Ten Point Programme or about women's rights. So I started traversing the district, combining the NRM message of unity, security and development with the call for justice and emancipation for women. I was really driven to talk to as many people as possible. As people heard about my work, there were invitations from other districts beside my own. Of course women's rights was a controversial subject that was capable of raising feelings of resentment from men and even from many women. Somehow I wasn't too concerned about what people thought as long as I had the opportunity to talk about the inequities and injustices women were facing both in public and, in secrecy, in their homes.

By that time I had attended some seminars and workshops on gender and development issues and, in the process, had started learning the language of gender. Also I was beginning to use the new knowledge I was acquiring to translate what I knew by intuition and conviction into timely messages for women's advancement and into carefully designed strategies to address the problems that hindered women's progress.

Meanwhile, ACFODE had succeeded in attracting many women to join. Just after my election to Parliament, ACFODE elected me as Chairperson, a position I held from 1989 to 1993. When I was first asked to run for the position of Chairperson of ACFODE to follow Maxine Ankrah, I declined for two main reasons. I really did not feel adequate to fill that important position and I didn't think I could find the time. I was finally persuaded to run for the Chair and was elected. Somehow people find time and energy for the things they care about the most, and that was the case. So there I was, very strongly rooted with one foot in the state through Parliament and the other foot well placed in the civil society through ACFODE.

Since its founding, ACFODE has served as a catalyst to reawaken hitherto dormant women's organisations to mobilise women around the issues of equality and development. ACFODE grew in numbers and strength to the extent that it was working in collaboration with government offices and officials for the advancement of women. At its first national conference on women held in Mukono in 1986, ACFODE had recommended to the establishment of a ministry for women government.[1] In 1988 the government set up the portfolio for the Minister of Women in Development in the President's Office and appointed Hon. Joyce Mpanga to head it. This led to the establishment of the Ministry of Women in Development in 1991. (The name of this Ministry has changed several times; for clarity I will refer to it as the Gender Ministry.) ACFODE worked in close collaboration with this ministry and other organisations, especially the University Women's Association (UWA) and FIDA (women lawyers), to make gender issues visible.

Being the Chairperson of ACFODE provided me with valuable experience and contacts. It seemed my constituency knew no boundary. ACFODE worked to change women's lives wherever the women were located, whatever their circumstances. It is because of my experience in ACFODE that I call upon women politicians to participate in NGO activities. When you are involved in the NGOs, you become stronger politically.

Based as I was in both Parliament and ACFODE, I felt that the sky was the limit. I just threw my heart and soul into the struggle for women's liberation. It was just like when Jesus said that the harvest is plenteous but the labourers are few. My wish was just to spread myself as far as I could, all over the place. I wanted to talk about women, their potential, their wisdom, their talents and their contribution to the nation. We had been silent too long about the oppressive situations that women faced in patriarchal society. It was time to talk and yes, even to shout if necessary, to wake people up to see how badly women were treated. In a variety of public settings I would talk about the factors that undermine women's status and hinder them from realising their potential, and then suggest strategies that could be employed to remove those obstacles.

I must say that 1989 was the most extraordinary year for me. It was in that year that God not only opened all the doors and windows for me, but the main gate as well, for my full entry! Following my election to Parliament in early February 1989 and to the leadership of ACFODE later in that same month, in March the President appointed me to the Uganda Constitutional Commission.

The Uganda Constitutional Commission was a twenty-one member body established by an Act of Parliament in 1988 to draft a new constitution for Uganda. According to the Uganda Constitutional Commission Statute, the Commission was mandated to study and review the constitution with a view to making proposals for the enactment of a national constitution; and to formulate and structure a draft constitution that would form the basis for the country's new national constitution. The new constitution would establish a free and democratic system of government to guarantee the fundamental rights and freedoms of the people of Uganda; develop a system of government to ensure people's participation in the governance of their country; and create viable political institutions to maximum ensure consensus and orderly succession to government. That was a very big job.

The possibility of my serving on the Constitutional Commission had never crossed my mind! All I had dreamed about and longed to do was to make good laws for women. Now here I was, not only in Parliament, but also sitting on the body that was to draft the most fundamental law in the land, the foundation on which laws made in Parliament were to be based! The Baganda have a saying, *Kyembadde njagaliza embazi, kibuyaga asudde*, meaning, 'The wind has blown down the huge tree which I needed an axe to cut down.' My desire had been to become a parliamentarian. Little had I known that I was to be chosen to play a role in drafting this most important of all legal documents!

My appointment to the Constitutional Commission gave me the opportunity to change the existing situation that was discriminatory against women in so many ways. This was the greatest joy of my life. For me, I was ready to do my part to construct a gender-sensitive and gender-responsive constitution that would guarantee equality for women, in fact for all people. This was an opportunity that comes only once and I had to embrace it fully. I remember thinking that only God and I could know the joy that was in my heart. I saw the beginning of the journey to real liberation, based in law, for the women of Uganda.

Of course, at the time I wondered what could have possibly led to my being appointed to the Constitutional Commission. Let me relate here what I think some of the factors were that led to my appointment, although I may never know the real story or the whole truth.

Many people have assumed that since President Museveni and I come from the same district, somehow we have been connected for a long time. That is far from the truth. Since early 1986 when the NRM government came to power, I had been publicly advocating equal rights for women - for three full years - while the circles of power were somewhere else. My work at the grassroots had not been connected to those top people in any way.

I remember very well my first personal contact with President Museveni. It occurred in February 1989 when he called the parliamentarians from Mbarara to a meeting at his home in Rwakitura about a particular problem in the district. After addressing us at the meeting, the President called for a discussion. I put up my hand, and he said, 'Mrs.....' and I said, 'Matembe.' He said, 'No, you are not Matembe.' I said, 'I am the one,' but he refused to accept that. He asked again, 'Are you really Matembe? Are you not a doctor?' I told him that I was not. He said, 'Anyway, make your point.'

When the group dispersed to the compound for lunch, the President said to me, 'So you are Matembe.' I replied, 'Your Excellency, you do not know me? I have been working so hard in the LCs. I thought you knew me.'

He said, 'You know, I know the name but I was mistaking the person with someone else.' Of course, I was disappointed that he did not know me, but this gave me a chance to thank him for what the government was doing for women. The fact that he didn't know me was soon to change. The next day when I reached the Institute of Bankers in Kampala where I still had an office, I found the Minister of Justice looking for me. He informed me that the President had directed him to appoint me to the Uganda Constitutional Commission. I think that when the President saw me the day before, he had realised that this was the woman he was hearing so much about.

My next contact with the First Family occurred about a week after my appointment to the Constitutional Commission. In this case, Mrs Janet Museveni, the President's wife, sent her private secretary to ask this woman Matembe to come to see her. Mrs Museveni thought I was a lecturer at Makerere so she told her secretary to go and look for Matembe there. How she got my name or what she thought of me I did not know.

The secretary finally located me at my home and invited me to State House. This was my first ever visit to State House. During our meeting, Mrs Museveni told me she wanted to send me as her representative to a meeting in Minnesota in the United States. I remember saying, 'But how can you send me to America? I have never been there and I don't have any experience in travelling abroad.' At that time there were nine women ministers. I wondered why she wasn't sending one of them. In fact, I asked her, 'Why don't you send one of the ministers instead of me?' I remember feeling scared of traveling to America.

She said, 'It is you I want to send and I know why I want to send you. I will get somebody to travel with you.'

I told her, 'Madam, I do not know much about America'.

She said, 'Don't worry. I want you to articulate on the national policy.' The conference organisers had invited her, but she had decided not to go. She thought I would be the most effective person to represent Uganda. And so I had my first trip to the United States. The other person to go to this meeting was the late Diane Lule, the Chairperson of UWESO (Uganda Women's Effort to Save Orphans), an NGO that Mrs Museveni had co-founded. Since that time, I have continued to serve the First Lady in this way, representing her on a number of different occasions. She has told me that when she sends me, she knows that I will represent the country well.

In fact, when I was walking out of State House that day, I met the President for the second time. Later my driver told me that the President had seen my small personal car which I had bought on credit, and he asked the driver whose vehicle it was. I don't know why he asked. Perhaps my humble vehicle looked a little out of place there at State House. The driver told him it was Matembe who was inside seeing Madam. The President then went to the front entrance of the house and told the guards on duty there that when Matembe came out, they should tell her that the President wanted to see her before she left. As I came out of my meeting with the First Lady, the guards gave me that message.

I tell you I got worried. I knew this man was very sharp. Now, I thought, what does he want to talk to me about? I was anxious whether I would measure up to whatever his expectations were for me. I sat in a chair in one of the front rooms, waiting for him and worrying.

When he walked in, he said, 'Ah, Matembe, you are here'.

I said, 'Yes, Your Excellency'.

He said, 'Sit there and tell me all about yourself'.

Now, I thought, how do I begin? Do I start way back by saying I was born in Rutoma? I was having a difficult time deciding what to say. You know, he was so widely travelled and knowledgeable, and of course, he was the President of my country. Finally I started. I said, 'You see, I was born at Rutoma to Mr Samuel Rukoza.'

He said, 'Oh, you mean this man...' Imagine he knew who my father was. Then we had a nice chat. I told him I had been working all along since he had come from the bush. I took the opportunity to thank him again for liberating us and for giving women a platform. Then he said, 'You know I put you on the Constitutional Commission.'

I said, 'Yes, Your Excellency. I thank you very much. I have already taken the position and have started to work.'

That's when he told me that his wife had been invited to America, but she thought she would send somebody to represent her. He said he had told her to send a capable, effective woman, and she had chosen me. I said, 'Does that mean that I am one?' You can see that by that time I had relaxed, and I was trying a little joke.

He looked up, smiled and said, 'I think so!' I have included this whole conversation because it shows that in 1989 we were just getting acquainted. Before this, the President had only heard about my work. He had never seen me in person until the recent meeting at Mbarara. Until this time I had never been in close contact with those powerful people.

Immediately after my appointment to the Constitutional Commission, I reviewed what I knew about the Independence Constitution which had been written in 1962 and amended in 1966 and 1967. That document was discriminatory against women in various ways. First and foremost, the old constitution failed to specifically prohibit discrimination on the basis of sex. Whereas it prohibited discrimination on certain grounds like race, religion, tribe and so on, sex was not mentioned. One could have thought that this was a mere oversight, but in fact Article 20, Clause 4, expressly allowed the enactment of laws that were discriminatory relating to family matters. Also there were provisions supporting the application of customary laws. According to this article, women were not allowed to inherit their fathers' or husbands' property, nor were they allowed to become heirs to their fathers' estates. In fact, women were not allowed to own land. On the whole, the old constitution treated women as minors and not as full human beings in their own right. It was now our chance to ensure that the new constitution did away with such odious articles and provided equal rights for women.

When I joined the Commission, it had already started its work. I replaced Hon. Gertrude Byekwaso-Lubega who, after serving only a short time, had left the Commission because she was appointed Minister for Women in Development. The Commission consisted of 21 Commissioners, only two being women. Although the Commission could not claim to be gender balanced, it might be assumed that the appointment of two highly qualified women lawyers demonstrated an intention to ensure that women's concerns would be seriously addressed. Before we completed our work, one male commissioner resigned due to ill health. He was not replaced so we remained twenty in number for the rest of the time.

Mary Maitum was the other woman Commissioner when I joined. As it worked out, Mary's expertise and mine complemented each other well. Mary was also an activist. Among other things, she had served as Chairperson of FIDA.

While I had concentrated my work on the issue of women's basic human rights and how those rights were often denied, Mary was quite knowledgeable about the implementation and interpretation of the existing international legal conventions on human rights. There was also a real contrast between the two of us in our individual styles and approaches to our work. Mary is soft-spoken and elegant, loving, clear-headed, and very patient. She's truly a gentle lady, surely a contrast to the public persona I have chosen for myself.

When I joined the Commission, I noticed right away that the issue of women and the constitution was not featuring prominently. As a newcomer to the group, I mostly kept my thoughts to myself while I learned about the workings of the Commission and the role a commissioner was supposed to play. However, I was ready to call attention to this oversight as soon as the opportunity presented itself.

The Commission had broken down its programme into three stages: first, sensitising the people about what a constitution was and the need for a new one; second, collecting and analysing people's ideas about the constitution they wanted; and third, writing a comprehensive report and a draft constitution. Fr John Waliggo (1996), the Secretary to the Commission, has argued that the constitution-making exercise, as it was devised, served a greater purpose than merely the forging of a new constitution, for it provided a country-wide programme in civic education within the history, cultures and context of Ugandan people.

It had been decided to employ a participatory approach in the making of this new constitution. To start the process, seminars were to be conducted in the districts with all the district leaders invited to discuss the important constitutional issues. In fact, all the constitutional issues that finally found their way into the 1995 Constitution were drawn from these district seminars.

It was obvious that most of the people invited to attend these district seminars for leaders were men, simply because the participants were invited in their leadership capacities, and most leadership positions were held by men. The categories of the invited participants included: district councilors (with very few women, less than 10 percent per district), head teachers, heads of department in the civil service, chiefs, and religious leaders. The large majority of leaders in all these categories were men.

I think it was taken for granted that when the Commission invited people in those categories that all Ugandans would be represented. Until I arrived on the scene, nobody, including the two women Commissioners, had asked the question that I had been asking every day in my advocacy work for women – where are the women in this thing? Are the women included or left out? In whatever I did, wherever I was involved, gender equality was always my main focus. Unless special notice is taken, it may not be clear whether the equal participation of women is catered for or not. Of course, there was nothing that was saying, don't bring women, nor was there anything saying, be sure to bring women. From my experience working in the gender struggle, I thought that women in numbers might not show up for the meetings the way arrangements were being made. So, I wondered, where are the women? When I raised this question, Mary was immediately supportive, and the Commission adjusted its programme to bring in more women.

After noting the low percentage of women at the first seminars, the women Commissioners convinced the Commission to invite all women leaders in a district to the seminars, irrespective of whether they were LC leaders or not. I wish at this stage to commend our male colleagues on the Commission who were very co-operative and supportive on the gender question. In fact, some of the male Commissioners played a lead role on this issue.

In the early stages of our work, the topic, 'Women and the Constitution' was chosen as one of the four main topics to be discussed in the seminars. The others were 2) What is a constitution and why does Uganda need a new one? 3) The historical context within which the new constitution was being made, 4) What are the major constitutional issues Uganda should focus on when making a new constitution?

The topic 'Women and the Constitution' never ceased to be controversial, and it was always hotly debated. Everyone, including the youth, paid their full attention during that part of the discussion. If that topic was discussed first, it would consume almost all the time set for the debate, leaving other topics little or no time at all. When we saw the interest the subject generated, the Commission decided to schedule 'Women and the Constitution' at the end of the meetings. This way people would know it was coming, and because they were so interested, they would sit and wait, even if it meant staying very late in the night. Oftentimes we would conclude the meeting even though many people wanted to stay longer and continue discussing this hot subject.

The Commissioners divided into groups of three, with each group visiting specific districts allocated to it. During the district seminar stage, I was in a group with Justine Okot and Colonel Kale Kayihura. Very soon in the process I realised that, in spite of our efforts, the women who came to the meetings were very few. I could not just stand by when the women of Uganda were being left out of this critical political exercise, so I devised a strategy to get more women to attend the meetings.

I would arrive in a place before the day fixed for the seminar and move around the villages to mobilise the women. Going to trading centres and nearby villages, I would introduce myself and ask the women if they had heard about the meeting on the constitution–making exercise. The women would tell me, no, they had not heard, and, no, they had not been invited. I would say, 'Don't worry, I am now inviting you. You simply come. If there are no seats for you, you can sit on the floor.' So these women would come and I made sure they had space to sit and an opportunity to participate in the seminars. I would invite any women I came across, whether educated or not, whether leaders or not.

In 1989, the northern part of Uganda was experiencing insurgency and insecurity when we went there for those district meetings. I remember when we reached Kitgum, the leader of my team, Justine Okot, a very loving and fatherly man, pleaded with me. He said, 'I know you, Matembe. I know your love for women, but please also have love for yourself. You know it's not safe here to travel in the villages and to move at night. You may be killed. Please just be content with the number of women who were invited to this seminar. Don't go to the villages in the night to look for more. Remember, as the leader of this team, I am responsible for you.'

I would promise him that I was taking his advice seriously, but when he went to his room, I would quickly set out to look for women. When next day he saw the hall filled with women, he could not believe it. He said, 'You mean you went against my advice?'

I would laugh and say to him, 'What did you expect me to do, to be content with just a few Kitgum women taking part in this debate?' To me women's liberation was more important than my life. Besides, I had a strong belief that God who had blessed me with this assignment would protect me and see me through it. I told Justine to just pray for me and leave everything to God and He would protect us. In fact, on the day following the debate in Kitgum, our party narrowly escaped death. On our way back to Kampala, we reached a certain place just five minutes after a group of rebels had crossed the road.

When I was able to contact local women ahead of time, these meetings took on a different dynamic. Now, in contrast to the previous male dominated meetings, local women invaded the hall. The idea of an invasion is fitting. It was as if the women were invading foreign territory. However, when they did come, there were no chairs for them. Therefore, under my direction, the women would be advised to occupy the space on the floor right in front of the speakers' table while men sat on benches or chairs facing the front. The women would sit on their mats and listen.

There was no problem with this arrangement anyway since, according to tradition, men usually occupied the chairs and women sat on the floor. This was the custom in any situation where there were not enough chairs, even if the men and women involved were equal in power and status. You would not have seen a woman seated on a chair while men were standing. Good enough, in recent times this pattern has broken down.

Of course, when it came to questions and debates, men tended to dominate the discussion. Part of the problem was that women were not used to speaking in public, especially in the presence of such large numbers of male leaders, including the elders. So at first, women would be afraid to raise their hands to ask for the floor. In that case, I would encourage them to participate by asking the audience to let women speak. Sometimes I would just choose some women to talk, even when they were not asking for the floor. Eventually, after a few women had raised provocative questions, others would start giving their views. During these debates, I became more aware than ever before that women know a multitude of important things and possess a great deal of wisdom. When women are quiet, it does not mean they are ignorant or have nothing of substance to say. It is because they have not been given the opportunity and the space to talk. Given the chance, women know what they want and they certainly know how to speak up for themselves.

Indeed, during the constitution-making exercise, women were given the opportunity to speak in these public meetings, maybe some of them for the first time in their lives. And the women of Uganda talked. They articulated their interests and needs with insight and intelligence. As a matter of fact, the women constituted a force that really embraced the constitution-making exercise. I came to believe that women viewed this exercise as their main hope for liberation. Gauging from the questions they were asking, their contributions to the debate and their level of mobilisation, one could argue that women believed that the constitution was going to be their saviour, a panacea for the many problems they faced. People will recognise the trust the women placed in the constitution-making process if they know one fact, that is, that almost half of the 26,000 memoranda collected by the Commission came from women or women's groups. This volume of memoranda is quite remarkable when women constituted only 2-10 percent of the participants at the district and sub-county educational seminars. Passive women? Silent women? Women with no opinions on public issues? That was certainly not the case!

This educational exercise of informing people about the making of a new constitution was taken to all the districts and sub-counties in the country, and, further, to all the post-secondary educational institutions. Apart from the official seminars organised by the Commission, any educational institution, any religious organisation or, in fact, any group of people which chose to, could organise their own seminars and invite the Commission to facilitate them. Women NGOs utilised this avenue very well. Organisations like ACFODE, FIDA, the Muslim Women's Association, the Catholic Guild, the Mothers' Union, and many other women's groups from different parts of the country organised seminars and invited us to facilitate. Mary Maitum and I, and male Commissioners like Fr John Mary Waliggo, Prof. Edward Kiddu-Makubuya, Prof. Phares Mukasa Mutibwa, among others, were frequently invited to address women's groups in various parts of the country, especially on the topic 'Women and the Constitution.'

After the opening educational exercise to inform people about the constitution-making process, the next phase of the Commission's work was to go out to the people a second time, this time to the sub-counties to collect people's views about what provisions they wanted included in the constitution. From these views, a draft constitution would be written. Every Ugandan was encouraged to contribute his or her views. This could be done either at public meetings where people's comments were recorded by Commission staff, or people could send their written memoranda to the Commission. Some of the people's comments were tape-recorded. Memoranda were received from district councils, county councils, sub-county councils, parish and village councils. Some memos came from NGOs and other organised groups including associations of professionals. In addition, a very large number of individuals submitted personal memoranda. Before this stage of constitution making was completed, it was clear that women in Uganda had a lot to say about the possibilities for a better future based on law. However, two questions needed to be asked during stage two, and their answers taken very seriously: did women have sufficient knowledge about constitutional issues to state their opinions, and would women find a way to state their views so that their views would be catered for in the draft constitution being constructed?

When women leaders and activists from Parliament, the Gender Ministry and women's NGOs recognised that only a small percentage of those attending the organised seminars were women and that women were not submitting memoranda in large numbers, they agreed it was time to take action to remedy this situation. Surely, for as long as we could remember, it had been considered a normal state of affairs that women were mostly excluded from this kind of public decision-making. But now, in this case, were women failing to participate because they accepted the idea that, as tradition would suggest, this whole public process was mainly the responsibility of men? It was time to go to work to change the political culture. Here was a great opportunity for women to influence the future constitution. But what needed to be done? An action plan was soon devised.

In collaboration with some of the leading women's NGOs, namely Action for Development, Uganda Women Lawyers Association and the University Women Association, the Ministry of Gender designed a Constitutional Consultation Project. Funding was supplied by DANIDA (Danish Development Agency). The Consultation Project, which complemented the work being done by the Constitutional Commission, was composed of the following activities.

Brainstorming Workshop
Before it embarked on its educational programme, the Ministry organised a national workshop for women on the theme 'Women and Constitutional Reform'. The objective of the workshop was to enable the Ministry to work out an educational programme based on the needs, interests and aspirations of the women of Uganda. Participants were chosen to represent different groups of women, that is, different ages, different

ethnic groups, different regions, and different religions from around the whole country. Then on the basis of the workshop recommendations, the Ministry produced a training manual on Women and the Constitution and designed an educational programme.

Research on Women and the Constitution
In a parallel activity, ACFODE was commissioned by the Ministry to conduct a pilot survey to obtain baseline data that would assist the Ministry in determining how women could be involved in the constitutional reform process, especially women at the grassroots. It was believed that to fully involve women in the process, there must be some basic understanding of women's status and socio-economic realities. The overall goal was to design an appropriate educational programme which would enable women to understand the importance of their participation in the process and its relevance to the conditions of their lives. The research was conducted in Mbarara District targeting rural women, and in Kampala District focusing on women traders in slum areas and women professionals. The survey was also used to pre-test the training manual on women and the constitution produced by the Ministry. The report of ACFODE's findings was also used by the Constitutional Commission in designing its educational programme that targeted women.

Recruitment of a coordinator and a trainer
The Ministry recruited a project coordinator and a Trainer, both of whom worked under the Management Committee constituted by the Ministry, ACFODE, FIDA and UWA to implement the project.

Educational Programme
The project organised a number of informative meetings for women at different levels. Special meetings were held for women MPs and the Secretaries for Women's Affairs at the LC5 (district) level. Next, two trainers from each district were given special training and mandated to organise educational seminars for women in their districts. The project also ran regional

seminars for women in each of the five regions of Uganda. A media contact group was appointed, given special training and commissioned to spread information about the constitutional reform process throughout the country. Constitutional committees were formed at all levels of LCs and charged with the responsibility of stimulating debate on constitutional reform and collecting women's views to be incorporated in the Ministry's memoranda destined for the Commission. In all these activities, the Ministry was preparing and equipping women with the necessary information and skills to be able to give their views on the new constitution to the Commission.

The special seminars to sensitise women on constitutional matters and to facilitate collecting women's views on the constitution gave women an additional channel for expressing their ideas and concerns to the Commission. The result was a very comprehensive memorandum drawn from women all over the country, with the title 'The Recommendations of the Women of Uganda to the Uganda Constitutional Commission.' Some of us thought of the report simply as 'The Voices of Women.' Anyone reviewing the Ministry's report can see the issues that women brought to the Commission's attention, including, among others, harmful cultural practices, maternity rights, affirmative action, equality, and discrimination on grounds of sex. Going a step further, one can then find provisions addressing these issues in the draft constitution, showing that the Commission paid careful attention to the women's views.

During the final stage of the Commission's work, that is, completing the draft constitution and compiling the report and the recommendations, the two women commissioners never hesitated to draw the attention of the male commissioners to the women's voices memorandum. Whenever they were reluctant to accept provisions in the draft that would fully ensure gender equity and protection for women's rights, we would point to that extraordinary report of what women expected from the constitution, and remind the Commission that women constituted more than half of the country's population. The report proved to be a very useful tool to direct discussion on the drafting of provisions on women's rights.

Of course, the project faced severe shortcomings. This very ambitious project lacked adequate funds to accomplish all its objectives in the short time available. For instance, the training manual used for educational programmes was in the English language which limited its use with women who did not understand English, and there were no funds to translate the manual into local languages for more accessibility. Additionally, the training received by the two district trainers did not prepare them sufficiently so that they could effectively explain the complex constitutional issues to their fellow women. There was just not enough money or time or proper training for them to fulfil their mandate.

Additionally, due to lack of funds, the national trainer was not able to follow up and monitor the work of trainers who were located all over the country. However, it should be said that the tremendous effort put forth by the Ministry-led group certainly had positive effects. Some have called the Uganda Constitution one of the most pro-women constitutions in the world. To give just one example, an article in the *Chicago Tribune* in December 1996 described our constitution as a 'Women's Constitution' (Tamale 1999).

We should all be aware that the gains for women in the new constitution were not granted on a silver plate. They were hard earned. Great numbers of women at all levels of society were involved in various ways in constructing the new constitution. In this case hard work yielded results. It is in this regard that I applaud the efforts of all Ugandan women who in one way or another participated in this exercise. What Ugandan women are enjoying now in the Uganda Constitution are fruits of women's own efforts, though the full harvest will be in the future. To be fair, I cannot fail to acknowledge the contribution of many forward-looking men who supported women's efforts in this cause.

According to the report of the Commission, women participated actively and enthusiastically in all three stages of the Commission's work. Indeed, many observers believed that women were the most united group embracing the exercise. For example, Commissioner Fr Waliggo says that women knew what they wanted, displayed a unity of purpose and submitted sound proposals for inclusion in the constitution (1996:38).

Women leaders participated in all the district and sub-county seminars organised by the Commission. Women were also able to organise their own meetings through the LC Secretaries for Women's Affairs, inviting the commissioners to facilitate these meetings and to help educate women on the constitutional issues. Although we recognise that the percentage of women attending the district and sub-county seminars was small compared to the men, it should be noted that women who did attend the seminars helped to provoke lively debates on the issues concerning 'Women and the Constitution'.

As has been stated, when peace and order returned to most parts of Uganda in 1986, women re-activated their old organisations and formed many new ones. Also, the proximity of Uganda to the UN Conference to mark the end of the UN Women's Decade held in Nairobi in 1985 led to a new awareness and interest in gender issues. Since the Nairobi conference there had been a gradual shift in emphasis away from a welfare approach to women's problems toward a new focus on women's emancipation for development. A number of these women's NGOs were national, some with international affiliations, while the majority of them operated locally within their own districts and sub-counties. This last category included women's community-based organisations (CBOs) and clubs. A large percentage of these women's groups at all levels participated vigorously in the constitution-making process.

The leading women's NGOs, like ACFODE, FIDA and the National Association of the Women Organisations in Uganda (NAWOU), took every opportunity to act as facilitators in these activities by conducting seminars and workshops for women's local organisations and clubs around the country. Many of the NGO memoranda commended ACFODE, FIDA and NAWOU for the assistance these organisations provided.

The massive participation of women in the educational programmes yielded at least three important results. First, women were able to influence the constitutional debates by making the gender question a very prominent constitutional issue that was discussed at all levels of the debates. As reported in *The New Vision* Newspaper of 12 June 1991,

> As the debates on the new constitution for Uganda became a common phenomenon on every social gathering, be it wedding, burial, RC meetings and even in local drinking spots, the issue of equality for women has hit the ceiling (Mugisha Rwabwoogo).

The Commission report added this insight.

> As a result of the intensive activity of so many women, the idea that women should receive fair treatment in the new Constitution obtained support from many people from every level of society and every major group and institution (Report of the Commission 1992:148).

Secondly, having understood, at least to a degree, the importance of the constitution and its relevance to their emancipation, large numbers of women submitted their own views about the constitution by using all channels available. In addition to all the memoranda officially submitted to the Commission from all levels of LCs, women submitted their views through the comprehensive memorandum drawn by the Ministry, 'The Voices of Women,' and through other organisations, and clubs. In addition, many individual women submitted their own views to the Commission (see Index of the Commission Report on Sources of People's Views 1992). Women gave more memoranda than any other single group and as Waliggo observes,

> Most of their submissions repeated the same points and arguments without any marked differences between educated and illiterate, urban and rural, rich and poor women. This was the greater success of the Uganda women. Disadvantaged people usually are very prone to divisions

among themselves and in what they want. This time those divisions were fully contained so as not to undermine the unity of purpose (1996:38).

All these memoranda described the concerns expressed by Ugandans on the issues of equality for women contained in paragraphs 7.62-7.70 of the Commission's report.

> Both men and women want to see an end to the discrimination and marginalisation of women in every sector and aspect of life. They have great expectations in this regard, of the new constitution and the new society governed by it. Unless this basic concern is fully resolved by the new constitution, the majority of Ugandans will remain frustrated and disappointed (Report of the Commission 1992:150).

This statement sounds a bit utopian. Surely, if Ugandans, both men and women, truly wanted to see an end to discrimination against women, things would be better today than they are. Perhaps one problem is that different people have different views of what discrimination against women entails.

The third and last important result of the women's massive participation in the constitution-making process could be easily overlooked, and it could well be the most significant. Recalling how new women are on the scene of public politics, the question needs to be kept in mind: how do people learn to do what they don't know how to do? This entire political exercise was a valuable training ground for women to learn how to get involved in the political process. To get more women actively involved in politics, what do we have to know, and what do we have to do? During the constitutional making exercise, many women learned new skills and pertinent information that can continue to be used each time these things are needed for the women's cause.

The issues of discrimination against girls and women and the need for gender equality were the main topics of women's memoranda. Women also submitted views on other topical constitutional issues, such as, the political system, the presidency, and the separation of powers. Based on these submissions, I believe that many women understood that issues of equality can only receive adequate attention by gender-sensitive leaders under gender-responsive political systems and structures. Evidence that women had participated fully in the country's constitution making could be found in the abundance of provisions for the promotion and the protection of women's rights enshrined in the draft constitution.

It is not surprising to learn that the work on the Commission did not always go smoothly. Initially, some of the commissioners serving on the UCC were not at all sensitive to the women's cause. It took a good amount of persuasion on the part of the women commissioners and some sensitive men to educate and convince those male commissioners who held traditional views, on the importance of the gender factor to the constitutional exercise. Indeed, a handful of the commissioners resisted some of the more progressive proposals such as the importance of gender-neutral language, the affirmative action seats of district women representatives, and even the representation of people with disabilities in Parliament. Progressive proposals on these matters were fortunately secured in the final constitutional text.

I want to say how important it was that some of the men on the Commission were already committed to gender equity when the Commission started its work. Hon. Kiddu Makubuya, who is presently Minister of Education, was always with us. This good man was also an active supporter of ACFODE's work. Another fair-minded man on the Commission was Captain Kale Kayihura. Kayihura was one of those men who joined the NRA in the bush early in the struggle. Many of those army men came out of the bush committed to bringing women up. During the Commission debates Kayihura would talk and talk on the side of women.

From the very beginning, the Secretary of the Commission, Fr Waliggo, was a strong advocate for women. Even up to now, his heart is with the women of Uganda who he feels have suffered too long. Father Waliggo also played a key role during the Constituent Assembly which debated the draft constitution leading to the promulgation of the Constitution. He chose not to run for the CA, but stayed intimately involved in the body's proceedings. His weekly column in *The New Vision* kept the public informed about the important issues under debate. One thing he managed to do was to demystify the complex and controversial gender issues involved. I can say that by the end of the Constitutional Commission's work, almost every commissioner was truly gender sensitive.

The Draft Constitution, consisting of 20 chapters, and a 750 page report was presented to President Museveni on 31 December 1992 in Mbarara. To show the reader how anxious the President was to see the product of the Commission's work, let me describe the scene when we turned these historic documents over to President Museveni. Most of the commissioners had arrived in Mbarara, but Fr Waliggo and the official bound copies for the President were still on the way. As the Chairman, Justice Ben Odoki, was presenting the President a set of the documents, although they were not bound and therefore not the official ones, Fr Waliggo arrived. When the Secretary arrived with the bound copies, Justice Ben Odoki handed them to the President. At that point Odoki made a gesture as if to take back the first set of documents that he had given the President. Using body language along with his words, the President said, 'No, let me keep both of them.' Everyone laughed and laughed. Everyone knew that both sets were the same, but it was clear that President Museveni wanted to possess all that was given to him and was not willing to give any part back. It was a wonderful moment for Uganda and for the President whose government had kept its promises.

The Commission had taken almost four years to complete its assignment. There was a certain amount of relief that the draft constitution was finished, and a large amount of satisfaction for what we had accomplished. However, we were all aware that much work remained to be done to take this draft to the next stage where the new constitution would become the law of the land. The Commissioners had to decide whether they wanted to participate in the next part of this work in the Constituent Assembly, or to allow others to complete that task. Although I would have liked to take some time off, I found that I could not let go of the responsibility that had come to me, to see that the new constitution was as 'women friendly' as we could make it. No, it was not yet time for Miria Matembe to take a holiday.

When I went to contest the election for the CA, I thought, really I must win. I prayed every day. I would wake up in the morning, and say, 'God, you know if I don't go to the Constituent Assembly, I will die. Please help me.' I thought to myself, what will I do if I don't win? I would be so upset. Maybe I would just leave the country. I could not imagine being in the country while the draft constitution was being debated in the CA and I would not be there taking part. I just didn't know how I would manage in such a situation. If I heard that the CA wasn't defending the gains for women, would I go and break into the hall and yell at people and get arrested? Of course, I knew that if I lost, I had no right to be there in that assembly. But, if I wasn't there in the CA, what would happen to all our efforts, to all those provisions for women we had fought so hard for? Would they be lost in the CA? Would women have to go back to the old days and the old ways? This was unthinkable. I had to win.

There were three of us running for the one woman's seat in Mbarara District. This time the women with whom I contested were colleagues and friends. I like to campaign, and when I talk, people give me their full attention. I am known as an articulate and dynamic public speaker, and I bring a lot of humour to the campaigning. In this election, there was a new element that was certainly unexpected to me. Some men candidates began to refer to me during their campaigns. At their campaign rallies, they would tell their audiences something like, 'When you send me to represent you in the CA, I will be like Matembe in articulating your interests, and I shall support her in promoting women's rights.' Can you imagine? In this way some men actually campaigned for me, knowing that, in the process, they would get more support for themselves from women voters. This showed that in these elections for the CA the women question was really something to reckon with.

I won my seat, and was soon on my way to the next challenge – to work with other enlightened people in the Constituent Assembly to see that gender equality and protection for women were enshrined in Uganda's new Constitution.

What Others Say *(Rev. Father John Mary Waliggo)*

On 8 July 2000 Nancy Dorsey met with Rev. Fr John Mary Waliggo at the Uganda Human Rights Commission in Kampala where he serves as a Commissioner. Nancy Dorsey asked Fr Waliggo to describe his work with Miria Matembe during the making of the 1995 Uganda Constitution

Dorsey: Anyone who knows about the constitution-making process in Uganda has recognised that something very special went on here. To start, please describe this process briefly for the readers.

Rev. Fr Waliggo: Yes, about the new Ugandan Constitution, there is an important background story. The independence Constitution of 1962 was made by just a few people, and mainly in London. In February 1966 one man, Milton Obote, the Prime Minister, overthrew it. From that time onwards things went terribly wrong in Uganda. There was no legitimate constitutional order! Obote's 'pigeon-hole' Constitution of 1966 was not accepted. The Constitution of 1967 was just imposed by a parliament whose term of office had already expired! There were riots, fighting and emergencies here and there.

When Idi Amin seized power in 1971, he ruled without any reference to the Constitution. When he was overthrown in April 1979, a lot of groups of people began to analyse what had gone wrong in Uganda. Most people in these seminars and workshops concluded that our problems were not essentially military nor economic. They were political and constitutional. People had not agreed on how they wished to be governed; power was not evenly shared; resources were unjustly distributed. That is why we have had wars, battles, insecurity, instability and the gross violation of human lives, human rights and property.

Many people hoped much in the general elections of December 1980. But these elections were grossly rigged by Obote's party, UPC, assisted by the soldiers. Yoweri Museveni clearly warned before these elections that should they be rigged, he and his men would go to the 'bush' to fight for democracy. He founded a political party, Uganda Patriotic Movement (UPM). When indeed the elections were rigged, Museveni and his men, both civilian and military, went to the 'bush' in early 1981. As soon as they had gone, they issued a promise to all Ugandans that should they win and remove dictatorship, they would invite all Ugandans to contribute views in the making of a new constitution, to establish agreed-upon rules for everyone. It is this promise that kept some hope in the hearts of people. Of course some were doubting whether such a promise would be kept after victory.

It is a credit to the NRM/NRA that when they captured state power in January 1986, they kept that vital promise and the detailed programme of participation and consensus in the exercise as they had conceived it in 1981. By immediately appointing a Minister for Constitutional Affairs in January 1986, and choosing a very well-known lawyer at its head, Sam Njuba, it was clear that Museveni and his NRM were committed to keep the promise for a people-made constitution.

This was the first time we had a Ministry for Constitutional Affairs, and immediately, good enough, people began to go to the Minister and to the Ministry putting in a few of their views. So the mandate of the Ministry was to try to put in place the necessary logistics so that the constitution making could begin in earnest. Having done some research, they started to recruit legal officers. Then in 1988 the bill establishing the Uganda Constitutional Commission was tabled in the NRC which was the parliament at that time. It was passed in December 1989. There were liberal democratic principles in the statute. There were about eight pillars on which to build the constitution, with the intention to involve as many people as possible in the constitution making, with the Commission knowing that it was autonomous. The law-makers said to the Commission, 'You are autonomous and independent of government. Your only masters are the people, and let the people speak.'

That is the background up to 1989 when the Commission began its work. Now the Commission had originally been given two years. However, it was stated that if the Minister of Constitutional Affairs found that two years were not going to be enough, he had the power to extend that time. So we joined together with Miria R.K. Matembe in March 1989. And from there we worked together and the programme continued until we completed the work in June 1993 with the *Draft Constitution,* the *Main Report,* and the *Index of Sources of Information* that people had given to us. (Fr Waliggo pointed out the 3 volumes on his desk.)

I had been in exile from 1983 until I came back at the end of 1988. I had been approached from the very beginning in March 1986 about working on the Uganda Constitutional Commission. The first time I met Miria Matembe, in March 1989, she was a newly appointed member of the Commission. At the same time, she was doubling as a member of the NRC, so she had that double work. Many of us were full time, but there were some members who were members of Parliament at the same time.

Our opening exercise was very good. We said, if we are going to be together for all these years doing this work, let us first know each other, academically and socially. So, each one of us was asked to present a paper which would then be discussed by the others, what we called internal seminars, to be able to know and appreciate each other. There were only two women out of 21 commissioners, and both women were lawyers. The other one beside Miria was Mary Maitum. Both of them took the themes of women. Miria chose to discuss the fundamental rights of women and Mary Maitum gave a presentation on women and international human rights conventions. So straightaway we knew that the women agenda was going to be very important. And we had already seen of course that in the NRM this was an important issue.

I became interested to know more about this issue because of the energy and strong expressions with which Miria brought out her remarks. I had to ask myself: 'Who is this powerful woman?' So, you know, through daily friendly interaction, I got to know where she comes from and her family background. Then we would talk, talk and talk during breaktime. Very often at this initial period I used to sit next to Miria. One thing I may mention is that I was the only religious leader inside the Commission. Miria was always very respectful. However much I said I wanted to be called John Mary, she always called me Father.

Something special happened during our initial sessions at the Commission. During one of these sessions, Miria said to me: 'You, Father, if you are a genuine religious leader and you don't fully support the rights of women, then you will be betraying your ministry (*laughter*). You must be a friend of women on the Commission.' This was a very challenging message to me which I reflected on very often whenever women's issues and issues concerning other vulnerable groups were being discussed.

Okay, I will say, although there were two women out of 21 commissioners, one thing we have to appreciate, is that we did not find, even me, big obstacles or opposition to women's rights. We said we want to make the women's rights an agenda for progress. No one on the Commission had any objection. We moved together on it. Oh, you could find one or two of the men who jokingly would begin making some jokes on women, but Miria made it clear from the very beginning that humiliating jokes should be out! Sometimes during a tense discussion, you would get something, one male commissioner, thinking he was bringing in a good humour with a point on women, but if that point undermined the status of women, then you would see Miria intervening strongly and saying, 'No.' (*laughter*) So gradually we learned how to discuss with humorous jokes that would not offend anyone. I think that was a major issue. And that is exactly what the Chairman did in the CA in 1994 when some male member made a joke, 'You know that when a woman says "no," she means "yes."' And the women in the CA walked out, to show their dignity and call on members, 'Please, let's be serious.' So I think that was a good lesson women Constituent Assembly delegates (CADs) gave to the men!

Now I will just briefly pass through the processes and show the role of Miria in the constitution making. As I have said, the first part was getting to know each other during the internal seminars, and we got to know Matembe. She had a very clear agenda, and her clear agenda was mainly on women and children, and nothing but full liberation for them was acceptable. She got together well with people who had a strong sense of social justice, who had a strong sense of gender sensitivity, who had a strong sense of liberation, and who had a historical mind to know what women and children have gone through. In short, people who were for a new order. But if you were conservative, you would get a few bullets of words from that corner there, where Miria sat (*laughter*).

After the internal seminars, the next step was to get together and make out the programme of our work. We unanimously decided that the agenda of the constitution-making exercise should come from the people, if the process was to be true and genuine. We organised to go to all the existing 34 districts and to the major organisations of civil society: women, youths, workers, professionals, religious leaders, political leaders, persons with disabilities, universities and other tertiary institutions of learning, and to the security organs, civil service and the like. These workshops were either for one or two days.

After brief presentations by the commissioners on: whether Uganda needed a new constitution; a historical background of

Uganda's governance; what is a national constitution; what usual aspects are covered by most national constitutions; outlines of the 1962 and 1967 Constitutions; the mandate and time of the Commission, then we would ask people some crucial questions. Do you want a new constitution for Uganda? If so, what type of constitution do you want? What items should it address? How should the new constitution bring an end to dictatorship, wars and instability? How can every Ugandan fully participate meaningfully in the making of the new constitution? What are your views on the proposed programme and timetable of the Commission? What are the main controversial issues you want the new constitution to resolve or address? Do you have any other points on the entire agenda and exercise?

In these workshops, I sometimes paired with Matembe to go to districts such as Tororo, Mpigi, and so on. Two or three Commissioners went to every such workshop. It is during such workshops that you would see Matembe with all her power of expression, the ability to arouse the sentiments of people, her power to make women participants happy for having an outspoken woman in the group of Commissioners, a woman who spoke and everybody listened. Participants would laugh, ululate, shout, and clap as she challenged the old-fashioned male domination and oppression! In some places you would find people who were a little bit conservative who would say: 'Oh my goodness, she's saying things which are not usually said.' But that was her work and mission.

In every such seminar or workshop, Matembe very much insisted on finding out how many women were in attendance. She would then challenge the male organisers, 'Where are the women? Where are they? You have chosen as usual to leave them in the kitchen, haven't you? Out of 5000 participants, you could invite only these few women? Yet we are your mothers, your aunts, your sisters, your wives! You should be ashamed! How do you leave your mothers out of this every important exercise?' She made a very important point which really challenged the organisers. As more seminars were held, more women were invited. That was a score to which Matembe richly contributed.

Everywhere we went, the TV, radio and print media followed us. Each seminar was widely reported on. For five years the media and people were never tired of the constitutional process.

It remained very popular throughout. I think this media influenced the kind of words Miria would say. It influenced her call to women to fully know that the constitution making was their unique chance for liberation!

Throughout this period, Matembe utilised her various positions of leadership to advance the cause of women. As a commissioner she fully participated in workshops. As a member of NRC, she mobilised all women in her Mbarara district constituency. As the Chairperson of Action for Development, she organised women seminars on the constitution. Many women began to say, 'The constitution is our saviour. If we don't fully participate, we shall never, never achieve equality.' Through the Ministry of Women in Development, women received grants from DANIDA to organise their own constitutional seminars in all the 167 counties of Uganda, and for the various civil society organisations of women: women journalists, judges, lawyers, politicians, etc. Women tried hard to have a common agenda, to make sure they were not left out of the constitution, and to encourage all women groups to submit memoranda to the Commission.

Now, I should just mention that, on the Commission, each of us had an interest in special categories of people. I was committed to having schools fully participate and all religious groups in Uganda: Muslims, Protestants and Catholics. Whenever they invited me at weekends, I would go, to make sure they fully participated in the constitution making. Miria Matembe and Mary Maitum did the same for women. Through the Ministry for Women in Development, the women of Uganda came up with a united memorandum to the Commission in 1991. This was a powerful document which was presented in style to the Commission. Among the 26,000 memoranda to the Commission, almost half came from women's organisations and individuals. This was a great achievement of women for a common liberation. Miria made a great contribution to it. She succeeded in convincing women that it was a question of either now or never. If women wanted their aspirations and desires to be included in the constitution, then they should not miss this rare chance that comes once. Her emotional and emphatic call bore many fruits!

Let me now mention another contribution of Miria in constitution making. Some people in the seminars tried to be wiser than Miria, especially those who were lawyers! When women would be asked what they wanted the constitution to address, they would give their views from their everyday experiences. One woman wanted wife-beating to be abolished by the constitution. Then a 'wise' lawyer would stand up and say that is not a constitutional matter. Then Miria would jump up with an angry expression on her face and say: 'Ah, ah, ah, stop that nonsense! Anything that any person brings up here is a constitutional matter. To decide what is constitutional or not constitutional is not your affair. Let everyone tell her own story in her own way.' This message from Miria was very empowering and liberating. The people who would come to workshops, perhaps afraid and wondering how they could contribute to constitution making, found an able defender and empowerer. Miria would say: 'You just explain your concerns, your worries, your sufferings, your difficulties and you express your aspirations and your desires. What is it that you want to see in the Uganda of tomorrow? What type of Uganda do you want yourselves, your children and grandchildren to live in peacefully and happily?' This message liberated many people to express their real from-the-heart feelings and daily experiences. In all these workshops, Miria was a much more powerful speaker when she was speaking from the heart. She is not the person who would communicate enthusiastically from a written paper to be read to the audience!

Another thing I have much valued in Matembe in sensitisation seminars is her expertise in pedagogical or well designed shocking exaggerations! To make an impressive point when talking about a section of people who have been for a long time oppressed systematically by culture, laws, religions and patriarchy, you need to exaggerate a bit if you want to make a point. You need to know how to shock people in order to make them grasp the point you wish to make. This is one of Matembe's tricks or methods of making an impact, an impact which cannot be easily forgotten by both men and women! She has the power to revolutionalise an issue so that everyone can see the point she is making.

I am not saying she is an extremist. I am only saying that if something is crooked on one side, *(demonstrated his point with his hands)*, to put it straight, one has to bend it in the other direction so that it can come out in the middle. This strategy made Matembe one of the most media focused persons throughout the constitutional exercise! She uttered the quotable quotes loved by the young, free-roving media! The more she protested against media reporting of her remarks, the more the media became attracted to her!

Having sensitised people and having received a 29-item agenda for the constitution, we settled down for a few months to do what the people requested us to do. They wanted us to give them educational guidelines on those 29 items, which included the specific rights of women, children, workers, persons with disabilities, etc. They wanted us to reproduce copies of the former constitutions and produce brochures on how they should prepare and submit their memoranda to the Commission. They also wanted to know the existing laws which offended against human rights, and particularly the rights of women in inheritance, marriage and at the dissolution of marriage. Miria contributed much to this exercise, using the many research assistants we had to develop the section on women rights and the laws which discriminated against women. She was working hand in hand with Mary Maitum and other commissioners. The UN Convention Against All Forms of Discrimination Against Women (CEDAW, 1979) was the key test. After publishing these educational materials, the Commission went back to the people.

The next phase for the Commission was to tour all the 900 sub-counties in Uganda, giving a one-day workshop in each on the constitutional issues identified by the people, and receiving their views. During the sensitisation phase, people had warned us: 'You are our sons and daughters; if you let us give views out of ignorance and we make a bad constitution, you will be accountable. Your job is to enlighten us so that we can contribute intelligently rather than from ignorance!'

And this is what we were telling people: 'Contribute out of knowledge, not ignorance. When ignorance is shared, it multiplies. If we share knowledge, knowledge is multiplied.' Miria empowered people to offer intelligent views. Apart from the North, Miria was not afraid to go anywhere else in Uganda to give these sub-county workshops. A few commissioners exhibited a lot of fears to go to the insecure areas of the East, Karamoja and the North.

In our final year of work, Miria managed to go to several areas of insecurity. She came back with lots of new insights about the sufferings of women and children in those areas of the North and East. These trips brought a new theme into her life: women and children in areas of conflicts. Apart from those areas, Miria worked more in the areas of the West and Buganda. To understand Miria's contribution, you have to know that when she's speaking, she goes beyond just women issues to all other issues for empowering every one of the vulnerable groups. In her view, whatever enslaves any category of people must go. Whatever policy the government chooses, whatever structure it wants to set up must be completely sensitive to the majority of people, who happen to be women and all other vulnerable groups. Having completed the 900 sub-counties, the Commission came to the next phase.

The next step was to receive views and memoranda as they came in and to translate all those memoranda which were written in local languages. As I have already said, there were a total of about 26,000 memoranda, some as long as 300 pages and others as short as one page or one-half a page. A lot of memoranda came from grassroots people in Ankole where Miria comes from. Occasionally, Miria helped in translating the meaning of some of these memoranda.

When the Commission embarked on the exercise of collecting all views, oral and written, from all the 900 sub-counties, again Miria fully participated. People had requested the Commission to collect their views to ensure that government did not interfere with them! The Commission honoured this request. Miria was overjoyed when she discovered women had submitted a lot of views, both orally and in the written form. This meant they had heeded the call to fully participate, and tell their own stories, and articulate what they wanted in the new constitution.

The next major task was to divide work among ourselves, for the analysis of the views submitted and then writing draft chapters. Matembe was in the group to analyse views on Parliament, the Executive and Judiciary. All views had been summarised under the 29 agenda topics. What did the people say about citizenship? You would find their views in a summary of say 400 pages, people's views on Parliament in a summary of 600 pages, etc. This was a very challenging period. In Miria's committee of four, two members were also members of the NRC. Very often they would finish their NRC meetings at 5.00 or 5.30 p.m., and then they would come to the Commission to begin work on their assignment. Sometimes they would work up to 9.00 or 10.00 p.m. I really think this type of work challenged Miria very much, but she made a real contribution.

After every committee had agreed on the contents of the chapters under them, each commissioner was asked to write one draft chapter. Miria was given the chapter on Parliament. We then conceived a plan to move away from the Commission premises to a hideout at Nabugabo Lake, 150 kilometres from Kampala. At this place there was no electricity, no flush toilets, but it had plenty of monkeys and birds! Miria joined the group for some days. As you know, Miria is mainly for active life, not secluded intellectual retreats! She felt as if she was in a cage! But she worked hard. We hired a generator to be able to work beyond midnight!

One of us, the late Lt. Colonel Sserwanga-Lwanga, used to work until 3.00 a.m. and be the first to get up at 6.00 a.m.! We had a good life there, socially speaking, always being jolly. One person would write the first draft of the chapter by hand, pass it on to another for comment, then to another, and the last person wrote the final text of the draft. Then a driver would take those handwritten draft chapters to Kampala for typing! During this exercise I discovered Miria could adapt herself to every situation, however hard it may be. She is very good in creating a friendly atmosphere for teamwork. She has a rich collection of real experiences about the suffering of women and girls which remain in the minds of her listeners.

Back in Kampala the entire Commission studied every draft chapter, paragraph by paragraph and approved the final chapter. There were 26 chapters in all. These made the Main Report of the Commission, entitled 'Analysis and Recommendations.' It ran to 900 pages. Each chapter ended with the recommendations which were used in the draft constitution. During this period, Miria was very attentive and powerful to ensure that we respected people's views, and particularly the expressed desires and aspirations of women. She was keen to ensure that the entire women agenda as expressed in the memoranda was fully respected. Women and children were to get equal rights. On citizenship she once again stood for equal rights for men and women. She was an enthusiastic supporter for special sections on the rights of women and children, and she found no objections from the other commissioners, who were all fully committed to the fundamental rights of all citizens and all vulnerable groups. Up to this moment Miria had not taken seriously the need to emphasise the rights of persons with disabilities, youth and workers and minorities in the same way as the rights of women and children. But gradually she understood the need for liberating all vulnerable groups and creating an effective collaboration among them. Once she was convinced of this, then in the CA she was to champion a lobby group of all vulnerable groups and their CAD representatives.

Having completed the main report, the Commission worked on the draft constitution. Much of the work had already been done in the recommendations within the Main Report. Yet knowing that the Constituent Assembly was to discuss only the draft constitution, every commissioner was alert and active to ensure that the draft constitution contained all the major recommendations in the Main Report. Despite her busy schedule of work, Miria tried her best to be fully present in the discussion of every article in the draft constitution. Our work ended very happily although everyone was tired. During the month of December 1992, several commissioners and staff worked many nights beyond midnight to meet the deadline of 31 December. This was the day the Commission was to submit the Main Report and the draft constitution to the President. Up to midday of 31st December, some of us were in the printing and binding houses trying to get the texts ready for presentation to the President at 2.00 p.m. at Mbarara, 300 kilometres from Kampala. But we squarely met and beat the deadline! (*laughter*)

The remaining months of 1993 were for publishing the draft constitution and distributing it widely to the people; the final editing and publication of the Main Report, as well as distributing copies to the districts and other organs; and completing the editing and publication of the Index of People's Sources and statistical analysis of controversial issues. To keep our promise to the people that the government did not tamper with anything we had done, we had to do all the above ourselves.

Matembe was very happy with the entire work of the Commission. In the draft constitution she saw all the rights of women and children she stood for. All that she had been fighting for all her life was now part of the constitutional draft. That is when she conceived the idea that she should stand for election to the Constituent Assembly to go therein and defend the draft constitution she had been involved in putting in place. I wished her well and promised her my moral support.

The Commission let Miria down on some issues. When it came to the issue of representation of interest groups in Parliament, some commissioners were against special representatives. Those who supported the principle were a bit concerned on the numbers of such representation. By the time the constitution-making exercise started, there were 34 districts, and each district had a woman representative in the NRC. At the conclusion of our exercise, there were 39 districts. Some felt that perhaps we would be accused of favouring the Movement system which had introduced the affirmative action by allocating one seat in Parliament for a woman district representative. Some Ugandans saw this provision as a tactic of the Movement to get votes from women. In the end we decided that women should be represented by 15 members in the new Parliament, chosen on the basis of regions rather than districts.

Miria Matembe, Mary Maitum and a few other commissioners were not very happy with this proposal, but gradually the consensus emerged for 15 women representatives in Parliament. Matembe took this issue to the Constituent Assembly and won an overwhelming support for the principle of one woman representative in Parliament for each district! She did not achieve this alone, but in intimate connection with all CAD women and many CAD men. The principle enshrined in the Constitution is that every district is to have a woman representative in Parliament. Today, Uganda has 58 districts, and each has a woman representative in Parliament.

The other issue on which Matembe and the majority of commissioners lost out at this stage was the requirement of the draft constitution to be written in non-sexist language. Most of the commissioners wanted an inclusive language throughout the text of the draft constitution. But the expert drafter did not like the cumbersome nature of this, and he thought that such language would make the draft longer than necessary. The consensus that gradually emerged was to allow the expert drafter to do what he was most used to. Of course Miria and others were not completely happy at this consensus, but Miria became determined to fight this issue, in case she was elected to the Constituent Assembly. And once there she did just that so energetically that our new Constitution is written in non-sexist language throughout!

The third and last idea on which our Commission did not pay enough attention was the representation of interest groups at the local government levels. The memoranda we received did not call attention to it. In the Constituent Assembly, this representation became a real issue. Working with the CA women caucus, Matembe was able to put this issue on the constitutional agenda. At the conclusion, women had been given an affirmative representation of one-third on all local councils. The improvement on the Constitution chapter on local government owes a lot to the women CA delegates, and Matembe played an important role there. The Equal Opportunities Commission was not fully developed in the draft and it remains vague even in the Constitution. Because of that vagueness, this commission has not been established, five years after the promulgation of the Constitution! Many of its duties seem to be carried out by the Uganda Human Rights Commission or the Inspectorate of Government and the Leadership Code.

So what I can say is that during the five years I was with Matembe on the Commission, I found her very resourceful, and very friendly, especially if you were a good listener and if you had a liberated mind. She has a good sense of humour and a loving heart, especially when deep down you shared what her life was. I got to know much more about her family background. For example, the mother was sick and I used to go there. When the mother died, we went to bury her. I got to know how Miria grew up, why she decided, 'I must make a mark'. From time to time, she would just give me a whisper, and say, 'You know, Father, when my name is in the newspaper and I'm doing something good, I want my mother to read it.' That motivation to achieve something. She always wanted to be remembered for her small contribution to the women's movement, to women's rights, and her contribution to the Constitution. You know the NRM movement can go but they will certainly be remembered for the Constitution.

Now after we parted, she came and discussed running for the Constituent Assembly, and whether members of the Commission should try to go there. I decided that I would not go to the CA, even if I was nominated. We discussed this at different times, many of us, whether to stand, having done our work, or whether we should leave that work to others. We did everything, even this whole report by consensus, every paragraph, and every paragraph of the draft constitution by consensus. So that even now when I talk about the Constitution, there is no gentleman or gentlewoman who was a member here who would say that we were interested in anything other than respecting the people's views. There wasn't any cheating. There wasn't any manipulation. So from that point of view, nobody can say there was anything there forced by strong arm. Whenever we disagreed on anything, we would consult again. If Matembe, after missing two meetings, found that we had passed a provision she did not agree with, then she would say 'I don't agree with this.' Our Chairman, Justice Ben Odoki, who always sought our consensus, would then say, 'We'll go back to reconsider the point raised.'

When Matembe decided she would run for the CA, the commissioners did not have objection. When the election campaigns for the CA began, four other commissioners also chose to stand as candidates and they all passed through. We regarded this as a good point, because these members would be able to explain fully how we had come to the decisions we made, basing them on the people's views and wishes.

As a member of the CA, Matembe came to see me with Hope Mwesigye, woman member for Kabale. They wanted to discuss how to set up a women's caucus within the CA. My view was that this was a very good idea, but such a caucus should include all CA representatives of vulnerable groups: youths, persons with disability and workers. Such a caucus would then be bigger and more powerful, with one voice for liberation. I recommended the caucus to receive funds from an Austrian organisation run by Ursula Steller, and this fund helped the caucus to set up an efficient secretariat, which did a lot of good work on research, lobbying and training members how to lobby for their interests. I continued to interact with Matembe to discuss new strategies in the CA. The work of the women CADs was so successful that women, children, etc., got all they demanded in the new Constitution. The Movement caucus could not afford to antagonise women.

My only contribution in supporting them was a weekly column every Thursday in *The New Vision* from 1994 to the promulgation of the Constitution in October 1995. In that column I dealt with many constitutional issues which were being debated in the CA. Matembe and many other CA delegates said they much valued the views and guidance in that column.

That is how I have seen Matembe and worked with her for all these years since early 1989. I have visited her home to meet her husband and their children. I was very warmly received. When she was going to stand for Parliament in 1996, after the CA, she told me she was a bit worried since politics in Mbarara were taking a religious sectarian line. She feared some Catholic women might reject her. I told her, 'Never fear or be worried as long as you yourself completely avoid that religious sectarianism.' I assured her, most people were no longer electing people along religious lines. They were now electing good people, efficient people, people who were determined to serve all in justice. Matembe was elected Member of Parliament in June 1996. She was very happy.

She has learn that in politics not everyone will love you or appreciate your work. What is most important is to know the motivation you have in seeking a leadership position. As a member of Parliament, she decided to do her Master's degree in law in England where she had gone for medical treatment. When she completed her Master's degree she was very happy and appreciative of all the advice. I was very happy with her performance as well. Since she was appointed Minister of Ethics and Integrity, she has been involving me in her workshops to work out the mandate of the Ministry and on the methodology to take in advancing ethical and moral and cultural values among all Ugandans. I am convinced she is doing a very good job.

Overall, I find Matembe a woman who has a clear purpose in life, and is determined in achieving that purpose. And she has gradually grown, especially in knowing how politics is played. At first she used to be so disappointed if something failed, but now she knows that that's the life. Even if you are failing, you have to fight, and you shouldn't just give up or feel miserable. You learn to say, we used one strategy and it failed, now take another strategy. That's what really shows that someone has grown to political maturity. The journalists and the media have a special interest in her with her bombastic words, somehow. But she seems to know how to enjoy it and the journalists know how to enjoy it as well. She has begun saying, 'Ah, those people, they can report what they want. They're not taking me away from my agenda.' So there is that love/hate relationship. When she is not in the daily papers, many people ask 'Where is Matembe these days?'

So, Miria has achieved her mission which she aimed at. She has seen the best of it. She has also seen the weaknesses within even the women's movement, the jealousy, the disunity. But you know, to unite the women's movement, you have to sacrifice some of your views, so that you move together as a group. I think she has seen that. Now she is happy to know that the issue of women's rights is not simply in the hands of women, but there are many men out there who also support women's rights now that these rights have become constitutional.

Note

1   At the Mukono conference ACFODE also made other timely recommendations: that every ministry should have a women's desk; that more women's representatives be mandated at all levels of government; and that the NCW (National Council of Women) be replaced by a more representative, more independent umbrella organisation for women's NGOs.

CHAPTER 5

Women in the National Resistance Council and the Constituent Assembly

I t may be hard to comprehend that at the same time I was working with the Commission to create a draft constitution, I was also serving in the newly expanded National Resistance Council (NRC), and as Chairperson of ACFODE. It is good that I was a younger woman. These days, more than a decade later, recalling my hectic schedule during that period makes me ask, how was I able to do all I did? It seems that my dream of a better world for women sustained and inspired me, and the God whom I depend on and trust provided the strength and guidance required for the work.

Before continuing further with the story of constitution making, this time in the Constituent Assembly (CA), let me describe my experience in the NRC where for the first time a good number of women became members and participants in the activities of that House. This milestone of women entering parliamentary politics in large numbers should be understood and celebrated. First some background.

When the National Resistance Movement (NRM) took over the government in 1986, it established one of its existing organs, the NRC as the legislative assembly (parliament) for the country. This assembly consisted largely of people who had participated in the bush war and a few others appointed from the general public as ministers. In 1989, the NRC was expanded and elections held, elections which brought into the NRC women in numbers that no previous government had seen, as well as members from other formerly unrepresented groups. In fact, 1989 was a defining moment in the political history of Uganda. In that year Parliament was opened up to be more representative of Uganda's population (Tamale 1999).[1]

Thirty-six women were elected to the NRC in 1989, 34 as district women representatives and two others (Rhoda Kalema and Victoria Sekitoleko) in open seats. In addition, three women were appointed by the President, and two others were part of the original NRC who participated in the bush war. Though the total number of 41 women was quite small in an assembly of 270 members, their presence in Parliament was a big step forward for the women of Uganda. One woman, Hon. Victoria Sekitoleko, was appointed the Minister of Agriculture, a very important portfolio, bearing in mind that women in Uganda are the backbone of agriculture. Three women, Hon. Gertrude Byekwaso Lubega, Hon. Betty Bigombe, and Hon. Joyce Mpanga, were appointed Ministers of State. Five women, Hon. Gertrude Njuba, Hon. Betty Okwir, Hon. Dr Wandira Kazibwe, Hon. Florence Nkurukenda, and Hon. Rhoda Kalema, were appointed deputy ministers. Since the affirmative action seats for women were based on one per district, every time a new district was created, another woman joined Parliament.

By the 1996 elections, the number of district women representatives had risen from 36 to 39. In that election, 26 women candidates ran for mainstream seats with eight of these, almost one-third, being successful. Four women were chosen to represent special interest groups: one from the youth, one from the army, and two from people with disabilities. One woman was appointed as a minister, and became an ex-officio Member of Parliament, making the total number of women in Parliament 52 (19 percent). Yes, Uganda was experiencing a new phenomenon, that is, a large number of women legislators in position to influence the political process at the national level.

Since the 1989 elections, a lively debate about the effectiveness of women Council Members (CMs)[2] has taken place around the country, especially in the media and among academicians. In developing countries like Uganda, a member of Parliament is expected to play a wider role than simply sitting in Parliament to make laws. MPs are expected to mobilise the people in their constituencies for development. To this end, they are expected to conduct educational programmes, organise people to participate in self-help projects, and to contribute funds to the developmental and social projects in their local areas.

In fact, women MPs face a dilemma which has been much discussed but has certainly not been resolved as yet. The dilemma is, who exactly does a woman representative represent, everyone in her constituency, or mainly the women in her constituency? One could say that each woman MP in Uganda has two kinds of responsibilities in two different fields of action as stated above for all MPs, first, in the parliamentary body itself, debating and influencing the laws and policies of the government, and second, back home in the constituency, listening, advising, and solving problems at the local level. But what is the main work of women MPs in the House, representing women? And what is their main work in their home districts, sensitising the public about gender issues and organising their fellow women to participate in public life and exercise their rights, or something else? In my own case, I believe that I serve my constituency – families, communities and the district - best by focusing considerable attention on helping the most vulnerable members of society, women and children.

It is not surprising that, in Uganda's patriarchal society women representatives in the NRC were criticised whatever they did. A statement from *The Weekly Topic* (16 March 1990) shows the kind of mind-set that was frequently reflected in media comments on this subject.

> [W]hat they should remember is that they have made very few lasting political and economic gains. The place of women

in public life today was given to them by men. Tomorrow a chauvinistic government can amend the law and remove NRC representatives for women. ...

An implied threat appears to underline this entire statement. In this writer's view, women do not have a right to a place in public life unless men have given it to them. And it is further implied that men's permission for women to participate could be withdrawn at any time, if... if... if what?

This short-sighted view leaves out the historical fact that Ugandan women joined men in the armed struggle that we know as the bush war. This participation of women in the resistance against political oppression became the basis for their claim to increased participation in the future politics of the country. During those years in the bush, gender questions began to be consciously addressed by the National Resistance Army (NRA) and the (NRM).

Women entered the bush war for different reasons: loss of husbands, children and other relatives; political harassment and intimidation; or being caught in the war zones. As part as my MA dissertation research, I interviewed Major John Kazoora and Captain Gertrude Njuba. Kazoora told me,

> Women had grievances. Their husbands were killed, others jailed. Women and their daughters were being raped. So generally women were antagonised and anguished, in some cases, even more than the men (1997).

Kazoora said that whereas some men deserted, he did not recall any woman deserting. He hailed women's tenacity, honesty and dedication to the struggle.

Ankrah gives the categories of women who went to the bush this way. The first consisted of ordinary women, housewives, traders, and farmers who secured food and cooked it for fighters and supplied them with information needed for planning. The second category included cadres, propagandists and recruiters to the movement and the NRA, who worked outside the camps but serviced the guerilla infrastructure. The third category consisted of professional fighters, mostly young women, trained in the tactics of guerilla warfare. All the women played vital roles that led to the success of the NRM/A.

Byanyima (1992), herself a participant in the guerilla war, says that women's involvement in this war constituted an important stage in their history of struggle for equality. She argues that this struggle provided women with unique opportunity to engage in political governance at the same time they were challenging the tradition of male dominance. Another warrior in the bush war, Gertrude Njuba, says,

> Women's support was so crucial that if a woman of the home did not support the struggle, we could not occupy the forest of that home or the neighbouring forests. However, once the woman consented, we would be assured of accommodation, safety, food and information (1997).

Njuba says that women were also very influential in persuading their husbands and sons to join the struggle, and once these joined, the guerillas were assured of food supplies and protection, since the women were eager to provide food for their sons and husbands, and to conceal them from government forces.

According to Njuba and Kazoora, affirmative action, the principle which later became a cornerstone of women's participation in the new politics of the country, was born out of the necessities of life in the bush under wartime conditions. These two bush warriors argue that when men and women lived as colleagues in the bush, everyone came to appreciate women's potential, their special needs, and the constraints on them that needed special attention. I want to make it clear that, as these stories show, the women of Uganda themselves *earned* their place in public life. It was not simply given to them by men as this uninformed chauvinist suggests.

Returning to the statement above, that women have made few lasting political and economic gains indicates a very traditional, out-dated view of the economic realities in Uganda. These days it is widely recognised that women in Uganda produce an estimated 70 per cent of the agricultural output of our predominantly agricultural economy. The question here is, if women perform a good percentage of the work involved, why have they not made more substantial economic gains? The truth is that our archaic socio-cultural system is structured so that women perform much of the work that leads to economic gains, but their contribution remains largely invisible, and they, the workers, are often excluded from the benefits their work brings to families, communities, and the nation.

Tamale raises a very interesting question regarding the 1989 elections, that is, whether the term 'representative' is misleading since each representative was elected by an electoral college. And then, most of those voting to elect women district representatives were men. When the upcoming elections were announced, in some districts men quickly became what Tamale called 'self-appointed hunters of "appropriate" women' to fill the newly created seats. Ninety percent of the women who joined NRC in 1989 told Tamale that they had been approached by male 'elders' (1999:118). It is good to see that this phenomenon of men being the ones to choose women candidates has faded to a good degree in subsequent elections.

I was not aware until I started serving in the NRC how very progressive the male councillors in Mbarara District were. Instead of choosing a 'proper,' polite, soft-spoken woman to run for the women's seat in their district, they had chosen me, in part because of my outspoken ways and non-traditional views about women's place in society. In fact, it was men in Mbarara District who had sought me out and encouraged and supported my candidacy, although, as the reader knows, I had been waiting for years for this opportunity and was determined to contest the first parliamentary election open to me.

It should also be recalled that at the time this affirmative action (women's seats in the NRC) was introduced, the women's movement in Uganda was in its infant stage and its influence had not yet been widely felt. It is hardly surprising that since women had been historically left out of national decision making, when the doors were suddenly flung open for them, the majority of the women were not really prepared to participate in politics at the national level. Tamale (1999) makes an interesting comparison that helps us put this issue of inexperience in perspective. She says that women joining the NRC were as unprepared as men would be to tend homes. The fact is that some of these women had not been at all interested in politics, and had been all but dragged into running for election by men. In contrast, some women CMs had played leadership roles in NGOs and CBOs in their communities and had gained recognition and valuable organisational experience in those groups (Tripp 2000:74). In a few cases, women were chosen because in their districts there were very few women with enough education to qualify, as any candidate was required to be at least a Standard 6 graduate. In addition, it should be noted that the space into which women were being pushed (NRC) was both compositionally and institutionally a male one. Tamale describes the parliamentary culture as having a 'men's club character' where women are treated as intruders (1999:118). In that sense, this parliamentary body could be seen as territory foreign to women.

These difficulties notwithstanding, it is evident that the women in the NRC were able to make an impression on the political scene. Bearing in mind that the percentage of women was very small compared to men - less than 20 per cent - and that the majority of the women were newcomers to the political scene, sitting in a male-dominated assembly of mostly veteran politicians (that constituted group of 'historicals') these women did an admirable job. A sizeable number of them were professional women, who were gender-sensitive and committed to the women's cause. These women ably and effectively contributed to debates in the assembly, and in the meanwhile, the newcomers were watching, listening and learning.

Hon. Victoria Sebagereka, a CM from Mukono District, noted that although most of the women council members were inexperienced, they were inspired and encouraged by NRM's policies and the Movement's determination to groom them into leaders. She recalls the training courses organised for women by the NRM Secretariat and the Gender Ministry, which training helped them to improve their leadership skills and build their confidence. Sebagereka comments,

> In spite of the constraints we had as pioneers such as big
> geographical constituencies and limited logistics, we were
> able to make an impact (1997).

When I was doing research for my M.A. dissertation in 1997, I
had the opportunity to interview both Professor George
Kanyeihamba and Professor George Kagonyera, CMs
themselves, about their perceptions of the women's
participation in the NRC. Kanyeihamba (1997) described the
first batch of women in the NRC as dedicated and nationalistic,
as able to highlight the plight of women and enlighten the men
on the extent of women's marginalisation. In his opinion, these
women were convincing because they based their contributions
on conviction backed by well-researched information on
important issues, unlike some male CMs who, he suggested,
were mostly interested in addressing the gallery.

> This trend created a culture of seriousness in the NRC
> nurtured by women because their contributions were well
> researched and scientific. Some of the women like Sekitoleko,
> Kazibwe, Matembe and a few others were sophisticated and
> were able to present their case effectively. (Kanyeihamba
> 1997)

Kagonyera (1997) remarked that women like Sekitoleko,
Rwabyomere, Matembe and others were articulate, confident,
and knowledgeable, and that these women made high level
contributions to the debates. He further noted that women
were so influential in the House that men had to change their
condescending ways of using language and analogies
considered by women to be sexist and offensive.

While some female newcomers sat and listened as they
gained confidence, other women were ready from the beginning
to articulate on the gender question and influence decisions
made in the house. In all, there were about ten women who
talked on a regular basis. Those of us who did stand and
contribute could expect to be attacked in that formidable, male-
dominated environment.

In my own case, since I had been on the political circuit for
some time, I had learned how to deal with the boisterous,

sometimes rude opposition of men. Having had experience at the LC5 level, and having strong convictions and an agenda to pursue, no one was going to keep me from standing up and talking in the House. It was interesting, whenever the Chairman of the NRC, Hon. Moses Kigongo, would say my name, granting me the floor to speak, that even those who were dozing would wake up. Not only that, but no sooner did I start to talk than some male CMs would call out, 'Point of order,' or 'Point of information,' in an attempt to intimidate me and shut me up. But I would shoot back something like, 'You shut up. I am already informed. What do you want to inform me about?' It was like real fighting.

In contrast, when another woman would catch the Chairman's eye and he would call out her name, and then men would start to shout, 'Order' and 'Information,' the Chairman would quickly address the men, 'No, let her present her argument,' and the men would quiet down. Yet the Chairman never did that for me. The Chairman and I liked each other very much, and whenever I stood up, he would let me talk, but then, when the men started shouting, he left me on my own. One time I asked him, 'But why don't you protect me like you do the other women?' He laughed and said, 'Ah, you, you can manage on your own.'

Of course, outside the assembly, all the women CMs were able to lobby their male colleagues and solicit their support on the issues of interest to them. Kagonyera observed that on matters of gender, these women CMs would act in unison, even when they had not agreed prior to the debates. (I'll argue later in this chapter that women CMs were not always ready to act in support of a common front.) Kagonyera believes that because women acted together, they were able to influence the NRC to pass a number of laws for the protection and promotion of women's rights.

The remarkable influence of women in the NRC was particularly notable during the debate on the Penal Code Amendment Bill 1990, when the women CMs led the way in raising the penalty for the offences of rape and defilement from 14 years imprisonment to the death penalty. Women's influence was also apparent during the debate on the CA statute when NRC women succeeded in raising the number of designated women representatives to the CA from 15, as originally proposed in the bill, to one woman representative per district, making them 39. They also secured International Women's Day (March 8th) as a public holiday in Uganda, and influenced Parliament to enact a law establishing women's councils.

One woman CM who made a particularly notable contribution to the country during the NRC period deserves a special mention. As Minister for the Pacification of the North, a position specifically created for her, Betty Bigombe worked for the return of peace in the troubled northern part of Uganda. A commitment to peace and reconciliation and enormous personal courage sustained Bigombe as she travelled the length and breadth of the northern region, negotiating with the rebels in a bid to return the area to normalcy. Her openness, flexibility and sensitivity made Bigombe an outstanding negotiator. One important result of her work was the successful return of the ousted former head of state of Uganda, the late Tito Okello Lutwa, and other prominent personalities who had gone into exile. As *The Monitor* newspaper observed,

> This was a remarkable achievement for a 'mere' woman whom the old hands in northern politics once dismissed for a 'political upstart' doomed to failure (4 January 1993).

Bigombe's success at mobilising the people of the north to reject rebel activities remains unsurpassed.

It is not surprising that at times women CMs contradicted each other on matters of gender. For those of us who had very progressive views about these matters, this lack of a united front was really frustrating at times. In any case, women in the NRC failed to form a solid women's front with a common purpose. On a number of occasions, certain women shied away when the gender issues on the floor became controversial. In such situations, these women would remain silent while one vocal woman pursued the argument amidst rude attacks and interruptions from male colleagues. As a woman who was comfortable in this public role as an outspoken advocate for women, I was constantly challenged to deal with this lack of unity and support among my fellow women.

This lack of unity among women was also apparent in a wider sense. Both Kanyeihamba (1997) and Tamale (1996) have observed that in general the women CMs were unable to successfully mobilise the grassroots on the gender question. As a result, what the women's movement was accomplishing at the national level, in fact the 'movement' part of what women were doing, had not effectively reached the grassroots in many parts of the country. This inability to sensitise and mobilise women around the country helps us understand the political fallout in the 1994 elections for the Constituent Assembly, when experienced and highly competent 'parliamentarians like Rebecca Kadaga, Joan Rwabyomere and Joyce Mpanga failed to win their bids for mainstream seats in the CA. In most rural areas, parliamentary politics has continued to mean 'men' to many voters, and women candidates are still regarded largely as intruders in the political arena.

This appears to be a good time to describe in detail an incident that has been inexorably linked to my political career, for better or for worse, an incident that has placed me at the centre of an on-going hot controversy. Let me begin at the beginning to tell this story.

In the 1990s, it was absolutely shocking how many rape and defilement cases were being reported in the press. Women were saying, this is just too much. We must do something. So the decision was made to demonstrate against rape and defilement. The organisational work and the actual demonstration were led by the women CMs from the NRC. We brought in all the related NGOs, the schools and many other groups to take part. It was decided that the demonstrators would walk through the city. Additionally, we would write letters of protest to be submitted to different authorities such as the Ministries of Education and Justice, the DPP (Director of Public Prosecutions), the Speaker of Parliament and the Chief Justice.

We completed the necessary preparations including making large numbers of posters to carry during the demonstration, posters that stated our intense feelings about the matter. On the designated day several hundred women and some men, including male parliamentarians, demonstrated through the city and delivered our letters. Some of the authorities came out and received the delegations and told us they were going to study the situation. Finally, we converged at our city square, now called Constitutional Square. Usually, when we have demonstrations or charity walks in Kampala, that's the place where we would end the demonstration by having different individuals make public statements. At the square, I was called upon to speak. I made quite a long statement. I covered several topics, among them, the commoditisation of women, the marginalisation of girls, and the fact that rape and defilement are rooted in our culture. I included several examples.

Then, as I concluded my remarks, I made a statement that has since taken on a life of its own, a statement that has been often quoted, but more often misquoted. What I said was, 'Finally, I wish to say this, that all rapists, defilers and all those people who in one way or another commit sexual offences, are in possession of potentially dangerous instruments which must be taken away from them if they can't use them properly.' I didn't use the word 'castration'. I should add that among the posters that day were some that said, 'castrate them'. When I finished my remarks, the women demonstrators on the scene cheered and shouted very loudly in approval.

The next day, the headlines in the press read, 'Castrate men, pleads Matembe.' Big headlines . An interesting scene took place at Parliament later that day. When I reached the House in the afternoon, I was running a bit late. I had not yet had a chance to look at the papers. As I was just sitting down, one of the Members of Parliament stood up and said, 'Before I make my point on the subject before the house, I'd like to make a preliminary observation.' He said, 'I have seen in the papers of today that Hon. Matembe is calling for the castration of all men. Surely, if this is true, then I think Matembe has gone berserk and she should be taken to the mental hospital in Butabika.'

Usually, when people say things like this about me, I don't keep quiet. I spring up, sometimes even before the speaker has finished. On this occasion my political instincts told me that I should defend myself, that I should set the record straight, but I was in a bit of a difficult position for two reasons. First, I didn't know exactly what had been printed in the papers. Secondly, I paused because of who was making the remarks. Actually, I knew certain things that if I said them in Parliament, this man wouldn't have taken lightly. Saying them would have helped my position, but I realised I would hurt him so much. God helped me control my tongue, to cool down. After all, there were many members with me at City Square who could stand and defend me. All the eyes of the NRC members turned to me for several minutes. The man continued to talk, and the women sitting there kept quiet. Not a single one said anything in my defence.

I remember motioning to some of the women to stand up and say something. After all, they were with me during the demonstration. They were there and heard what I said. I wanted them to stand up and say, 'Matembe did not refer to all men. She made her remarks about defilers and rapists.' But nobody stood up. They all kept quiet, and the memory of that moment brings me intense pain even today. I felt so lonely. I felt totally alone. In my heart I was feeling so hurt that I was struggling for these people and they couldn't stand up and defend me. This lack of support made me wonder if I was fooling myself. And I thought, surely these women have betrayed me.

While I was still in the house, some of the women wrote me notes, saying, 'Don't worry. We are with you.' They passed them to me where I was sitting. When I walked out of the house, some of them came to me and said, 'Don't be afraid. We are with you.' In my anger of that moment, I responded, 'You are rubbish. You can't be with me outside here when you couldn't stand up in there to defend me. You left me alone in there. Leave me alone now.'

The next day the papers had as headlines, 'Matembe kept quiet.' The papers reported that so-and-so said such and such, and Matembe was expected to make a reply, but instead she was mute. All the eyes in the house looked at her for several minutes, but she kept silent. The next day another headline, 'She said it.' I continued to remain silent on the issue. I never said a word about it. The papers continued to write on the subject, things like, although she keeps quiet, Matembe said 'castration'. From that time, people really abused me through the press and on radio. For all the time this controversy raged, I didn't respond. I didn't discuss this issue for about seven months or so. During this time, I was abused in the media and harassed at public meetings for having called for the castration of men. It was obvious that many men were really angry with me and most did not try to hide their harsh feelings towards me. It is interesting to note that all this time the media were condemning me in one way or another, rape and defilement were not condemned. What an absurd world we live in.

Finally, some months later, I broke my silence. After watching a programme on TV that disturbed me very much, I wrote a letter to the editor of *The New Vision*. The TV programme reported about a seminar in Kampala that the Catholic Church held for Catholic women from all around the country. At the closing of the workshop, the organisers told the women to condemn the use of condoms in the strongest terms. Women at the meeting stood up and read the resolutions which included condemning the use of condoms, and actually advocating the banning of condoms in Uganda. I felt absolutely terrible. Mark you, I had been at the vanguard of the struggle against AIDS for some time. That was the time when Uganda was at the centre of the AIDS scourge. The government was determined to employ any strategy available to combat that disease. Now this action seemed to be counteracting the benefits we were beginning to realise. Imagine. These women leaders had been called to the seminar and pressured to pass these resolutions to ban condoms, the church's position, when many of us had been out all over the country advocating the use of condoms as one means of protecting women from AIDS.

I knew that women have not just double or triple jeopardy, but, should I say, multiple jeopardy, where AIDS is concerned. Consider all these factors. During sexual intercourse with an infected partner, the female is much more liable to pick up HIV/AIDS than the male. Add that, because of culture, many women cannot refuse to have sex with husbands or boyfriends, even when they are convinced the man is infected.

Another problem comes from a polygamous marriage in which it is normal behaviour for a man to have multiple partners, and each wife has no choice but to have intercourse with the man. Look at this situation. The man brings four women to his home. Now they are told, stick to one partner, but how can a woman stick to one when the man is moving around to four women? It is a very dangerous arrangement.

But the problem is not just cultural. It is also related to the supposed economic dependency of women on men. I call it 'supposed' because in actual sense, everyone in society is dependent on the women who till the land, who grow the food, who store, process and cook the food, who manage the household resources, who care for the family, who nurses the sick and looks after the elderly and handicapped. In spite of these contributions, if a woman refuses sex with her husband for any reason, she will be driven away. She will lose her home, she will lose the land that sustains her and even her children. Yes, she can even lose her children. What an impossible, life-threatening situation! She has to say yes to sex all the time, whether the man is infected or not.

This brings up another kind of jeopardy women face, that of caring for the sick without appropriate protection. Performing the service, women are exposed to bodily fluids that may pass the HIV infection to them, the caregivers. Even blood transfusions like I had when I was given a caesarian section during the birth of one of my children can be deadly unless the blood supply is 100 percent safe.

In the case of this workshop I felt defeated and disillusioned to see that, due to religious and cultural beliefs, these women were taking actions that were clearly against their own interests. I didn't know what to do!

I thought about it for three days or so. Then I picked up my pen and wrote a letter to the editor of *The New Vision*. I remember saying that I had decided to keep quiet at one time, but now I was forced to speak up. I said that in the past when I had talked in defence of our little ones who were being defiled and raped, people's wrath was heaped on me. Now, just the other day, I learned about some women leaders being called to a workshop and then being sensitised to condemn the use of condoms to the detriment of their lives. I said, either society is mad or I'm living before my time. It was quite a long letter. Apparently, large numbers of people read it because many responded with letters, saying, 'Matembe was right'. This whole issue on castration has continued to resurface from time to time. First people condemned me. Then they hailed me. Then condemnation again.

At different times people have asked me if I regret saying what I said. Let me say plainly that I do not regret my strong statement. I must say that over the years I have found that many of the media people focus on a single remark I made in public, which was just an off-hand remark, a 'by the way'. Although I usually make extensive statements, the media tends to grab one remark, often out of context, like a dog grabs a bone and never lets go. Of course, I had no idea that this particular controversy and the confusion about exactly what I said would come up again and again. Since I didn't deny the misinformation, I was really condemned by some who did not know the truth. Some people were really very angry, especially men. Even my husband.

I need to describe the reaction of my husband who is generally not angry at anything I say. In all our time together, he had never expressed such anger. However, this time it was different. He had read what was in the paper, and I think he had been confronted by his colleagues at work. When I arrived home after this incident, he said, 'You should check your words before you speak.'

I said, 'So, what did I say now?'

He said, 'This thing about castrating men.'

I said, 'Were you there?' I could see that he was really angry. I said again, 'Were you there? If the press misquoted me, are you going to believe the press instead of defending me? Are you now joining my attackers?' So it ended there.

During this time, I devised a tactic to defuse some of the strong feelings against me over this incident. On different occasions, when I went to see some man at his office, as I was leaving, he would say, 'But, madam, you are scaring us.'

Then I would reply, 'But how am I scaring you?'

He would say, 'About this castration.'

I would say, 'Ay, do you mean that you are also a rapist?'

He would answer, 'No, me, I'd never do that.'

Then I would say, 'So, why are you scared when I was talking about rapists and defilers who are raping helpless women and girls?'

He would say, 'Oh, you were talking about that. Then it's okay.'

I remember one time, when I arrived at a sports club, a man said to me, 'madam, who do you think you are?' He sounded very annoyed.

I said, 'What is the problem?'

He said, 'How can you want to castrate us?'

I said, 'Eh, you people. I thought you were gentlemen. You mean you are also rapists?'

They said, 'No, why are you saying that?'

I then said, 'But I talked about rapists. Why are you nervous?'

'Oh,' they said, 'You mean those? Then it's OK.'

So that's how the whole thing died down at least a little. Of course, in the campaign for Parliament in 1996, my opponents really used this issue against me, making accusations against me during public rallies. Someone would ask, 'Why do you want to castrate our men?' Such charges I chose to answer indirectly.

I would say, 'Now, you men, do you have a girl of 6 or 7 years?' Someone would say that he did. Then I would say, 'If you found a man on top of that girl, tearing her to pieces, what would you do?'

Then all of them would shout in unison, 'I would spear him. I would kill him.'

Then I would say, 'Then I'm a better person than you are. The Bible says, "Thou shalt not kill." For me, I'm not for killing. The same Bible says that if any part of your body makes you want to sin, what do you do?'

'Cut it off,' they would shout.

'So,' I would reply, 'what wrong did I do? Conforming to God's word, I tell you, I'm a better person than you.'

Then they would say, 'Oh, Mama Matembe, go and castrate them.' So that's how I managed to counteract some of the anger directed at me.

What people think I said keeps coming back again and again and again. But these days it is starting to come back on the positive side. Recently, in Kampala a child of three months was defiled. I was aware of the case but I kept quiet. I didn't make any public statement or talk about the incident to anyone. Soon there was a public demand, 'Where is Matembe? Where is Matembe?' Because people were demanding a statement from me, finally I went on the radio to talk about this incident. And from that day forward, people seem to be saying, 'She was right. She was right.' So finally I felt I had been vindicated.

Returning to the NRC experience, one part that wasn't so positive was that we women CMs never managed to organise ourselves to talk and act with a common front. For instance, I would stand up and talk about women based on the work I had been doing, and some woman would stand up and argue against me. I remember a time when we had a meeting of women CMs, and I told the women, 'I'm determined to quit because I am tired.' I was tired of getting a standard negative response from many men without support from women. Many times I raised issues on gender equality to be harassed right and left by men. 'Information,' 'Order,' the men would shout. In my previous political work, the more men attacked me, the more determined I became. But these attacks by men were really detracting me so that I would back off. My main disappointment was that my female colleagues just kept quiet. Why were they not taking up the cause? Why were they not defending me? I wondered. Yes, many times I felt exhausted, worn out, and alone. Looking back now I can see that the lessons learned by women in the NRC were a key factor in women being able to do what was necessary to achieve our goals in the Constituent Assembly. Let me move to the story of the CA now.

On 18 February 1993, the Minister of State for Justice and Constitutional Affairs presented a bill to the NRC on establishing a Constituent Assembly. The Assembly would be given the mandate of debating the draft constitution and presenting a finalised version to the government and the people. There was heated debate in the NRC about how the CA should be constituted. It had been originally proposed that the CA would be composed of the members of the NRC. However, since the people of Uganda had been educated about the constitution-making exercise, they had taken their own personal involvement in the process seriously. The above proposal was rejected on the ground that if the constitution was to be truly the people's constitution, based on the people's views, the people had to be the ones to decide who would discuss the draft and promulgate the new constitution. Therefore the idea of a Constituent Assembly elected through universal adult suffrage was adopted.

The CA statute was passed in the NRC in April 1993. Section 4 of the statute stipulated the categories of people to be elected as delegates to the CA: first of all, delegates directly elected from each electoral area; and secondly, delegates representing interest groups such as women, youth, people with disabilities, workers, and the army. Some people criticised the inclusion of special seats on the grounds that this diluted democracy by bringing in a large number (about 25 per cent) of delegates to the CA who were elected indirectly. On the other hand, many believed that this proviso enhanced democracy by enabling groups that were normally marginalised to participate fully in the constitution-making process. In the absence of a provision of this nature, the majority of Ugandans would not have had a full voice in determining how they should be governed, for if men dominate public decision making, women, the youth, children and others are often overlooked and their voices unheard. The provision was in furtherance of the Constitutional Commission's observation that Uganda needed a constitution to which people would be sufficiently committed so that constitutional law would effectively control political action, the government and the governed. The participation of all classes of people in the debate, adoption, and promulgation of the constitution was seen as a way of realising this commitment.

A CA Commission appointed by President Museveni was given the responsibility of demarcating electoral areas for direct elections of CA delegates. The Commission designated 214 electoral areas, each of which was to elect one delegate. Seventy delegates were also to be elected to represent the special interest groups, making the total number in the Assembly 284. More than half of these special interest delegates, 39 in number, would be women, one from each district.

When it was announced that a Constituent Assembly would be constituted through a general election, the task of influencing the elections became the next challenge for Ugandan women. The Ministry of Gender quickly took a leadership role, designing and implementing a voter education project for women. Other women's NGOs such as the Uganda Gender Resource Centre (UGRC) and the Mbarara District Women Development Association also carried out voter education, in three areas, Kabale, Mbarara and Iganga.

The aim of voter education was to help people understand the importance of participating in the CA elections both as voters and as candidates. The provisions for the promotion and protection of women's rights in the draft constitution were highlighted as the call went out for women to play an active role in defending those important provisions. Appeals were made to women to offer themselves as candidates and also for voters to vote for gender-sensitive men and women for the CA. Surely, this was the first time in the country's history that gender concerns were a major campaign issue.

When the CA elections were held in 1994, it was obvious that the political landscape had changed a great deal in the five years since the NRC was expanded in 1989. There was evidence that with each passing year women were gaining in access to political participation and power as well as in political experience and expertise. Gains were noticeable but there was no time to sit back and enjoy them. The struggle was ongoing. The reality of the situation was that, to put it simply, it was time to go to work again.

The new phenomenon, starting with the NRC in 1989, of a good number of women serving in Parliament has had a major impact on parliamentary level politics since that time. It is obvious that never again will women be excluded from politics at the top, unless women let down their guard. Historical barriers to women talking in high level public fora were broken in the NRC, and it is no longer acceptable for someone to suggest that women were not fit to take part in such bodies. Having women in Parliament had become a fact of Ugandan political life. Yes, women are in the House to stay. From the time that women went to Parliament in 1989, a growing number of women began to say, 'If so-and-so can go there, then I too can go there.' This opening up of possibilities for women was a major achievement of the NRC, and especially of the pioneer women who served there.

Also, having one woman representative from each district in the NRC and the CA was an idea that caught on. After the NRC elections in 1989, the argument could be made that anything less was unacceptable to all but the most unenlightened. The NRC adopted this formula for the CA. Then in the CA, the women delegates led the fight to ensure that one woman parliamentary seat per district became part of the new constitution, although the draft constitution had included only 15 parliamentary seats for women.

The results of the elections in April 1994 were cause for women to celebrate. Fifty-one women would be serving in the CA. Thirty-nine of those were district representatives elected through affirmative action. Nine women out of the 36, a quarter who ran in mainstream seats against male candidates, were victorious. One woman was chosen to represent the National Organisation of Trade Unions (NOTU) and two women were nominated by the President.

Now when the CA opened - President Museveni officiated at the function on 18 May 1994 - I thought, we cannot have this problem of women working against each other in the CA. There were many provisions in the draft constitution that had been included only after a determined struggle inside the Constitutional Commission. I could not accept the possibility that if the CA women were in conflict with each other, they might cause us to lose what we had gained by hard and persistent work. I decided that even if it meant quarrelling with other women delegates, I didn't care. I would do what was necessary.

In the CA, there were many men who had not been in the NRC. Right away I became aware that some of them were saying, 'Where is Matembe? Which one is she?' It was obvious that some of them really thought I was a monster. It seemed that many people wanted to see who I was, and it was clear that some of them intended to silence me. 'We shall manage her,' was what some men were saying. Where did they get such ideas? Surely it was from the media and from the negative things that were being said about me around the country. From day one I was thinking about strategies that would help us break through this kind of bias.

When the CA opened, one of the first things the House did was to establish a Committee on Rules. This committee presented a prayer for approval, but this prayer was certainly not gender neutral. The prayer was focused on praying for 'men, men, men.' This could not go unchallenged. When the prayer was tabled, I rose to speak. I said, 'Yes, I have something to say about the prayer.' I said, 'We are here, both men and women. We came in our own right, we were elected, and therefore we must all be prayed for. This prayer which prays only for men is not a suitable prayer.'

Oh, such an explosion followed. 'Information.' 'Order.' Someone shouted, 'Is Matembe in order to bring matters of God up in this house?'

Then I said, 'By bringing prayers into this house, you have brought God. Therefore I must be prayed for. I need God also.'

What perturbed me was that, in spite of my urging, the other women in the CA did not question this sexist prayer that left women out. The other women delegates kept quiet. Only one woman, Hon. Rhoda Kalema, whom I respect so much because she's our grandmother in the struggle for gender equality, spoke. She said, 'My sister, Hon. Matembe, is going too far. In these matters of God, there's no way you can bring in gender, women and men.' She said, 'It's just too much. She should drop it and let us continue with our prayer.'

I thought I might be losing. I felt so bad, almost like I was going to cry. Then I shouted, 'Look here, I represent one million people from Mbarara and I must be prayed for in my capacity as a woman. Therefore I demand that this prayer includes women.' The moment was very tense, but God was with me. When we went to voting, a gender-neutral prayer was accepted. This business about the prayer convinced me that I must devise a strategy to bring the women delegates together to take a united position.

The proceedings in the CA started with a general debate. Each delegate was given thirty minutes to state her/his concerns and discuss her/his positions. Yes, people would have a chance to talk, talk, talk. Now, because I had seen how hostile some people were to me on the first day, I carefully devised a plan. I decided that I would talk towards the end, after most others had made their statements. Then I decided that in my talk, I would concentrate on just two points, where we came from and where we wanted to go as a country of peace. After providing a little historical background, I would call upon people to really be mindful of our nation, of our destiny, and to leave selfish interests out of these proceedings.

Of course, I wanted to spend most of my time on the topic nearest my heart, that is, the gender question. When it was my turn to talk, first I made a point of introducing myself to the House in a way that I hoped would break through some of the biases against me. I said, 'Mr Chairman and honourable delegates, I am Miria Matembe, married to Mr Matembe. We have four sons and we are living happily in our marriage.' And I said, 'The reason I am introducing myself like this is because many of you here think that I am a cantankerous woman who is working to destabilise society and destroy marriages and destroy our culture. But,' I told them, 'for those of you who think like that, I want to tell you that I am a very, very kind woman who loves the family, who respects the family. But I am a woman with a cause.'

I continued, 'I am glad you are all here today because I want to woo you to my cause. I want to share this cause with you, so that the misunderstandings about me can be dismissed, because you will have known what my cause is and I will win you over to espouse this cause with me. Therefore, please listen to me and listen to me without a bias. Listen to me, at least those who are seeing me for the first time. Listen to me so that you may change your attitude towards me.' People were very quiet, just listening. So when I came to the gender question, I really talked, I really talked. I quoted statistics about women's contribution to development, about women's lack of income, about women's hardships. I talked to them about what gender equality means. In fact, I demystified the whole issue of gender equality.

Near the end, I was aware of a powerful moving spirit as I said that the women of Uganda were waiting. I asked the delegates, while they were listening to me, to cast their minds to their constituencies to visualise the situation of women and girls there. While I was talking, I really felt like a poet expressing my deepest feelings in a poetic style. I said, 'Look at Kapchorwa and the practice of female circumcision. Think about the girls who continue to have their bodies mutilated in the name of a culture aimed at gratifying the sexual interests of men.' I went on, 'Look back, you who come from Kabale and Mbarara, and those areas which continue to give away those young girls of 12 or 14 years to marry, girls whose lives are shattered while they are still children. These girls have babies before their young bodies are ready for childbirth, and of course some die giving birth. You people from Lira, Apac and Gulu, look at these widows inherited against their will only to contract and die of AIDS.'[3]

People were paying close attention as I talked on. 'Look at those women who carry water on their heads with children at their backs and those who deliver babies by the riverside or in the bush as they fetch firewood. They are crying to you. They are crying to you for their liberation. And will you really put cotton wool in your ears so that you don't hear this cry?' At the end I called upon them to participate in this cause which is for the development of the country, for better homes and for equality for all Ugandans.

When I was talking, it was so quiet that you could drop down a needle and hear it fall. When I concluded, people stood up and clapped and clapped. Can you imagine, I got a standing ovation for my speech, the first one in these proceedings. Since this was the start of the CA I really felt great about this breakthrough. Some men had tears in their eyes. I saw Mr Chinery Hesse wiping his eyes, and Hon. Onegi Obel, too. My speech had gone right to their hearts. Many of the male delegates seemed to be looking at this whole issue of gender inequality for the first time. It seemed that my words had really begun to sensitise them on this important matter.

After the session many of the delegates sent notes to me. They wrote things like, 'Oh, so that's what you mean. Ah, fight on. Now we are with you.' And, 'Oh, Matembe, now we understand. So that is what you mean. I will fight with you.' And, 'Now that we understand, we are really sensitive to this thing. Don't fear. We are going to help you.' You know, quite a large number of notes were written to me. I'm sorry to say that I didn't save any of those notes. I wish I had. The response that my comments brought gave me energy for this next fight. From that time, I knew that achieving our goals would not be a problem if we did our part.

Early in the proceedings, a meeting was called for all women delegates. This first meeting would be very important. I was not the only woman delegate who was determined to see that the women in the CA form a united front so that we could act as a powerful voting block. So we went to meet for the first time to see how we would constitute ourselves into a women's caucus.

Some women entered this meeting with little understanding of its purpose. I remember one woman who said, 'You people, who are you to think that you know more? We all came here. We are equal. We are representing our constituencies. Therefore, you should not appear to be teaching us, to be thinking that you know more. We are all equal.' She said, 'Some of you are even going to make us lose out, because you are just bringing emotions, you are even bringing non-issues. The other day we almost lost out. Some of you are going to make us lose out on this gender question if you continue to push these equality issues. You are too much.' It was not surprising to find that there was a tension between the more experienced delegates and the political newcomers who were happy just to be there in that prestigious body. But this tension must be addressed.

I was ready for just this kind of challenge. I stood up to speak, 'You ladies, I am going to talk now without fear or favour. Those of you who said that some of us did certain things, I know you mean me, about the prayer. And I want to tell you, I never lose.' I said, 'I'm not going to lose now because I've never lost.' I said, 'Even with that prayer, which you call a non-issue, which was about gender language, I won it. So I don't intend to back off. Let me say that some of us have been in this struggle for a long time. In fact, many of you are here because of our struggle. Therefore you must learn from us.'

And I told them, 'This question of being equal with each other, forget it. How many of you have traversed the whole country educating people on the constitution? How many of you gathered people's views from all parts of the country about the kind of constitution they wanted? How many of you helped to write the draft constitution that we are here to debate? How many of you have ever left the borders of Uganda to talk on behalf of women? How many of you have stood and talked about Uganda's progressive record on integrating women into development at an international conference and received a standing ovation? How many of you have been received at these conferences the way some of us have? Therefore we are not equal. Although all of us were elected to this Constituent

Assembly, we are not all equal. Some of us are more experienced. We know more. Some of us have been in this field of gender struggle for a long time. Some of you have just come in here.'

And I told them, 'I am not going to see what we have fought for so long lost, such as these important provisions for women's rights in the draft constitution. I am not going to see these provisions taken out simply because everyone wants to be heard. We are here to talk seriously and to achieve as much as we can for women in this constitution. Therefore we must create a forum where we can articulate our views. We have realised that many of us here are not knowledgeable about gender and other constitutional issues. That is understandable since some of us are coming into the political arena for the very first time. Since we are coming in at this high level, against our eloquent men, some of whom have been politicians for so long, we must have skills-development seminars so that we educate ourselves. We must do research, and we must learn to work together.'

When I read this last section, as I am writing my life story, my words sound a bit harsh and uncaring, and yet I remember I said those words. Was I being a monster as some people thought I was? Should I regret being so 'unladylike?' When I look back at the challenges we faced and what has been accomplished in the last decade and a half, I don't regret my toughness. Was I rude? I do believe that in Uganda, 'being a lady' has generally meant remaining silent about the oppression of women in patriarchal society.

You know, since long ago I have had this dream that some day women would be liberated from the most oppressive conditions of their lives. That dream drove me to start to battle the system in hopes of causing change. As change occurred, I was encouraged to believe that some kind of parity or gender equity was really possible if we didn't let up the pressure. How could I have been 'agreeable?' Agreeing with the system? Agreeing with being treated as a second class citizen? Smiling? Happy? How could I act 'like a lady' and at the same time take a leading role in the struggle to change the unjust system?

Because we, the women in the CA, recognised our situation as a minority block, we formed a non-partisan coalition called the CA Women's Caucus. We developed a number of structures and services to support caucus members and caucus activities. We also developed strategies to counteract our two main weaknesses.

The first weakness was numbers. We were 52 women out of a total of 284 delegates. If our weakness is numbers, we said, then why don't we boost our numbers by forming alliances with the other interest groups, the workers, the youth, the army, and people with disabilities? So, although we were called the Women's Caucus, we were actually a block of special interest groups who joined forces to forward our common goals. When we brought these others into our caucus, we became 72, an expanded block of delegates, and this opened up more possibilities. Additionally, we began to look for progressive male delegates who would support constitutional provisions that addressed gender balance and gender equity.

Our second weakness was that many of us were not experienced in the art of politics. We lacked political experience and the arts of politics, like public speaking, like lobbying and coalition building. In addition, since we were not knowledgeable about some of the issues, then we had to be better informed. To remedy this second weakness, we embarked on a programme of skills-development training. To this end, the Ministry of Gender (funded by DANIDA), in conjunction with the Uganda Gender Resource Centre (funded by Austria's North South Institute for Development), organised regular workshops and seminars in which the caucus members were educated on the procedures and rules that governed the CA, on negotiation techniques, coalition-building, debating skills, utilisation of the media and the art of lobbying. Through the workshops, women acquainted themselves with salient provisions of the draft constitution, their relevance and the gender implications. In addition to the training sessions, a series of other timely initiatives were instituted that supported caucus activities.

With funding from the Fredrick Ebert Foundation, the National Association of Women's Organisations in Uganda (NAWOU) established a Gender Information Centre at the conference complex where the CA meetings were being held. The Centre channelled information and services in two directions. Through the Centre, caucus members gained access to research, consultation, lobbying efforts, secretarial assistance, and facilities for meetings. Additionally, a radio programme produced by the Centre provided information on CA activities from the women's point of view for the general public. On these weekly broadcasts, women delegates were invited to discuss the most critical issues being debated in the House that were of special concern to women.

ACFODE initiated the Link Programme (funded by the Ford Foundation), a programme of civic education, the goal of which was to enhance the civic competence of citizens. The programme conducted activities including seminars and workshops in 20 districts and at schools and institutions of higher education. These aimed to link the public with what was taking place in the CA where the new constitution was being formulated. Other organisations carrying out civic education programmes included the Department of Political Science at Makerere University, FIDA, Uganda Human Rights and Youth Centre, Uganda Civil Servants Association, and the Association of Public Administrators.

⋅ Under the Link Programme, ACFODE also used the media to spread the word about CA proceedings. Informational radio programmes were broadcast in six major languages. ACFODE published *The Link Bulletin* about what was happening in the CA. *The Bulletin* reported the ongoing debates between the key political actors on important issues, and provided in-depth articles on relevant constitutional issues. ACFODE did not limit itself to presenting only the women's perspective on CA proceedings, but presented broad-based analysis and commentary.

The caucus also devised a strikingly effective lobbying device called 'Gender Dialogue'. We knew that we had to win many people to our side, but how could we win them? NAWOU again supported by Fredrick Ebert Foundation funding helped us to establish a public discourse. This meant that whenever there was an amendment which we wanted to bring to the House, we would initiate this dialogue. We would identify the most eloquent speakers, whether they were on our side or not on our side, people like Hon. Elly Karuhanga, like Hon. Omara Otubo, like Hon. George Kanyeihamba, like Hon. Sam Kutesa. These men were chosen because, once they stood and articulated on an issue, it would usually go through. It was necessary to get them involved in our cause, even those who originally did not support it. We said, let us include them in this dialogue, and then we can lobby them. This process made it possible for the caucus to be an effective minority and succeed in shaping the CA agenda.

So, when there was an important issue to debate, we would schedule a public dialogue. The Sheraton Hotel was the favoured venue. You know, if you invite people to come to a meeting after a heavy day, and at the end there is a cold drink and some bites, they will come and then go home nicely. All of us in the caucus, other CA delegates and a variety of interested people, especially women activists, would come to these sessions. We would arrange for a spokesperson to put forward an amendment we wanted to move and then everyone in attendance would discuss it. Part of the purpose was to convince the male CA delegates about the importance of that amendment.

Then afterwards we would decide who should move the amendment. We agreed that under most circumstances women should not move amendments. Our procedure was to identify those men who spoke with eloquence, men who were listened to by the whole House. We would ask them to move the amendment and then maybe a woman would second the amendment. Then a debate would ensue. For me, because I am always so controversial, I decided to come in only when I saw any of our amendments going astray. It was a good strategy for Matembe to work behind the scenes and be silent in public most of the time. So if an amendment that came up was on track, I would not comment. However, if I saw something important being diverted, then I would come in to bring it on course. So we designed that strategy to influence the heavily male-dominated assembly, purposely avoiding clashing with the men whose support we needed. You see how pragmatic we were. Very, very practical. Very realistic.

Another of our strategies was, when an amendment we favoured was raised, even if a woman delegate didn't support it, she was expected to just keep quiet. She was not to oppose it, because the moment any woman opposed it, some man would say, you see these women are not united. As if the men were united on everything! To succeed we needed a high level of united action. Women delegates would be reminding each other, let's make sure we don't lose. We came here to struggle and win for women. Of course, some women would want to talk, just to talk to the gallery, so that they could be reported in the press as having contributed to the debate, just like many men delegates were doing. We said, you talk on other things, but when it comes to the gender question, if you don't agree with it, just remain quiet. And, good enough, that was done.

To provide oversight of the various activities, the Gender Ministry instituted a Monitoring Committee within the Ministry, a committee composed of ministry officials and some women delegates to monitor the proceedings in the CA. We were extremely serious about following those provisions that applied to women. Were these provisions on track? Were they likely to pass? What did we need to do to support their passage?

In summary, a whole series of initiatives were put in place to support the women's caucus and its work: supplying information on important issues to delegates and the public; providing skills training to delegates; overseeing all relevant activities; and initiating dialogue on current debates but dialogue from women's point of view.

There were other things during the CA proceedings that worked in our favour. For example, I was elected to the Legal and Drafting Committee, one of the four standing committees. This was the committee that vetted amendments. This committee was charged with the content and wording of the constitution. Amendments would be presented to the committee, and then it was the committee's responsibility to look through them and harmonise them. If there were a number of amendments on one topic, we would look at the different ones and discuss them until we reached agreement on the best compromise. Then we would table that amendment.

Can you see how advantaged I was? I truly believe that when I am advocating for women, I can never fail to convince people. So in the end, all those amendments that women favoured were included in the Constitution, including some provisions which were not originally in the draft. For instance, the stipulation that there would be one-third women on each local government body came in by way of an amendment. The gender-neutral language, that is, 'he/she,' came in by way of an amendment. Also, a very big victory, the provision of one woman representative in Parliament from each district came by way of an amendment. It should be remembered that the draft constitution had set 15 as the number of women to be in Parliament for the entire country. You see, in the CA we achieved even more for women than the draft constitution included.

I should add here that women found it easier to participate in committee work. The CA actually started out with the idea that every debate would take place in plenary sessions in the entire House. However, very soon it was realised that this approach to the work was completely unmanageable. That's when the decision was made to form five select committees. Women played much more active roles in committee sessions than in the plenary proceedings. In these small, less formal settings, women felt more at ease to take part. Tamale's research revealed that women spoke two and a half times more in committees than in the House. One of the real breakthroughs on gender balance came when the women on the Committee on Local Government introduced the idea that women should be automatically given 'a third' of the seats on any local government council. These bold women not only devised and proposed this plan, but they fought for it until it was adopted.

One constant in the NRC and in the CA was what Tamale (1999:128) describes as 'anti-woman sentiments'. A good number of male delegates and some women behaved as if women didn't really belong in such bodies, and that no one should expect women to be treated as full and equal participants in politics at this high level. For the progressive women working on the front line for gender equality, it was hard to tolerate statements sometimes made by female delegates who were willing to accept second-class status for themselves and other women. Also, no matter how well women performed their duties, there were invariably some men who looked for opportunities to ridicule and embarrass the women delegates present.

One rather interesting incident shows something about how gender politics were being played in the CA, and how women delegates were ready to fight for their rights in the House. The incident started when a male delegate made the following statement.

> Mr Chairman, I am speaking as a career diplomat, and when I was learning diplomacy, my professor told me two things. He said there is direct line up between a diplomat and a lady in the use of words except that they are in the opposite direction. In that what they say is always the opposite–what the diplomat says will be the opposite of what the lady will say. When a lady says 'no,' she means 'perhaps' (laughter), and once she says 'perhaps' she means 'yes,' and when she says 'yes' then she means 'no' (laughter) (Ogola, CA Proceedings, July 12, 1994).

The sexual overtones of these remarks were outrageous. In addition, other men were laughing, stamping their feet, and obviously enjoying the discomfort of the women delegates. Women CADs began to demand that the Chairman call the delegate to order. The man defended himself by saying that he was only cracking a joke, and added, 'A country which has no sense of humour is no worse than an atomic bomb.' A number of women delegates were very angry by now. Hope Kabirisi was the first one to raise a challenge.

> Point of order... Is the speaker holding the floor in order to impute that we ladies do not normally mean what we say?

> At least that is what I understand him to be saying and I
> wonder whether that is in order, Mr Chairman (CA
> Proceedings, 7/12/94).

This man had certainly insulted women, and to make matters
worse, other men were joining in to support his attack. I was
the next one to speak.

> Is he...in order to sit in this hall and rebuke women...by
> implying that they just do not know what they want, they
> do not know what to say, they do not mean what they do? Is
> he in order Mr Chairman to use even sexist analogies in this
> hall (CA Proceedings, 7/12/94)?

As male delegates continued to laugh and stamp their feet,
women's anger had risen several levels. Another delegate, Hon.
Winnie Byanyima, rose to say the following.

> I do know how to take a joke on a good day, but Mr Chairman
> I find the comments...offensive. Is he in order to suggest
> that I do not mean what I say simply because I am a woman
> (CA Proceedings, 7/12/94)?

The Chairman, Hon. Wapakhabulo had not accurately gauged
the level of the women's outrage. He was reluctant to rule the
delegate out of order. Instead of disciplining the male delegate
and bringing the Assembly back to order, he made the following
ruling.

> The honourable made a joke...the ladies in this House were
> disturbed and a point was raised. I asked Honourable Ogola
> whether that was what he meant to say. 'In other words, do
> you intend to crack a nasty joke at the expense of ladies?' I
> asked him and he said he did not intend that. Then he
> proceeded at one stage to say...and he was actually
> interrupted as he was finishing to say that which more or
> less could have been an apology. So could you say it so that
> we hear it (CA Proceedings, 7/12/94).

When the Chair finally yielded to the overwhelming pressure
from the women and ruled the delegate out of order, the delegate
reluctantly withdrew the offensive words, but substituted other

remarks that were even more offensive, included below. The instigator of this unpleasant scene was obviously enjoying his moment in the spotlight, urged on by some of his colleagues. His remarks appeared to be directed at women in general, but most of the women delegates felt that he was directing a nasty attack at the women sitting right there in the House. Next he said,

> If somebody has not got a wide scope in life, I am not going to apologise for her ignorance... There is a Russian saying (laughter) that a frog in a pot can only see the size of the sky which is equal to the mouth of the pot... some of us have lived in a pot with a larger mouth; therefore we are able to see a large part of the sky (Ogola, CA Proceedings, 7/12/94).

At that point, the women decided they had had enough. Most of the women delegates 'walked out' of the House, giving a clear warning that they meant business and demanded seriousness in the assembly. *The New Vision* of the next day, 13 July 1994, under the heading 'Matembe leads a walk out,' reported that all the CA women delegates, except five, walked out in protest against the use of derogatory, sexist, offensive language by one of the male delegates. Support for the women's walkout came quickly. In his weekly column in *The New Vision*, Fr Waliggo made a timely and accurate observation about the women's action.

> Their 'No' was to be taken as 'No', their 'Yes' as 'Yes'. They were not going to tolerate a few men who thought women's issues were issues of fun. That day they gave a clear lesson not only to the CA and the mass media but to the nation as a whole (1994).

Hon. Karuhanga from Nyabushozi County, Mbarara District, a strong ally of women in the CA, had this to say in the House.

> Mr Chairman, the issue of sexist language in this hall which tends to demean other members of the other sex should be taken very seriously by the members... When I was elected, I was elected among others by women and my job here is to make sure that their dignity is preserved in this Assembly.

Any words which imply their demeanour or continued situation as they are should be resisted and should be avoided... I really would like to appeal to members in future to use a language that does not offend members of the opposite sex (CA Proceedings).

This was clearly a situation where men who were used to behaving as they pleased in what they considered to be male space learned that the times were changing and that such offensive sexist behaviour was no longer acceptable in the House. Over all, this was a victory for women. The following day the women delegates were given a platform in the assembly to present our protest against derogatory language and insensitive attitudes toward the women there in the House. The issue was debated and it was agreed that such language and behaviour were unacceptable in the House. No such incident ever occurred again in the CA.

At the same time that 52 women in the CA were learning the art of politics as delegates, one woman was playing a pioneer role as Deputy Chairperson of that body. Professor Victoria Mwaka, a distinguished academician from Makerere University, was elected to that position during the opening exercises. Women in the NRC had realised the disadvantages they faced when both the Chairperson and the Deputy in that body were men. Among other things, this gender inequity seriously affected whether female delegates felt free to contribute to the proceedings. So it was agreed that the CA would have one male and one female in those two leadership positions. Women lobbied outside the House in an effort to influence the nominations by the President who was responsible for proposing names to the CA prior to elections for these two positions.

I had worked with Professor Mwaka on a number of programmes and projects and regarded her highly. For instance, she and I had worked together on the development of a population policy for Uganda. The Population Policy Secretariat within the Ministry of Planning had a team of people who visited every region of the country to educate people about population issues, and Victoria and I were assigned to the team working on the topic, Women, Population and Development. We worked together in different districts and different fora.

Victoria was one of only two women professors at Makerere and Head of the Department of Geography, as well as being active in the University Women's Association. When her name was suggested, I said, 'Good,' although she was not a lawyer or a politician. Some of us lobbied for Mwaka's nomination for the post, agreeing that we would guide and help her.

There was some opposition to her nomination since she was not a lawyer and at the time she was working on a short-term project in Dar es Salaam, Tanzania. In fact, she arrived in Kampala just the night before the election of Chairperson and Vice-Chairperson were to take place. Hope Mwesigye and I met her at the door. There was no chance to really prepare her. We told her to just go in and show her confidence. Good enough, she was elected.

In comparison to the Chairman, James Wapakhabulo, who knew parliamentary procedures through and through from longtime experience, Victoria was a real newcomer to this role. She was expected to perform well even though she was learning on the job, not an easy thing to do. While many male delegates tried to make her uncomfortable, others gave her their support and worked to help her. The newspapers attacked Mwaka relentlessly (Tamale 1999:140). In fact, she was in an untenable position, being new in a complicated, difficult position, and constantly being compared by unsympathetic male critics to an experienced male professional. It is my wish that people could appreciate the work that pioneer women do as they break open old all-male systems for women.

I cannot stress enough that women managed to achieve what they did in the CA because of successful coalition building. Those of us who had been in the NRC had faced the problems of lack of co-ordination and unity. But in the CA we managed to work with a common purpose. The success of the women's caucus was recognised by some prominent male delegates. In an interview the CA Chairperson, James Wapakhabulo, told Sylvia Tamale (1999:109):

> At first when women came in they...didn't know each other
> really...but as time went on, they began forming into a caucus
> and I dare say that that caucus achieved a lot of things. If
> one reads the Constitution in areas of property,... divorce or
> death of partners, in areas of establishing affirmative action
> institutions like the equal opportunities commission, [in the
> area of children, these things] came straight from the pressure
> from women... [T]he [Constitutional} Commission had
> recommended 15 parliamentary seats for women but this
> group lobbied quite effectively and it was reinstated to 39–
> one woman from each district. And they even went beyond
> that and insisted on having a predetermined share of seats
> in local councils so that... one-third of seats in a district
> council is reserved for women, which...is no small
> achievement.

CA delegate George Kanyeihamba observed that women played
such a vital role in the CA, that by the end, men were frightened
to oppose amendments moved by women (1997 interview). In
fact, some women delegates threatened to decampaign male
delegates in the next general elections if they did not support
the provisions on women's rights. Yes, women were learning
to play politics, and to play tough.

Of course, there were men who, for whatever reasons, did
not recognise what women had accomplished in the assembly.
This is evidence of the persistence of the patriarchal mind-set
in Uganda. David Mukholi, the chief librarian of *The New
Vision* and a regular contributor to the newspaper on Uganda's
history, wrote a book which he *titled A Complete Guide to
Uganda's Fourth Constitution* (1995). In his 'complete guide'
he mentions that caucuses were very important in the CA, but
somehow fails to mention the women's caucus at all. Using
traditional sexist language, he describes a 'nine-man' committee
and lists women committee members along with the men (p.44).
From his book, one would learn nothing about the historical
negotiations that took place in the CA around the gender
question. Women scholars now call such history 'his story.'
Shouldn't women ask hard questions about why we are so often
left out of the historical record? Where is 'her story?' I must

say that this neglect and lack of recognition is one of the main reasons that I feel compelled to write this book. How else can people learn about the contribution of women to this gender sensitive constitution?

The new Constitution was enacted on 22 September 1995 and promulgated on 8 October. It contains 19 chapters and 287 articles. In the end most of the critical provisions concerning women made it into the Constitution. These things were not just given, and it is clear that what was accomplished for women was not a one-person matter. To achieve what we did needed real unity, collaboration, strategising, and lobbying. Women delegates learned new skills and then used them on the job. When the CA ended, there were many more women experienced in the political arts at this high level.[4]

After managing to get this 'pro-women' Constitution, what remained was to translate the constitutional provisions into reality, to get them transformed into actual laws that would bring protection to women and their rights. This continues to be the challenge ahead of us. That challenge is there. It is ahead of us. It is not insurmountable.

What Others Say *(Justice Dr G.W. Kanyeihamba)*

On 17 July 2000, Nancy Dorsey met Honourable Justice Dr George W. Kanyeihanba of the Uganda Supreme Court in his chambers in Kampala. She asked the Justice to describe his work with Miria Matembe in the NRC and the CA.

You have asked me to say a few words about my friend, Honourable Miria Matembe, the Minister of Ethics and Integrity in the present government. It's a very interesting subject to talk about. Certainly Miria is a very exciting person. She's got a very charming and vocal personality. I must say that wherever she is, Matembe is a performer and must be noticed.

I came to know Miria Matembe when we were both members of the legislature, which was then known as the National Resistance Council. She found me there when I was also a member and Minister. Initially, I was Minister of Commerce, then Minister of Justice and Attorney General, and later on, I sat there as Senior Presidential Adviser. That's where I knew her longest.

We were closest in the Constituent Assembly, where we were both delegates. I represented Rubanda County East and she represented Mbarara District. While we were there, we were both members of the Legal and Drafting Committee, of which I was Chair. She participated very effectively, in both the committee and in the Constituent Assembly. She was often heard, making a lot of points, points of order, both in the Resistance Council, and in the CA, particularly about her very favourite subject, the championing of women's rights and their protection.

Now, as I said, Matembe is a very engaging personality. She could be a very formidable opponent if you are not on her side. She will not hesitate to stop you in your tracks, if she thinks you are either opposed to women's rights or you are being flippant about women. This became very evident in the National Resistance Council. Whenever issues relating to women's rights came up, Honourable Matembe would be at the forefront, championing those rights, suggesting improvements in the law, proposing amendments which were often adopted. It did not matter whether it was a man or woman who came up with an idea to advance women's rights, Matembe would jump in and also champion the idea.

So I would say that her influence in the National Resistance Council was considerable. She was of course assisted by other women who thought the same way, people like Joan Rwabyomere, Mrs Joyce Mpanga, people like Winnie Byanyima, Cecilia Ogwal, Margaret Zziwa, people who were in the CA, some of the names I can't remember. But they were very vocal like her. But she always seemed to have the loudest voice amongst them. If Matembe started speaking and said, 'I'm standing to support this motion,' or 'I'm standing on a point of order,' whether you are a Minister or an opponent of that idea, you'd better listen, because she would make very formidable comments on that issue, and if you were not careful, by force of argument, she could divert attention from your own idea to her own. That is how I remember her in the National Resistance Council.

While we were in the NRC, I believe Mrs Matembe earlier on would have wanted to be minister, in the earlier days of the Movement. She often said so to some of us. Often I sat next to her in the NRC. She would sit next to me, and she always wanted to be minister to contribute to the development of this nation, and she always took the issue philosophically. At one time I think she looked a bit bored in the National Resistence Movement. I remember we were talking about it, and she said, 'Look George, I know you are familiar with universities. I would like to go and do a higher degree.' So ultimately, after we had discussed it, I recommended her to my former university, the University of Warwick in England. And I actually wrote to my former colleagues and associates there, and eventually she was admitted to do an LL.M degree.

I visited the university while she was there and discovered that she was well liked there, and many people asked her to talk about women's rights in Uganda. And also, I guess she was a popular participant in seminars on her favourite subject. I once went there as a guest speaker at the university, and Miria was among the audience, and the people who talked to me said, 'Eh, did you know that you have a very famous person here, one of your MPs, do you know her?' I said, 'I know her.' She came to the seminar and she contributed, and I was very delighted to see her. She was there with my son. My son was doing his first degree in mathematics and computer science.

So Matembe, wherever she is, she is the centre of attention. She's also the centre of controversy where women's rights are concerned. She does not compromise. Her view is that women should be equal, and there cannot be any compromise on that issue. So when talking about their voting rights, about their equality in government, their equality in business, or land rights and inheritance or anything else, Matembe cannot compromise. She will insist on her point.

Then in CA, there I knew her much more intimately. When she came there, she was, shall I say, a 'warmonger' against men. I want to put it that way. She immediately declared that war in her major statement. Most people know that I am a very sympathetic to women's rights, and I was an ally to them, including Matembe in the CA. So I saw that the way she was going to approach the subject of women's rights was going to be very controversial, very confrontational and unproductive. So I pulled her aside with one or two other colleagues who were also very sympathetic to women's rights, and we said, 'No, Miria, that is the wrong approach. You must be diplomatic. These men are the majority here, and they are still capable of rejecting any provisions about women's rights in this constitution. So let us be diplomatic and take it softly. Try to convince them, rather than harangue them.' And Matembe agreed that this was the way.

This advice is one of the few points that she accepted, and I think it became very effective. So she took a more diplomatic approach when advocating women's rights and their protection, and her colleagues also collaborated with her. Some delegates had been alienated by her oratory which was so vocal and controversial. So she sobered down and sat down on the ground but firmly on these rights.

I can tell you that on many, many issues which relate to women in the Constitution, Matembe's contribution was significant. On issues like equality between men and women, that men are equal during and after marriage, that spouses have equal access to children, and on the affirmative action - especially affirmative action - Matembe really scored a great deal of marks, especially in articulating the ideas of affirmative action. She and Winnie Byanyima were almost single-handed, or perhaps I should say, double-handed, responsible for putting in the Constitution this idea of affirmative action, and having a commission for equality, although we haven't had it yet. Nevertheless, that really was their child. I would say that the women in the CA, Matembe, Winnie Byanyima – incidentally Byanyima is not always talked about, but she did a great deal of lobbying as well, Cecilia Ogwal – did contribute equally, usefully to the projection of women's rights and their protection that we now have in our Constitution.

I think Matembe also, although she may deny it, likes a bit of publicity. She would like to say and hear herself say that 'Matembe said this,' that 'Matembe proposed this,' and so forth. And often, even when other people may have shared her views, may even have spoken first on the issue or contributed more, she seemed to like saying, 'It is Matembe who did this.' Well, that is part of her fighting spirit, that 'what I fight for must be seen through successfully.' Some people might regard that as a weakness, failure to recognise the contributions of others. Certainly, in some of the areas where she has spoken or written, she has given the impression that rights of women were articulated and insisted on by women in the CA.

However, I can tell you that without men who were committed to that view, if they had not also championed and supported the Matembes of this world, we wouldn't have had this Constitution as it is. And I can enumerate dozens, dozens of men who used to come in the Legal and Drafting Committee, together with women, to make sure that the rights of women were protected. And I would like Matembe sometime to acknowledge that. She doesn't often do so.

FIDA, the women lawyers' organisation, when I was Attorney General, awarded me an honorary membership. And I'm always proud to say, when I'm talking about women's organisations and so forth, to say I'm speaking here in my capacity as a woman. (*laughter*) But Matembe has not often alluded to that. I cannot remember her saying, 'In the CA people like Aggrey Awori (who was one of our supporters on women's rights), or Kanyeihamba, or whoever, did assist us.' And I think she should bring that out much more, because our view was that the genders are equal, and people can only achieve development and respect for each other if they are regarded as equal, rather than one despising the other or saying, we are now going to get on top of you, to use a euphemism that is sometimes used.

I don't know what else I can talk about in relation to Miria. One thing I've heard. Many people are thinking that since Matembe, who is so vocal, who is so dominant in public life, and we never hear anything about her husband, he must be a henpecked man. That one I can quickly dispel as not true. I have met Mr Matembe. Mr Matembe is a master in his own home, and he will tell you so. He says, 'My wife is a politician, but when she comes home, we are a married couple, and I have no problem with her.' And Matembe respects her husband. As I understand, she cooks for him and serves him, and certainly I want to dispel that idea.

Honourable Matembe, since she became Minister, from time to time she calls me, and we exchange views. Recently, I was made, by our colleagues in the Judiciary, Chairman of the Committee on Integrity. Matembe welcomed the idea and wrote to the Chief Justice, thanking him for having allowed this committee to be set up, and she also sent me a copy of it, which is very complimentary. I look forward to working with her in this area.

She certainly needs, like so many ministers, to learn more about the intricacies of law. I think she's a bit weak in that area. She is regarded in legal circles as a basher of the Judiciary. As a lawyer, she should know better, that to make a blanket accusation against any group of people, without identifying individuals who are culprits, without investigating them, does ultimately undermine the institution you are trying to protect. There has been a lot of that. I think Matembe is one of those who can be accused of having made over-generalised statements, accusing the Judiciary. And the Judiciary at the moment is at a crisis because of that. I'm not saying that some of the weaknesses which are being pointed out are not true, or that they couldn't be eliminated somehow, but I think the accusations have been grossly unfair and out of proportion with what the Judiciary stands for and what its members do for this country.

I can condemn many ministers in the present government and in US governments, but for me to stand up and say, 'The whole 'executive is corrupt,' knowing that my friend Matembe is there, and Matembe is not corrupt, is not fair. So she should always think that, 'If I have friends like Kanyeihamba,' - she thinks that she knows me; surely she knows that I am not corrupt, but to say the whole Judiciary is corrupt, knowing she's including me, that is unfair, just as it would be unfair for me to say the whole executive is corrupt when I know she's there and she's not corrupt. So she needs to moderate her language.

She's still young. I'm sure we are going to get a lot out of her, both in leadership and as a citizen, and as she matures, it's very important for her to modify her verbal, shall I say, missiles, with the ones she regards as the enemies of human rights. Recently, we honoured a man, one of the greatest civil servants we ever had in this country, Canon John Bikangaga, who was for a long time an educationalist, Public Service Commission Chairman and has served his country with distinction. And yet you can hardly say that in the last thirty years you have heard anything being said about Bikangaga blowing his trumpet in public. But he has achieved the leadership of this country. His Excellency, the President who had another Head of State as guest made it a point to be present when the people of Kigezi and Uganda celebrated Bikangaga's 80th birthday. The Vice-President, the Prime Minister, judges, diplomats, ministers and other dignitaries were there on this occasion. It therefore shows that you can also achieve matters silently, and quietly by diplomacy and dignity. So there are other people who are achievers but who do it quietly. And my friend, Honourable Matembe, should also realise that. That you don't have to always be very verbal and confrontational and combative and shout loudly about your achievements, but that is her method and it works, but we could say, lower it a bit.

Miria Matembe is a very warm person. She is a likeable person, and she wants to achieve. And she uses methods which are considered boastful and controversial, but they often work.

Dorsey: *I had let Justice Kanyeihamba make his comments without interruption to this point. After we turned off the recorder - I thought perhaps we were finished - he mentioned an American film about the struggle for equal rights by African Americans in that country, a film that had impressed him very much. He saw similarities between the story of African Americans demanding equal rights in the United States and women in Uganda struggling for their equal rights.*

Kanyeihamba: I think that the story of Miria with her fight for equality and human rights accorded to women, can be compared to a film I saw some time ago, called 'Separate But Equal,' which is about equality of schooling of the races in the States. In the deep South, they believed that you could provide separate but equal educational facilities for the education of children, until one man was angry that white kids had buses and black kids were walking. Black kids didn't have good textbooks, the white kids did. So, he said, this is not good, this is not equal.

So he decided to challenge the system. When he decided to challenge the system, people were shocked. Even black people were shocked. They said you cannot challenge the system. This is the way things have always been done, they've always been done this way.

This man, the principal of one school, decided to challenge the system. He got signatures of equally minded people and they took a test case to the court. In the first court, they lost, and they were laughed out of court. In fact, the white people said, we never want to see your black faces here again. But they persisted. They hired lawyers of the National Association for the Advancement of Colored People (NAACP). They came and fought the case. The white extremists (KKK) in the area burned his house. They sacked him from the job. However, he persisted with his court case. In the end, the case went to the Supreme Court, despite a lot of struggles and sacrifices, the burning of homes and the beatings. And the Supreme Court then decided that it was true, that you cannot provide equal facilities for people of different races when you are in separate schools, especially when the principal group, in this case the whites, are in charge of the funds. So they outlawed unequal treatment of the races, by law.

And ever since then, it opened the door for everything to change. And that was one single principal of an insignificant black school in the South who challenged the unequal system, vocally and persistently and succeeded. It's a film worth seeing.

There is one issue that Matembe has been involved with recently where there are some serious misunderstandings that are not being properly discussed. It is very important for Ugandans that the misunderstandings about the Land Bill are discussed. I think that originally, one of the reasons for the unresolved differences and misunderstandings is that women plunged into it very quickly without seeing fully the emotional and customary implications that it involves. Land, as you know, is the basic commodity in Africa, that every family is proud to possess. Over the centuries land has been the home, not only of the family rituals, but also the family salvation during the times of plenty and the times of scarcity, and so forth. And the ownership of land has from time immemorial been identified with the male line. In most of Africa, that's the case.

So this ownership is a customary thing. The word ownership is such an emotive word that you can't simply discuss it in social terms in which people have been discussing it. However, the same can be achieved if we talk about inheritance rights, what rights has a woman got during marriage, after marriage, and so forth. These are clearly set out in the Constitution of Uganda. After all, we know that women can inherit and can buy their own land, and it should be theirs by right. That one has not been affected at all. So I think that we should have looked at legal procedures and legal institutions through which a woman's rights can be guaranteed in land, rather than emphasising or focusing on the word 'ownership', which is very emotive. Or in a case, for example, where a man dies and only a widow is left. Then the widow should be entitled and her entitlement protected by law. Here we should emphasise inheritance which is soft, rather than 'ownership' which is emotive, but the results are the same.

The Constitution makes it very clear that the woman cannot be thrown off the land.

Chap 4, Article 31 (2) Parliament shall make appropriate laws for the protection of the rights of widows and widowers to inherit the property of their deceased spouses...

The Constitution says that a man and a woman are equal in marriage, and if the man dies, the property owned, which includes land, devolves to his children and the wife he leaves behind. That one, I don't know why people have interpreted it differently. I would like someone to bring a case to court in which, when a man dies, the man's brothers or someone else have refused this woman to utilise that land as her husband was utilising it. But that one is clear. We don't need a separate law to emphasise that the woman can't be thrown off the land. Of course, now comes the problem – enforcement. That's what I'm saying. I'm looking forward to someone bringing a case. You know it doesn't matter whether the man has left a will or not. The widow should be protected. Her rights are guaranteed by the Constitution. We have been hesitating to enforce these laws because of custom. But the Constitution says that where custom conflicts with the provisions of this Constitution, the Constitution shall prevail, at least to the extent of inconsistency. So I don't know why people are finding a problem.

The other thing that I wanted to mention is in relation to this emotion about ownership of land which I think we should minimise. In trying to project and protect the rights of women towards land, the word 'ownership' should be very lightly advanced because it is very emotive.

One of the problems that we have, particularly in Uganda, is that when you say a man and a woman own the land together, then you are faced with a problem. That apart from the legal marriages, where you are entitled to one wife, some men marry two, three, four wives. Now, which woman is entitled to ownership? That question has not been addressed. So, men objected to a number of these provisions. First, because of the customary concept, that the ownership of land is in the family, and the head of the family is the man. That has not changed. Secondly, when you tell me that this land belongs to the present wife and myself, what will happen to my other children if I marry another wife or two wives?

Our Constitution has not outlawed polygamy. So, let us start with the question of polygamy first. The social belief of our society with regard to the land belonging to the family, that the land belongs to the head of the family. He is the one who has ownership. If we have to tackle those at the social level, I would take this matter, not to Matembe, but to Dr Kwesiga at Makerere's Department of Women and Gender Studies. Use that one first. And then the issue of land ownership would be solved easily. But, if you can't solve it immediately, do not use 'ownership' as a champion of women's rights. Use other terms, inheritance, equality in marriage, exclusive user rights to land, but at the moment it is inopportune to say women now have the sole ownership of the land. They should minimise the word 'ownership' because of the points I have made.

In relation to land, when a man remarries, nobody worries about the land issue. But when the woman remarries and especially out of the clan, this is a worry. And that goes back to the question of what is the family. In Uganda the family is the family of the man. So when people think that if you allow the woman ownership, she can marry someone else and take your own land from your own clan, from your own immediate family, and it goes to the other man, that is taboo. So when these women campaigners come and say but we are equal, therefore if a man can marry, and bring a wife and the wife shares that property, I should also be able to marry and bring a man and the man shares. No, that is not possible. Because they are saying the land is our land. We are the Baganda of this or that village. This land has always been here. If she marries somebody from the Bukiga, from Kabale, who is not in our clan, are these people entitled to our land? This could upset the balance of society's equilibrium.

I believe I was once discussing with Miria about women's rights, particularly those which men conceive to be an infringement on their own rights and ego. And I think I mentioned this motto to her, which my landlord in UK had in his house when I was a student there. Written in very big red letters, it said, 'I AM THE MASTER IN MY HOUSE.' Then underneath that line, in small black letters which you could hardly read, it said, 'therefore whatever my wife says shall be done.'

And I asked Miria, who is master? Now we could use the same analogy in relation to land. Men, for the reasons I have given you, are very emotional about the word ownership. But is it ownership that matters to us or is it the rights that are derived under that ownership? Can't we distribute those rights, protect them, to benefit women, without having to emphasise that it is women in the family who own the land? I think we can.

This works okay if there is balance in society, that men respect the view that although they are their own masters that women have rights which must be respected and protected. But should that fail, we should make the law in such a way that when there is confrontation then the reverse is true. However, if you should not exercise your right properly as master of the house, then the woman will take over, and become mistress of the house. Then she can say, 'Whatever my husband wants shall be done'.

The point I'm making is for appearance purposes, for the ego of men, and for the reasons I have explained, like polygamy and so forth, we can continue saying the land belongs to the family and the head of that family is the man who is the owner of that land. I'm not talking about the land which the woman herself has acquired from her own relatives or the land she has acquired personally. That obviously is hers, and I would never accept that the husband should try to take it away from her. Having said that, if this equilibrium which is reflected in this motto I have given was not to work, then we should devise methods saying, but if you misuse your powers as master of the land, and your wife and children are deprived, the law is written in such a way that they can take away your powers in the way this land is utilized. So that the woman benefits best and her children. We surely can do that.

Notes

1   I have been aided in this section by the work of Dr Sylvia Tamale of the Faculty of Law, Makerere University, who has done extensive research on women parliamentarians in Uganda. Her Ph.D. dissertation served as the basis for her ground-breaking book, *When Hens Begin to Crow: Gender and Parliamentary Politics in Uganda* (1999).

2   The designation CM or Council Member was used to refer to members of the NRC, although MP, Member of Parliament, has been the generally accepted term used over time.

3   In some areas of Uganda, if a woman's husband dies, she can be 'inherited' by her deceased husband's brother or nearest kin. In the past, women have had no choice in the matter. These days change is coming, in part because this is an outdated practice and in part because of the threat of AIDS.

4   The members of the CA caucus agreed to carry forward their solidarity by forming a permanent organisation. Thus, the Forum for Women in Democracy (FOWDE) was born and, since its establishment, it has played a pivotal activist role in training and advising women interested in joining politics.

Miria celebrates her victory having been elected to the Constituent
Assembly in 1994

Miria addresses the Constituent Assembly at the International
Conference Centre in 1994

Miria poses for a group photograph with her colleagues, the members of the Legal and Drafting Committee of the Constituent Assembly, 1995. On her right is the Chairperson of the committee, Justice George Kanyeihamba and on her left is the former Attorney General, Bert Katureebe

Miria joins women of Mbarara in a Kinyankore dance after addressing a political rally on gender issues in 1995

Miria on the floor of Parliament debating the Penal Code Amendment Bill when rape and defilement were made capital offences

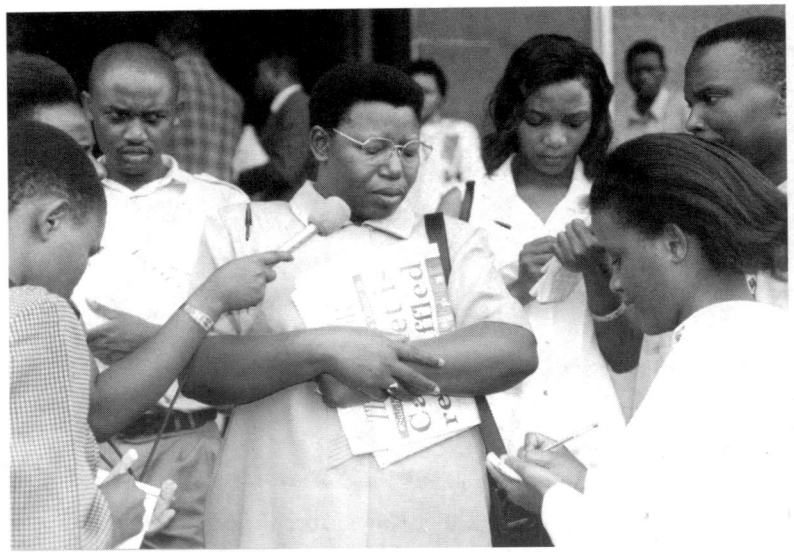

Miria meets the press

Miria in the International Conference Centre main hall during the
proceedings of the promulgation of the Constitution of Uganda, 1995.
On her right are her collegues Dr D. Matovu and C. Mavenjina

Miria, CA delegate for Mbarara District, signing the Constitution of
Uganda after its completion, 1995. Looking on is Abbasi Balinda,
Deputy Clerk to the National Assembly

Miria poses with a young admirer displaying the Constitution of
Uganda after its promulgation on 8 October 1995

Miria shares a joke with Nathan Byanyima, Member of Parliament for
Bukanga County and John Kazoora, her uncle, Member of Parliament
for Kashari County

Miria having a serious discussion with Cecilia Ogwal,
Member of Parliament for Lira Municipality in 1997

Miria representing Uganda at the Inter-Parliamentary Union in New Delhi, India

Miria shaking hands with A. Tandekwire after swearing in as a Member of Parliament for Mbarara District in 1996

Miria in a serious mood arrives at Parliament ready to present her amendment on the co-ownership clause in the Land Act in 1998

Miria inspecting a guard of honour by Uganda Police at Kibuli Police Training School when she went to address police officers on issues of ethics and integrity soon after her appointment as the Minister of Ethics and Integrity

Miria receiving anti-corruption petitions from Zie Gariyo, the Chairman for Uganda Debt Network, at the launch of Uganda's Strategy and Action Plan to fight corruption in 2000. Looking on is S. Madada, the Chairman for Anti-Corruption Coalition of Uganda

Miria addressing the second Global Forum to Fight Corruption in the Hague, the Netherlands in May 2001

Miria sharing a hearty laugh with Dr Speciosa Wandira Kazibwe, the Vice-President of Uganda, after the passing of the Referendum Bill 2000

Miria, officiating at Women's Day celebrations in Mbarara District, listens to a very emotional poem on domestic violence by a little school girl. Seated at her left is her friend and co-worker, Jolly Mugisha, the gender officer for Mbarara District in 2001

Miria on the floor with Wandera Ogalo, a member of the East African
Legislative Assembly to celebrate the election of Uganda's members to
the East African Legislative Assembly

Miria gets a congratulatory handshake from the President, Y. K. Museveni, after swearing her in as the first Minister of Ethics and Integrity in July 1998, at State House Nakasero.

CHAPTER 6

◆◇◆◇◆

A Feminist Lawyer in the New Millennium

U p to the time when I went to the UK to get my Master's degree at the University of Warwick, I had refused to be called a feminist. The reason was basically that the word feminist did not augur well in Uganda at that time. According to public perceptions of the period, 'a feminist' was dangerous, a terrible woman. If you mentioned that word, people would distance themselves from you. 'She's on the wrong track,' they would say, and they wouldn't listen. Part of the reason the term was really looked upon as dangerous was that it came from the Western world.

It is interesting to note that, in Uganda, men and people in general are encouraged to take up new ideas and innovations from the West. Many things from the Western world are promoted as progressive. However, patriarchal society, fearing its downfall, designates new (progressive) ideas about gender relations as 'foreign' and 'not suitable' for Africans. While the latest ideas about quantum physics, astrology, computer technology, etc., are welcomed, the idea of gender equality is most likely to be condemned.

Under the circumstances, I didn't want to be called a feminist. Many of us who were women activists knew that identifying ourselves as feminists was counterproductive. To do this would hurt our cause. Besides, I had my own way of defining myself. For some time, I had been very clear that I

209

was fighting for women, so I would say, 'Me, I'm not a feminist. I'm a self-styled advocate for women's rights.' That's what I called myself. But when I went to Britain for my Master's programme, I came to understand that a feminist is a person who is struggling to uplift women, someone who is challenging systems and structures that oppress women. There in Britain I decided, if that is the proper designation, then I must call myself a feminist.

There is another reason that I have now accepted this designiation. These days women in Uganda have reached a certain stage in public life so that we are able to say that we are feminists, and it doesn't get us into trouble as it did a decade ago. In the beginning of our struggle, it was a good strategy to vehemently deny you were a feminist and call your activism something else. If you can imagine, in those early days we didn't even use the word equality. Even that word, equality, sometimes caused us problems. So we would say something like, when women are doing so many things for the family, for the community, for the country, surely let them be entitled to certain rights.

When our point of view started to be accepted, the foundation was laid. These days we are in a different position. Yes, we can now say we are feminists without doing damage to our cause. Using that term now is not auguring badly because people have seen that, although we are feminists, we are doing certain things that need to be done and talking about things that need to be talked about. Don't you see? This change indicates that we have broken through and that many people now accept what we are saying and what we are doing. Most people are no longer scared of the word. So now I can say, easily, openly, without fear, 'Yes, I'm a feminist.'

There is another issue closely related to the one I have just described. When I went to do my Master's programme, I had a reluctance to take up feminist theory. I was aware that theory, any theory, is not some kind of truth that provides the answers to life's most difficult questions, but rather that theory serves as a framework within which to investigate something and then to analyse your findings. Yes, I knew that. However, I remember being concerned that I might get confused by someone else's line of reasoning, and that the result might be that I would be disassociated from my rural women. I was not willing to go in that direction.

Instinctively I knew what I wanted, in a straightforward manner, in a simple form. When a class I took began to take up some theoretical questions about, for example, how to define exactly what a 'woman' is, I was not willing to follow that line of inquiry.[1] I knew which women I was talking about. I was talking about the women of Uganda, my mother, my rural aunt, my rural women who were suffering. I wanted these women to enjoy rights over land. I wanted them to inherit property. I wanted them to have rights to education, training and jobs. I wanted them to assert themselves and to follow their dreams as I had followed mine. I felt those kinds of thing were what they wanted also, but that they might not be enlightened and empowered enough to speak about these things for themselves. I felt that they had paid fees for me through their suffering. Therefore, I felt I must take up the work of articulating for them.

At some point I told one professor that I didn't want to be confused by theory devised by others which might or might not fit our circumstances in Uganda. I told her that I came there to take a Master's in law and development, specifically because I wanted to do research about how law could be used as an instrument for the development and liberation of women, and I wanted to maintain my particular focus. I had certain questions that begged for answers, such as the following. How can we use the law to liberate women from all this bondage that denies them the chance to fulfil their potential? What kinds of laws are needed to enable women to empower themselves? How can law protect women from the worst abuses of patriarchal society?

At the end of the programme, I was very, very disappointed, not in any particular theory, but in the law itself. The only conclusion I could reach was that law is actually more of an oppressive instrument than a liberating one for women. I could say that was the major conclusion of my studies. Obviously, part of the problem is that in most cases laws are 'man-made'. Society continues to be patriarchal, mainly ruled by men, with laws being created by male leaders who may or may not consider women's interests when they create laws.

Another problem is that many people hold the premise that it is 'naturally' (God-ordained) men's responsibility to 'look after' women and girls. In other words, it is assumed that men will automatically, without question, provide for the needs of females in their care. Therefore, this thinking goes, laws to protect women's rights are not needed. In this argument, it is assumed that men will of course do what is decent and fair. We all know that the reality on the ground differs a great deal from this idealised view. We know that in very many cases, men not only fail to look after women and girls but, in fact, they are their worst oppressors. Perhaps the hardest part to swallow on this matter is that oftentimes it is within their own homes that girls and women are the most oppressed and mistreated. Imagine, the very institution – the family – that is supposed to be a refuge from harm. In fact, a recent study on gender violence in Uganda conducted by a coalition of women organisations in 2002, revealed that the home and the school are the two most dangerous places for girls. Now, I would ask my fellow Ugandans, what are we to think of this? The two places where girls spend most of their time are the most dangerous? Surely we are failing Uganda's daughters.

As far as oppressive laws are concerned, it is important to note that it is the poorest and the most vulnerable who suffer the most. From the time I became aware of the law, when I was still very young, I believed that proper laws, just laws, would be the solution to women's problems. During my Master's programme I reviewed the relevant literature and conducted in-depth research to learn how the law might be used to liberate women. I came to see that much of the time law is used in its most oppressive form *against* the vulnerable. From my study, one could easily lose hope in the law as a tool to spearhead women's development. Let me throw a little more light on the point I'm making.

If there is a law that states that a woman is supposed to have rights to some property when her husband dies, the reality is that if the husband dies, it is extremely difficult for this law to be enforced for the benefit of the widow. Yet, if there is a law that restricts the way women are supposed to dress, or states that women should not be seen in public doing a certain something, or that prostitutes should be arrested, if the law really takes away women's rights, it is enforced immediately, without any delay, and sometimes very harshly. But the laws that state that women should have equal opportunity to get jobs, that women should be treated equally at their workplaces, that women should inherit property, that women should be able to own land, I'm telling you, even if it is in the law books, enforcement of this kind of law is very difficult. So in the end the law is used more in its more oppressive and exploitative features against the vulnerable, and oftentimes it is women who are the most vulnerable. From my experience I would say that the law protects the rich and supports the status quo and the people in power. Although I have come to this conclusion, I have no intention of giving up the struggle I have undertaken.

In the passage that follows from *Song of Lawino* by Ugandan poet Okot P'Bitek (1972), a woman speaks to this issue.

> I have only one request.
> I do not ask for money
> Although I have need of it,
> I do not ask for meat...
> I have only one request,
> And all I ask is
> That you remove the roadblock
> From my path.

In the following section, I present three case studies that provide some insights about current realities in the legal system in Uganda and women's attempts to remove the roadblocks from their paths. These cases show that the legal system often fails women at the critical times when they need protection the most. The studies also show that if women are determined enough they may be able to find help in modern day Uganda. Sad to say, in each of these cases, a special intervention, yes, special help, was required to rescue the woman from an oppressive situation. Without the extra help, the outcome for the women would have been harsh indeed. I could call this section, 'Is the cup half empty or half full?' since it shows both the vulnerable positions of these three women and also the mechanisms that have been put in place in recent times to assist women in need.

*   *   *

Case Study 1: Mbarara District

After a legal education workshop conducted in a rural county in Mbarara District in 1989, a young woman (call her Kobu) approached me. No sooner had she started to talk to me than she was pulled off and rebuked by the Chairman of the area LC1 for 'disturbing big people.' At that time I was a Member of Parliament and a Commissioner on the Uganda Constitutional Commission, although I had gone on this programme as the Chairperson of ACFODE. I intervened and asked the Chairman to let the woman talk to me. After listening to her briefly, I handed her over to the Chairman and asked him to call his LC court to attend to the case.

About two weeks later, Kobu was brought by someone to my house in Kampala. They explained that Kobu had lost the judgement in the LC court. Her situation was as follows. Kobu's husband had recently died. According to the LC judgement, this young widow had to agree to be inherited by her father-in-law or she would be required to forfeit her children, her home and property. It was ruled that she was wrong to refuse to be inherited by her father-in-law, who, based on her refusal, had taken away her children and chased her from the home and property of her late husband.

Kobu was desperate. She was crying. On further interrogation, I learned that she had been married off when she was 14 years old to a young man of 18 years. The couple had lived together for four years and had three children when in 1985, during Obote's terrorist regime, her husband was shot dead by thugs. According to Bahima custom, as a widow, Kobu could either be inherited by a brother-in-law or her father-in-law. Since the brother-in-law was still young, the father-in-law decided to step in. Kobu refused. The old man chased her away, demanded a return of her bride price and took away her young children who were two years, one year and three months old. Unfortunately, the youngest baby died soon after being separated from its mother.

Up to 1989 when I met Kobu, she had nobody to help her solve her problem. She had lived in a state of misery and despair. That day at the legal workshop she first heard about a widow's rights over her children and property, and since then she had been looking for someone to help her see that the law was enforced. I took Kobu to the Administrator General who, on her behalf, applied for letters of administration of her deceased husband's estate and custody of her children.

This case took a long time to settle. One problem was that Kobu's father-in-law was very rich and he routinely used his wealth and status to get what he wanted. On the local level, bribes were a common practice, and decisions made by higher authorities oftentimes were not implemented down the line. This man actually had to be arrested and brought before the Administrator General before a final solution could be reached. Finally, Kobu was able to reclaim her children and property. However, that is not the end of the story.

The long period of struggle which exposed Kobu to offices of authority like the Administrator General, the district executive office, the police, and organisations like ACFODE and FIDA really empowered this young woman. Kobu had no formal education and was totally ignorant about how the law and legal institutions worked and was thus helpless inside the legal system. After the verdict in her favour, she had her home, property and children returned to her. In addition, she was now knowledgeable about things she had not known before, and she was a respected property owner. But there is more to this story.

Kobu has become known in her local area as a powerful woman who managed to do what had never been done before, namely to resist widow inheritance and all that it implies. As a result, Kobu gained political clout. She was later elected as leader of the Women's Council in her sub-county. In fact, she was my campaign manager in her sub-county during the parliamentary elections in 1996. Because she is highly respected in the whole sub-county, she often acts as an adviser to families with domestic problems.

Another interesting aspect of this case is that men in that area now respect women and widows' rights. In fact, Kobu's case discredits the argument advanced by some researchers that women are reluctant to take their cases to authorities for fear of being alienated from their families. On the contrary, her determination and persistence to claim her rights have made her a heroine in the village. Even her father-in-law before his death had such confidence in her that when somebody tried to encroach on his land, he approached Kobu for help and with her help his problem was resolved in his favour. The outcome for this intelligent and tough woman was that although she had no formal education, she has become economically, politically and socially empowered. It should not be overlooked that she is also serving as a role model for other women.

Case Study 2: Mbale

Mr Kalangala married his first wife Anna in church, and separated from her after a few years during which the couple had a few children. Like many couples in Uganda, the Kalangalas separated without going through legal procedures. Kalangala then started to co-habit with a second 'wife', Rose. This time there was no official marriage. Anna had left her children when they were very young, and Rose took over the responsibility for raising them. After living together for 18 years, Mr Kalangala died having written a will in which he left his property to Rose.

When Kalangala died in 1988, his relatives, led by his brother, who was then living with the first wife, Anna Kalangala (they had one child together), sought to bring Anna back into the deceased's home, claiming that as the legal widow she could reclaim her matrimonial home and property. The family threatened Rose with eviction, ignoring the deceased's will which, in any case, did not conform to the requirements of a valid will. Rose resisted eviction on the ground that she was the one entitled to the property. After all, she had lived on the property for a longer time than Anna, and she had cared for the deceased and his children all those years after Anna had deserted them. And, of course, Rose had nowhere else to go.

Rose first took her case to the LC1 court where she was referred to the Women Lawyers Association (FIDA). FIDA tried to resolve the case in the Administrator General's office. Finally, the case ended up in the Chief Magistrate's Court in Mbale,. where Rose won her case. She is now living happily in her home and enjoying her property. As in the first case, this case took about four years to be settled. It was Rose's determination, persistence and patience that finally led to a satisfactory solution for her.

As with Kobu, the process through which Rose had to carry her claim exposed her to legal knowledge and procedures, administrative and legal structures, and a number of organisations like FIDA and the Uganda Women's Finance and Credit Trust. In addition, a loan that Rose obtained from the Women's Trust had improved her economic situation. The challenges she faced only made her stronger and better prepared her to face new ones. Having won her case in the court system, she is now giving advice to other women who have similar problems.

Case Study 3: Mbarara

This case involved a 70-year old woman (call her Veneranda). Veneranda had never married, but continued to live at home and care for her parents until they died. Before her father died, he orally willed his house and land to his daughter as a gift for having taken care of him. After he died, Veneranda's brother evicted her from the land, on the basis of customary law that states that girls are not supposed to inherit their father's land and property. She sued her brother in the LC courts. The LC3 court decided in her favour. Her brother appealed to the Chief Magistrate's court in Mbarara Town as permitted by the LC statute (Judicial Powers Act, 1988).

Veneranda was living in Ibanda with a neighbour since she had no home of her own, and she had no money to go to the Magistrate's court which was about 80 kilometres from where she lived. At this point this old woman walked for three days to Mbarara Town because she heard about my work as someone who helped women with problems. After some searching, she found me. When she told me her story, I took her to FIDA. A representative from FIDA and I took her back home, where we called a meeting of residents and the LC3 court where we all listened to her case. All the LC courts, 1, 2, and 3, and many residents were in favour of Veneranda. After that, FIDA wrote a report to the Chief Magistrate on the basis of which he dismissed the case brought by the brother. After suffering mistreatment from her brother for a long time, Veneranda is now a very happy woman owning land and other property. Although she is old, she has also joined the women's councils, and in 1996 she fully participated in my campaign for Parliament. Other women now go to her for advice and she refers them to me or to FIDA.

*   *   *

One of the things that is so important about these cases is their multiplier effects. Through these women's struggles for their rights, many of the residents in their villages came to know more about the issues involved and how and where to look for solutions. In addition, since these women won their cases, other women have gained hope that if they struggle, they also can get a good result from the legal system. You see how important it is that women become empowered. One powerful woman serves both as a role model and as a leader for other women.

After relating the stories of these three women and the injustices they faced, I want to ask Ugandans to think about what kind of a country they want. How is it that women like these three are *routinely*, yes *routinely*, abused and exploited? Also, no one could miss the point that in each case it was family members who treated the women so badly. Is it right that most women live in jeopardy like this their whole lives? Does it really matter if these women were the ideal citizens or not, whether they were the perfect cooks or the best housekeepers or whether they 'pleased' their husbands 24 hours a day? Women in Uganda are sometimes beaten, sometimes severely beaten, for the above 'crimes'. Men are not beaten or otherwise abused in the same ways as women are, with the weakest excuses for the abuse.

This kind of unequal treatment has been called by feminists 'a double standard', that is, there is one standard by which women are judged and a very different standard for judging men. This double standard is arbitrary and inhuman. It gives males a considerable amount of freedom, at the same time it limits and restricts females. Under this standard, life can be good for males and 'hell' for females. One irritating part of the double standard is that males break social rules without facing serious consequences, whereas, if females break similar rules, there is a heavy hand waiting to punish them.

Let me tell you. The minute a woman enters public life, she is expected to act like an angel. She is supposed to be perfect, and she has to work doubly hard to be treated the same way a man is treated. A woman has to watch herself in public— she has to be 'good', whereas a man who is a public figure can go around drinking, or can go dancing every night. He can chase girls or have mistresses, in fact, do almost anything he wants. He can do all sorts of things that are unbecoming of a. leader, and society says, 'Well, that's how men are.'

Look at the women members of Parliament who have had the misfortune of having trouble with their marriages. They are looked at as if they are abominable, like they have done the worst thing, even when the marriage has broken up because of the man. But women are human beings. Why shouldn't a woman be able to go into a club and have a drink? The truth is that if people see this woman politician in a club with men other than her husband, someone will even say, 'Look at her.

She was drunk last night,' when she just drank one beer. It could be that there is no truth in the talk at all, and yet the lies damage the women's career.

Things that men do every day, if a woman does them, she is condemned. This kind of talk is used to undercut, to undermine women. For example, when Matembe goes to Parliament, someone might say, 'Look at that one. She was dancing with all the men.' This kind of public criticism then keeps other women from entering public life, since they don't want those things to be said about them.

I want to talk about the fact that women in politics are seen as breaking the social rules. It doesn't matter whether a woman politician is performing well or not, she is gossiped about. It seems that women are even worse than men in undermining the women. You know, if your marriage breaks down or if your children get in a bit of trouble, other women may say, 'It serves her right. Who is there to look after these children?' And they blame all the misfortune that falls in your family on the woman who has chosen this public life. They don't accuse the men in that way. I'm sorry to say that it is your fellow women who are the loudest in criticising you for this kind of situation, instead of giving you support.

In general women are blamed for everything and rarely given credit. If the children are good, who gets the credit? The man. If the children create problems, people say, 'Where was she?' Yes, it was the woman's fault. By the way, if a marriage breaks up, it's the woman who is faulted. A number of these marriages of women in Parliament which were broken, it's mainly because of the insecurity of the husbands. The husband might even make life hell for this woman. Then the woman may say, 'Why do I have to suffer like this? I can manage on my own.' The man may be impossible. Then the marriage breaks up, but I guess I would say, let it break.

Now, when you take the men in Parliament, they may do all kinds of irresponsible things. They may treat their wives and children badly, and yet, who cares? These are the double standards that make women so angry.

Even during the parliamentary campaigns these gender issues and these double standards are very prominent. First of all, the public asks, 'Is she married?' If you are married, where are you married? For example, look at my case, I contest in Mbarara and I am married in Bushenyi. Up to now.

Another part of the cultural double standard is that women are not supposed to complain. In fact, it is considered very bad behaviour for a woman to say anything unflattering about the men in her family. This taboo is even extended into society in general, that is, women are restricted from talking critically about any man, especially a public man. This is surely one reason that I have been so maligned and bashed. I am perceived to be the opposite of a silent and agreeable woman, because I don't just talk, I shout about the injustices I see, injustices that most people accept as normal because of the double standard that society accepts. I have broken an old taboo that says women should remain silent in the face of injustice from men.

Let me add another point about the double standard that has special meaning for women politicians. Just now I used the term 'public man'. When I talk about a 'public man,' who does that refer to? Of course, the answer is a politician. Now, if I say 'public woman', who am I referring to? The answer is a prostitute. One certainly wonders where these things come from. This incident of the double standard implies that women belong in domestic space, and that women who enter public space bring ridicule and humiliation on themselves. The argument we get is, you women, if you stayed home *where you belong*, none of this abuse would happen to you.

Yes, women politicians know this well. When women enter the public arena, people right away want to discuss the way they look, what they wear and their personal lives. Some people even suggest that when political women make public appearances, they should actually be somewhere else, that is, home looking after their husbands and children. No male politician is asked equivalent pointed questions about his spouse and children. What he wears is not an issue. Sometimes men in powerful positions even take on the role of sugar daddies, corrupting young girls, and no one makes a public issue of that. Yes, the double standard is a powerful tool of patriarchy. Don't question men about anything they do. Question women about everything when they dare to step into public life.

Returning to the three cases above, we should all be interested in what went on in those cases, and we should all be looking for ways to change society so that women are not vulnerable throughout their lifetimes. My conclusion about the whole matter is that it is very easy for men to abuse and mistreat women *with impunity*, meaning there are no consequences for the men who do these things. It is painful to add that, because some women personally benefit from the mistreatment of other women, women are often complicit in the mistreatment of fellow women. Men accuse women of not getting along with each other, but looking deeply at the circumstances, we find that women frequently align themselves with men because that's where power, resources and security reside. If sometimes women gain something, they don't seem to notice or mind that other women lose in the process.

There is a word used by feminists that helps us think about these issues - misogyny, which means 'hatred of women'. How else can we understand the epidemic of rape and defilement, of wife beating, of coerced, unwanted sex that leaves girls pregnant and disgraced, of child marriages where families agree to marry off girls of 12, 13 or 14 before a girl is old enough to speak for herself, and the humiliating public display of female bodies? At different times in our history, men involved in situations of armed conflict have captured and enslaved young girls and forced them at gunpoint to provide sexual services and do domestic chores. Sometimes the 'warriors' hack the girls with their machetes or otherwise brutalise them. Would these same men protect 'their own women' or would they abuse them too? The burning question here is, why do so many men treat women so badly?

There is another term that feminists use that uncovers another factor in the oppressive nature of our patriarchal society. The term is 'the male discourse'. It has been very interesting to me to find that a term has been devised to identify a phenomenon that I recognised some time back as a problem, although I had no name to describe it. Let me give an example of this phenomenon. When I hear someone say that a woman is nothing, or that a woman is useless, or that God put woman here on earth to serve man, I try to engage the people making such statements. I use this method a lot when I visit people at the grassroots. I ask people to tell me what words people use to describe men. They would list things like breadwinner, strong, fighter, master, decision maker, intelligent, etc. If I am in a situation where I can make a list for all to see, I do that.

Then I ask for the terms used to describe women. Often, in these encounters, there will be a pause, which I interpret to mean that mostly they don't even think about us. After the pause, they will say, women are weak, they are gossips, they are witches, they are disorganised, they are not clever, and so forth. And I list the things they tell me.

The two lists now give me a chance to make a point. 'Do you really think that women are weak?' I ask.

'Yes,' they say, 'they are not strong'.

Then I would say, 'Look at this woman, six-months pregnant, with a baby at her back, with a load of firewood and a small jerry can of water going home after four hours of digging in the shamba. Look at her,' I would say. 'Tell me, is she weak? How is she weak, this load she's carrying, the work she's doing?' And they would look at me. Then I would say, 'What weakness are you talking about? It is not physical weakness. It's the social role we play that makes us vulnerable, that leads you to call her weak. Look further,' I say. 'This child inside this woman gets everything it needs from the mother – protection, security, food, everything. That pregnancy makes her vulnerable, and you call it weakness.' Sometimes as I talk, it seems that people see the reality for the first time.

Recognising that we all use the male discourse when we talk aids us to understand what is going on. We all talk, both men and women, as if the way we talk makes sense, as if it is somehow the truth. Are men naturally the best decision makers and the best managers? Women make so many important decisions every day, by themselves, and the family depends on these being the right decisions. How much food to use each day in relationship to the resources available to the household. What to do when a child is sick in the face of limited money and limited time. When to plant seeds, how many seeds to save for the next planting, the careful weeding – all those decisions. They're based on intelligent thinking. Everyone should take note of what I'm saying here.

It is frustrating to think that women advocates like myself can help only 'some' women while other women never get the help and protection they need. It is discouraging to spend so much time and effort to change the laws and the system, and all the time the problem is so much bigger than our solutions. We never seem to catch up, or to have adequate solutions to problems as they arise. We seem to have solutions only after the fact, after women have suffered a lot. I would be grateful to anyone who could advise us what to do so that our solutions are equal to the problems.

Another interesting thing to note in the case studies above is that many of the structures where these women obtained help have been created since 1986. It is all too easy to look only at what remains to be done, 'the cup half empty'. Although I see enormous problems remaining for women, these days we can also see that there is some help available, as these cases show. When I am overwhelmed with the work that remains to be done, I can easily find myself asking, 'Are we really getting anywhere?' But I can also see what women in Uganda have gained. Let me now shift the focus from problems to solutions. It is time to revisit what's been happening in Uganda, this time to track the progress we have made in the legal field in the last 15 years or so, and to recognise some of the main players.

As I have said, the year 1986 was a turning point in the lives of women in Uganda. That was the year when the NRM government came to power through a protracted people's war. The NRM government changed the country from a state of lawlessness, instability and insecurity, and established a peaceful and democratic environment conducive to people's participation in the affairs of the country. Because women had participated in the bush war, fully proving their capabilities, the NRM leadership was prepared to give women more space in the new government, unlike any earlier time. This positive political will was demonstrated through the affirmative action of establishing a mandatory portfolio for women's affairs on the local councils. Other affirmative action initiatives would be added in the next few years.

This period coincided with the UN Women's Decade which had just concluded with the international women's conference in Nairobi, the proximity of which awakened Ugandan women to the global field of gender and development. Women in Uganda embraced this moment by either reactivating their old women-only organisations, such as FIDA, which had been stifled by the political insecurity of the dictatorial regimes, or forming new organisations like ACFODE, the Uganda Gender Resource Centre, the National Association of Women's Organisations in Uganda and others.

In a bid to mainstream gender issues in terms of development, the government established the Ministry of Gender. To further facilitate the democratisation process, the government expanded the NRC and initiated the making of a new constitution, through the Uganda Constitutional Commission and the CA. In short, this period from 1986 to the present has been a period of heightened activity in terms of mobilisation of the people to participate in the democratisation and development of the country.

A number of organisations involved in legal and human rights work have taken advantage of the new open environment to educate people about their rights. Notable among these are FIDA, ACFODE, Uganda Gender Resource Centre, the Legal Aid Project (LAP) of the Uganda Law Society and the Ministry of Gender and Community Development. Noting the gains women have made, Ugandan lawyer Florence Butegwa (1992) credits the government's leadership and the NGOs:

> The commitment of the present government and numerous organisations to facilitate the effective participation of women in the social, economic and political development of the country played an important role.

These organisations provided women with programmes in legal literacy, legal counselling, paralegal training and legal representation so that women would have access to information and advice. Legal literacy and counselling programmes have been spearheaded by FIDA and ACFODE while paralegal training has been conducted by the Ministry of Gender, ACFODE, the Human Rights Foundation and the Uganda Gender Resource Centre. The success of these legal education programmes reflects good planning and women-friendly training methods. One excellent strategy was for FIDA and ACFODE to integrate their legal programmes for women with financial assistance.

FIDA has so far opened three branches in the country. The one located in Mbale is partnered with the Ministry of Gender and the Uganda Women's Finance and Credit Trust which provides money management training and financial assistance to women. In this integrated programme, the Ministry conducts paralegal training while FIDA provides legal education, counselling and free representation of women in court. This innovative, collaborative and integrated approach has achieved quite a lot. Many success stories have been recorded, like the one in Case Study 2 above.

ACFODE'S multidimensional legal education initiative has been integrated with its other programmes such as those on reproductive health, family life education, and project management. ACFODE also operates a revolving credit fund to run in conjunction with its legal programme. From its beginning, ACFODE has made a point of avoiding top-down programming, but rather has brought women from all levels of society into the planning stage as full participants. This strategy of linking with rural women as equal partners is one thing that has made ACFODE uniquely effective.

ACFODE has chosen to concentrate its programmes in specific areas, one in each of the four regions of Uganda, and has been able to make a large impact. Here are some statements from ACFODE's 1994 evaluation report:

In Rubabo county of Rukungiri District men and women have realised and acknowledged women's rights to property and land in particular. Men now involve their wives in their dealings with land.

In Kioga county of Lira District, women and men have realised the importance of higher literacy levels of women in society. As a result more girls have been sent to school and widow inheritance has reduced.

In Kibuku county of Pallisa District a number of women now jointly own property with their husbands without any fear of legal manipulation. Incidents of child marriages have greatly reduced and bride price has also been generally reduced from 5 cows to 1 cow.

In Kiboga District, inheritance conflicts between mothers and heirs have to a certain extent been reduced by the Resistance Committee and Courts of Law.

The multidimensional approach adopted by some of these organisations and the technique of role plays, music, dance and drama as educational methods have resulted in a less legalistic way of implementing these legal programmes. Such methods have proved highly effective in grassroots education.

The paralegal training programmes have proved to be of great benefit to women in large part because the trained paralegals live and work within their own communities. This approach means that the paralegals are accessible to local women. Additionally, because the paralegals are known in their communities, their advice tends to be received and accepted without suspicion. An additional advantage is that these trained semi-professionals have been able to act as a link between lawyers and grassroots women.

These legal education programmes conducted by the Ministry of Gender, FIDA and ACFODE have gone beyond the giving of lectures and the distribution of pamphlets. Organisations now explain and interpret the law and give advice, solve specific problems, give financial advice and assistance, and represent women in courts of law when the need arises. Because these organisations have developed educational materials with the input of grassroots women, the materials are relevant and accessible to the women in the target group. Poverty is a major problem for many of those who are caught up in the legal system. The problem of poverty has been addressed by programmes that combine legal and financial aid. The three case studies show that it may not be possible to solve women's legal problems quickly. Invariably there is a need for money at some point, and obstacles that exist within the legal system, and other problems must be faced and overcome.

During the time that I was serving, first on the Uganda Constitutional Commission and then in the CA, I was devoting enormous amounts of time and energy hoping to produce a constitution that would truly change women's lives. A country's constitution is the basic law in the land. Wouldn't a gender sensitive, gender balanced constitution be the vehicle to lift the oppression off women? Wouldn't such a document at last truly liberate women? Fr Waliggo, (1996) Executive Secretary of the Uganda Constitutional Commission, called Uganda's new Constitution 'the women's constitution', stating,

> ... the Uganda Constitution of 1995 guarantees all the principles women need to spearhead their empowerment, development, dignity, and rights.

Of course, I realise that the Uganda Constitution is only 'a drop in the ocean' of what is needed. However, this grand document is there. Does this document give us a vision of what is possible, that is, a glorious society where women are located in the centre of all areas of life, *along with men*, as equals and partners? Surely this is something to work up to until we achieve it.

Let me say again that the constitution-making exercise was of tremendous importance in creating legal awareness among rural women. The workshops and seminars, the public meetings held in every part of the country, and the coverage in the media created opportunities for women to learn about their rights as provided under the law, as well as the inadequacies and the discriminatory nature of the law. Through this exercise women also came to know the importance of their political participation to their development. They learned the importance of their vote and the strength of their numbers - *more than* half of the population being women - in determining the political leadership of the country. Women were able to use this acquired knowledge to submit proposals for constitutional reform. The impact of these activities was also felt back home. More and more women were inspired to run for seats on local councils and gender issues became significant in every election manifesto, which had certainly not been the case up to that time.

As these case studies show, the existence of legal machinery within the communities is very important. The local courts are in the position to enforce women's legal rights. These courts constituted by an act of Parliament are composed of people living within their respective communities who are popularly elected by community residents. These courts, together with the legal aid clinics, have provided a non-legalistic forum similar to the old system of family structures traditionally used in Africa to settle domestic disputes. Historically, women have not been accustomed to going to state courts to enforce their rights but have traditionally chosen to use the familiar, tradition-based councils of kin and neighbours. If we truly want justice for women, it is necessary to make state institutions resemble these less formal, customary institutions (Armstrong 1995).

The LC courts and the legal aid clinics employ non-legalistic procedures in settling disputes. Many cases brought to these institutions end with a consensus judgement. The office of the Administrator General which, among other duties, is responsible for the administration of the estates of the deceased, has been very helpful to women. In collaboration with FIDA and LC courts, many women's disputes about inheritance have been settled at these sites without being subjected to the rigours of formal courts, for example, Case Study 1.

There appear to be five main constraints to legal strategies for the empowerment of rural women. First is the inadequacy of legal education. Although there has been a massive programme of legal and constitutional education throughout the country, no one believes that all the people have been reached. There are a number of factors which might prevent women from attending these programmes, such as, a heavy workload, living far from programme sites, lack of transportation or money for transportation, or needing a husband's permission to attend. The organisations conducting legal literacy have their own limitations such as insufficiency of funds and properly trained personnel.

A second constraint is the inaccessibility of legal services. Except for the LC courts which are accessible to everybody because they are situated within communities, other legal enforcement institutions may not be easy for grassroots women to reach. Out of 39 districts, FIDA currently runs its legal aid clinic in only three, namely Kampala city in the Central Region, Mbarara in the West and Mbale in the East. Indeed, the existence of these offices account for many success stories in these three districts as compared to other districts. Even then, these clinics are located in the heart of towns, very far removed from where most grassroots women reside. Although educational programmes are often taken to the women, counselling and individual or family legal advice are mostly provided at the clinics. This requires transport for these poor rural women who may have to visit a clinic several times before a case is settled, often because spouses or other family members refuse to honour FIDA's invitation. Let me explain further.

FIDA mostly depends on the goodwill of the person being accused. Once a woman lodges a complaint with FIDA, that organisation writes a letter 'invite' the person who is the subject of the complaint to come to the clinic office. If the person responds to the invitation by coming to the office, a discussion ensues and it is likely that a solution can be reached amicably. At times people refuse to respond to FIDA's invitation, or they may refuse to honour FIDA's settlement of a case. When this happens, there is a need for formal court procedures which tend to be frustratingly long, as seen in Case Study 2.

The third kind of constraint is customary and cultural. It constraints mostly affect the LC courts. The majority of the LC court members are men, who may have strong beliefs about local 'customs,' such as, that deceased husbands' land and property should pass to other male members of the clan rather than to the widow, or that the custody of the children automatically belongs to the clan. In many cases, these courts base their decision on customs and cultural practices which are oppressive to women. In Case Study 1, the LC court held that Kobu was wrong to resist widow inheritance by her father-in-law.

A further constraint of the LC court system is that sometimes court personnel fear rich and powerful people in the community and hesitate to rule against them. The man or family against whom a complaint has been brought may be someone who donates funds or basic services to the community, such as providing a vehicle to transport sick people to the hospital, or donating milk, sugar or food to needy neighbours. In such a case, members of the LC court may fear to decide against the community's benefactor. The important person may even stubbornly refuse to attend the court session. There is no mechanism by which such a person can be forced to attend. In other instances, the LC court officials may be corrupted with cash or other gifts to ignore the woman bringing the case to them.

The fourth constraint is perhaps the most frustrating of all. That is a total lack of enforcement machinery for the decisions reached through the LC courts and the legal aid clinics consensus procedure. Due to the principle of separation of powers, LC courts have no powers of enforcement. As a consequence, even when the decision has been in their favour, many women find they must appeal from LC1 court to the LC2 court and even to the LC3 court. In all three of these case studies, more than one court was involved before the final solution was reached. There is an urgent need to put into place an effective enforcement component so that court decisions are not ignored while women continue to suffer.

The LC court system would become much more effective if members of these courts were trained in the basics of law and the legal rights of women. At present there is no such programme. Often the LCs apply the principles of oppressive customary law because members are not aware of the specific law that is applicable to the case.

The last of the five constraints to the realisation of women's rights is corruption on the part of law enforcement agents such as police, judiciary and other officers within the Administrator General's office. Of course, corruption not only affects justice for women but for all Ugandans. This evil of corruption is rampant in all spheres of Ugandan life, and should be vigorously fought.

Notwithstanding the constraints which hinder the development of women's empowerment, what has been achieved so far shows that we are on the right track. When I am feeling optimistic, I believe that with the new Constitution in place and the continued political will on the part of government, the future of Uganda's women appears brighter. The women and organisations which have led this struggle need to continue with the same zeal and commitment in acting as watchdog to see that the law is obeyed and that women's rights are protected. The empowerment of individual women, as illustrated in these case studies with the multiplier effects they carry, can gradually lead to the empowerment of large numbers of women around the country. Let me quote here Gorrete Maida, Legal Officer of FIDA, who told me the following.

> What is certain is that the majority of Ugandan women have come to a realisation that they have been and continue to be unjustly treated, that they have been and continue to be robbed of their rightful dues. They are no longer contented with the status quo and can no longer tolerate the situation. It is mostly this realisation, the sense of injustice, which propels them along and makes those who come (to FIDA) to seek remedy demonstrate such patience and determination. They encourage us to push ahead in search of remedies for them.

In conclusion, let me say that the machinery for the administration of justice for women in this country leaves a lot of room for improvement. Unless something is done to domesticate and simplify the judicial system, women will not realise their legal rights.

Although tremendous success in educating society about women's rights has been achieved, Ugandan society continues to nurture customs, cultural practices and attitudes which are oppressive to women. These things are repugnant to fundamental principles of natural justice. In this country *the majority of the people know about the customs and they do not know the law.*

It is hard for customs to die quickly, especially so when those possessed with power are the ones to benefit from these customs. We shall continue to educate the people but there is a long way to go to effect a change of attitude. New laws alone without a change of attitude cannot work. It is in fact because of such attitudes that the LC courts have not helped women a lot. These courts tend to apply customs and cultural practices which are not only biased against women, but are inconsistent with the Constitution.

Note

1 Although at that time I was not willing to take the side route to explore some of these issues, I do admit that some of these debates are interesting and do have a connection to African life. To give just one example from a complex debate, if part of the definition of 'woman' is a child bearer, then childless women or women who choose not to marry and bear children are what - somehow not *really* women? Think about how childless women are ridiculed and humiliated in our culture. They are called barren or dry. Although it is sometimes the man that cannot produce children, the woman is always faulted. The situation is so bad that in some cases women pretend to be pregnant and may even steal a baby so they will not be treated as 'failed' women.

CHAPTER 7

A Moment of Reality: The Land Act 1998

Having gone through the constitution-making process, those of us who had worked so hard to write a new Constitution felt well satisfied with the finished product. Women activists soon began to ask themselves, but now, what happens next? Personally, I was interested to see that the words, statements and guarantees – the promises made – in this grand legal document be translated into better lives for people at all levels of society, but especially for the women who so often had been denied decent lives and legal protection. But what does it take to translate constitutional provisions into justice and equality for people in their daily lives?

In this chapter I am going to discuss the issue that is perhaps the most important for women in Africa – land. Land rights. Land ownership. Land security. The reader will quickly notice that I have very strong feelings and opinions about this issue. I have chosen not to try to hold my strong feelings in check, but to speak from my heart, in the name of all African women about this life and death matter. It seems to me that in this case it would be dishonest (un-Matembe-like) to try to write in an objective, dispassionate manner. I would ask the reader to think of the following as a plea to you to join this cause for women's rights, in this case, for secure rights to land, something that has been denied to most women in Uganda up to now. The Constitution contains a provision (Chapter 4, Article 32) which states that affirmative action would be deployed to help remove the imbalances created by history.

One area where there were major historical injustices and imbalances was in land policy. Because Uganda is mainly an agricultural country with the majority of Ugandans dependent on the land for their very lives, land issues are obviously of critical importance. Ninety percent of the population of Uganda live in rural areas, and the majority of these depend in large part on subsistence farming as the source of their livelihood. To this extent, having access to land guarantees a person daily food, and a surplus to exchange for essential products and services. The land also provides security for loans should one need money from the bank. It is clear to see that ownership and control of land is a matter of life and death for most Ugandans.

Knowing how people felt about land, the writers of the new Constitution decided that more equitable land laws should be a high priority. New laws on land issues were to be passed, and passed speedily, to promote peace and proper development in the country. Chapter 15, Article 9 of the Constitution obliged the government to pass a new land law 'within two years' of the promulgation of the Constitution. The Land Bill was tabled in Parliament in 1998. We, the women activists, thought this was our chance to secure land rights for the women of Uganda.

From the beginning, this bill was *very, very* controversial. Indeed, it was highly politicised. Different groups of people had a special interest in this Land Bill. Actually, there were three main groups which had what they saw as legitimate claims that needed redress where land law was concerned. The three were the Baganda, the Bunyoro and women. Although all the issues involved in the debate of the Land Bill were extremely interesting, I am going to confine my remarks to the struggle of women to secure land rights within that debate.

For me, I said, this is the time to clear up these problems, to resolve long-time grievances, and to make sure that the land tenure systems in this country will promote justice and development. Also I thought it was high time that women got land, too. We had just crafted what many called a 'women friendly' constitution, but did that actually mean anything?

During the time that I was serving, first on the Uganda Constitutional Commission and then in the CA, I was devoting all time and energy hoping to produce a constitution that would truly change women's lives. As I have already said, a country's constitution is the basic law in the land. Wouldn't a gender-sensitive, gender-balanced constitution be the vehicle to lift the oppression off women?

Now was the time to put these specific constitutional provisions to the test. It was time to use the relevant provisions to see that women were not left without land. As individual women and women's organisations began to organise in support of land rights for women, the following constitutional provisions served as a base for our advocacy.

I've already mentioned Chapter 4, Article 32 that was written with women in mind, as well as other marginalised people. Here is the entire article.

> Notwithstanding anything in this Constitution, the State shall take affirmative action in favour of groups marginalized on the basis of gender, age, disability or any other reason created by history, tradition or custom, for the purpose of redressing imbalances which exist against them.

Article 237 in Chapter 15 adds another important point, 'Land in Uganda belongs to the citizens of Uganda ...' (To see who is defined as a citizen, see Chapter 2 of the Constitution.)

Is this last provision a contradiction of the actual situation? Remember that women constitute more than half the population of Uganda. Yet, at the turn of the millennium, less than ten percent of women own land. One has to ask, does the land in Uganda really belong to the citizens of Uganda or only to men and a few fortunate women?

Chapter 4, Article 33 of the Constitution contains several provisions pertinent to questions about women's rights, as follows. As you read, please take special notice of clauses 5 and 6.

(1) Women shall be accorded full and equal dignity of the person with men.

(2) The State shall provide the facilities and opportunities necessary to enhance the welfare of women to enable them to realise their full potential and advancement.

(3) The State shall protect women and their rights, taking into account their unique status and natural maternal functions in society.

(4) Women shall have the right to equal treatment with men and that right shall include equal opportunities in political, economic and social activities.

(5) Without prejudice to article 32 of the Constitution, women shall have the right to affirmative action for the purpose of redressing the imbalances created by history, tradition or custom.

(6) Laws, cultures, customs or traditions which are against the dignity, welfare or interest of women or which undermine their status, are prohibited by this Constitution (p. 30).

To restate the central issue here, women in Uganda constitute more than 50 percent of the population and contribute an estimated 70 percent of the agricultural production, and yet less than 10 percent of women own land. The majority of the rural women who till the land neither own nor control it. They have only limited and tenuous access. To explain further, a woman does not have the right to decide which piece of land to till for her beans or other crops. It is either the father, the husband or the son who has the right (sacred right?) to decide how each section of land is used, and by whom. The consequence of this system is that women often end up with less fertile land to till while the best pieces are reserved for men to use for their so-called 'cash crops.' Looking further, we should not wonder that famine is endemic in many parts of Africa, including Uganda. The critical factor is that those responsible for food production are denied the rights to own and control land and its use.

The activism of large numbers of women and women's organisations that started in the constitution-making process continued as legislators started to consider the Land Bill.

Women organised their efforts under a consortium called the Uganda Land Alliance which mobilised the marginalised people who did not have land. The Land Alliance was constituted in May 1995 by 35 organisations and six individuals. This consortium of national and international groups was established to engage in advocacy work on issues relating to land policy. Its mission was to ensure that land policy in Uganda protects the rights of the poor, and that the poor gain and retain access to land and gain ownership of the land.

Women's efforts in the activity surrounding the debate of the Land Bill resulted in the creation of two main provisions for the protection and promotion of women's rights to land. These were the provisions that the women MPs introduced and supported in Parliament. The first provision concerned the consent of the spouse and children when one spouse wants to sell the family land. Hitherto, it was possible for a man to sell land without seeking the consent of either his wife or his children. In such a case, the woman and the children could wake up one morning to find some person chasing them off their land because the husband had just sold it out from under them.

We should ask, but who would do this kind of thing? Sometimes it was the husband, or the father or another male relative. Yes, men in the family were the ones to do this. A man didn't have to consult anybody before selling the family land. Of course, many men who became drunkards would just sell the land, and then drink up the money they received or maybe use it to marry another wife. Picture the poor wife at home who would find herself and her children without land, chased away by some person who had purchased the land from the husband. Of course, this meant that she had no home.

So, we were very interested in ensuring that the spouses, meaning mainly wives, were protected. Of course, it was mainly men who sold the land this way. We said, when a spouse wants to sell the land, he/she must get the consent of the other spouse and the children, that is, the children of majority age. If the children were not of majority age, then the LCs would be the ones to represent the children. So that was the first provision.

The second provision we wanted was to secure co-ownership of land for women, especially for land that is not registered. Mark you, the majority of land which is not registered is held customarily. Any customary land holding necessarily means it is either the man or the clan males who are seen as owning the land.

Let me explain more about why we wanted co-ownership of land. Now take the situation where this man is considered to be the owner of the land. In that case, whether he and his wife have been married for 20, 30, even 50 years, it doesn't matter, any time a man can just get up one day and say, 'Woman, I don't want you any longer. Pack up and go.' Actually, many men have been doing this, thereby rendering their wives homeless. Some desperate women in these situations have even resorted to hanging themselves. Some have even killed their children and themselves, since they had nowhere to go and no way to maintain themselves and the children.

Imagine that situation. This woman has been there for all those years. This land is where she belongs. This is her home. She has no other home. Since she came there to that home as a bride, she has been working this land, tilling it, producing the food, feeding the family. That's her life. And now one day, the man says, 'Get out of my house. I don't want you any more.' He doesn't need a reason. He can just do it.

Now the woman goes, either to her father's place where she is not entitled to any land because the land belongs to her father or her brothers or the sons of her brothers. Of course, she can go there, but she has no rights there. Perhaps she will be accepted as a squatter at her elder brother's home, but this brother is also married. He has a wife and a home of his own to think about, a home where his sister does not fit in at all. These people don't want this woman. And you know what happens? They may treat her as a servant, as a virtual slave. They don't recognise her at all as being anybody.

This property, her father's land, does not belong to this woman, and she does not belong to it. The land belongs to the brother, and in some sense to his wife. If she's going to live with them, this woman will have to work just to get food, – but she has no land. She has no rights. She has no status. Her father or her brother are likely to say to her, 'You, you failed. You failed to manage your home,' (just like my father used to blame my aunt for a situation beyond her control). This woman has returned to her natal home hoping to stay at her father's home or her brother's home. But her brother's wife is more entitled to this land and to this place than she is. In fact, this woman who was born in this place is not in any way entitled.

Remember that when this rural woman was married off at age 15 or 20, she had been working that land where she was born, her father's land, for many years. She had helped to make it productive. When she married, she was told, 'Go and make your home with your husband. You don't belong here anymore. You have no rights here. Your home is at your husband's place.'

So, this woman goes to her husband's place. She stays for 20, 30, 40 years. Now she is an elderly woman, aged. All her energy has been exhausted digging her husband's land, creating wealth from this land, feeding the family out of her labour. Then, at the end of it, this man says, 'Come on. Pack up and go away.' What choice does she have? She goes away. But where?

Now, let me tell you the worst situation of all. This woman may go to live with one of her sons. If that son is living on the father's land, and the father has chased the mother away, she is not allowed to go to live with her son either. Once the husband has said, 'Go away,' she cannot live anywhere on his land. The situation might be different if the son has his own land separate from his father's land. It is a possibility then that the woman could stay with her son, although the way patriarchal society is set up, she might not live peacefully with her daughter-in-law. However, if the land where the son resides is clan land, this woman can not be accepted, even in her own son's house, even if her son and his family are ready to welcome her there. The reality is that this is the husband's land and he is chasing his wife away, and there is nothing to prevent him from doing that, if he wants to.

So, our interest in securing co-ownership of land was against this kind of situation. So, we wanted this woman who has been living with her husband on this piece of land for these many years, together with her husband, to co-own the land. Her working the land should give her rights, but more important, her existence there should give her rights. She married when she was young, say 20, and now 28 years later she's 48 – that's my age. Can anyone imagine Mr Matembe telling me, 'Pack and go,' and nothing belongs to me. Yet it is possible here in Uganda for him to do it. It does not matter whether the wife is officially wedded (i.e. in church) or customarily married.

Now, you people of Uganda, all these years this woman has been digging. She has been creating wealth for her family, for her community, for her nation. Maybe she bought cows or goats, or made clay pots or wove mats to sell, or whatever else. Now at the end of it, her husband has seen a young girl, and he says to his wife of many years, 'I don't want you anymore. Pack and go.' Is this how Uganda should treat its mothers? Even porters are paid their wages, but what about the women of Uganda? What do they get for their labour?

So we were saying, since this is her matrimonial home, this place where she is, the place that sustains the family and herself, this home should be co-owned by a husband and wife. Where their matrimonial home is, the land that sustains them should also be co-owned by the couple. That's the second provision that we wanted to secure in this Land Bill.

So women mobilised themselves, held seminars and workshops, and even invited members of Parliament to attend. I remember one seminar organised by Forum for Women in Democracy (FOWODE) when we even invited the President, and he attended. We wanted to discuss the Land Bill and what women wanted from it. During that seminar women talked about what they thought was important. After the workshops, the women MPs drafted these two provisions about consent and co-ownership. We thought, if we can get these two provisions in the land law, then Ugandan women would be safe. We wanted this issue of land co-ownership, not only to use it so women could own land, but to use it to secure a permanent home for women.

For me, when I was arguing for it, I was actually arguing, not mainly from the perspective of land ownership, but mainly from the perspective of *'belongingness.'* That word may not even be in the dictionary, but it expresses this important idea so well. Where does a woman belong? Where is her home which she can claim as permanent? Home. Everyone needs a home. And the reason why I was determined to secure this provision is because of what I have described, this man getting up one day and saying to his wife, 'Get out of my home.' During my years of activism in my district, Mbarara, I have been constantly confronted with these cases, women being chased away, as in the three cases I have already narrated. This goes on every day and every day. Now, I thought, since Parliament is debating about land ownership, and land ownership gives a woman a permanent home, I wanted to secure land co-ownership for women because this would give them a permanent home.

You see, land in Uganda can be acquired customarily when you inherit it from a parent, but of course customarily women are prohibited from inheriting land. You can also acquire land in Uganda by buying it, but most rural women don't have money (men control the money in the family) and thus cannot buy land. Of course, women like me can buy land but there are very few in my category.

So, women activists and women MPs said, how can we secure land ownership for women? The majority of women are the rural women. Let us use their tilling the land and their long stay on the land as the basis for their owning the land. We said, Okay, if a woman has been married to this man, and she has been tilling the land, and that's where she has been growing food for the family, her very life depends on that land. Then both this land where her matrimonial home is, and the piece of land which she tills for sustenance of the family, belong to husband and wife as co-owners.

This provision would guarantee women a home so that they would never be chased away. That's what I wanted to secure.

If the wife co-owns this home and the land surrounding the home, and one day, the man says, 'Woman, pack and go,' the woman could say, 'No, I don't have to go anywhere because I belong here. I co-own this land with you. Therefore I am staying here.' So, I said, good. If I can secure these two provisions, I shall have secured a permanent home and a 'belonging' for the women of Uganda.

The procedure in Parliament is that when a bill is introduced for debate, it is sent to a particular committee. The committee is charged with the responsibility of discussing the bill, which it later brings back to the House for debate and adoption. The committee calls interested people to come to committee meetings to articulate their views about the bill. In the case of the Land Bill, a number of interested women's NGOs went to Parliament to lobby the committee. These women explained the two important provisions they wanted, first on consent and second, on co-ownership. This committee accepted the provision on consent, but rejected the one on co-ownership.

After studying the bill and receiving proposed amendments from interested parties, the committee made its report to the House. When the report was adopted, the committee started to read the amendments that were to be considered.

Needless to say, the women who had worked so hard to design these two provisions and lobby for their acceptance were broken-hearted about the rejection of the provision on co-ownership. Some disappointed women came to see me, and we talked. Me, I was not prepared to lose out on this matter. I said, I'm going to pursue this in the House, and bring this co-ownership provision in, by way of an amendment. Before doing anything in the House, I went and lobbied the Minister of Lands and the Chairperson of the committee in Parliament. These two officials were the ones spearheading the bill in the House. I told them why we must get this provision of land co-ownership for women. I described the conditions under which women live, as described earlier in this chapter. I talked and talked. Finally, they agreed that I could bring the provision on land co-ownership for women as an amendment to be debated.

After I had these discussions with the Minister and the Chairman, and they had said, Okay, bring it, I circulated the draft amendment to members. But who would support the amendment? Would the women MPs? At an informal gathering of some women MPs in the lobby of the House, the Vice-President, Specioza Kazibwe, raised the issue of whether women in Parliament should support this amendment. She said since the Land Bill was so controversial, maybe it was not the right time to bring in the co-ownership provision. Wouldn't it be better to reserve this issue for the Law on Domestic Relations at a future time? She knew that I was determined to bring it now but she wondered about the mood of the House at this time. What about the men, she asked. Will they support it? In fact, the VP was very aware of the delicate nature of the proceedings. She had a good point, especially on behalf of the government, since the government wanted to pass this law.

I want to say here that, although I know the importance of consensus building, and I can be a good team player, I have come to certain conclusions about the moment when someone says to women, 'Wait a little; we'll get around to you soon.' Or, 'Now is really not the right time; in future we'll attend to your interests.' In country after country in Africa, when a new government took power, the male leaders told the women that the really important issues demanded their immediate attention, and after that, women's concerns would be addressed – 'in due time'.

While we were still making the Constitution, I was invited to address a meeting of ANC women in South Africa. I told these women, please, when Mr Mandela says to you, 'Let's work on these "important issues" first,' you must not agree with him. I told them, when you get your majority rule, there will be so many problems to attend to that women's issues will never be considered. Even if you love Nelson Mandela – we also love him in Uganda, I told them – but you must keep the pressure on him to take up the women agenda straightaway. I am sure that I was only one of many voices giving them this advice. Good enough, they were wise. They constitutionalised women's rights and women's full participation in government, and I think they are even ahead of us. In one critical area, they are ahead of everybody, that is in terms of budgeting with women in mind. They have led the way on that one. The South African women learned from the experiences of women in other countries what women had not done right. The main mistake women in Africa made was agreeing to wait until the men got around to them, or until 'the time was right'. And time was never right anyway!

Now during the Land Bill debate in Parliament, I thought we must sort this out now while all the important issues are being sorted out, or there will never be 'a good time' for the issue of women and land. Once the 'important issues'– does that mean those of interest to men? – are settled, people will move on to something else. So I didn't hesitate. I said. 'Let us use every opportunity available. This is a law which is supposed to sort out problems of land ownership, and women certainly have problems of land ownership. Why don't we raise this amendment? Let's try. If we fail, then we can try again with the Domestic Relations Bill. Let's try instead of just keeping quiet as if we are not bothered by the problem of women and land ownership'. I told them, 'As long as you don't oppose me on the floor, let me go in there, raise this matter and argue for it. If you cannot stand up to defend it, please don't oppose it'. So we agreed to table the amendment.

So, the debate came to the House, and I stood to fight this next important battle for women. I moved my amendment which would provide for co-ownership of land between husbands and wives. The amendment consisted of four clauses, each important on its own, with the four combining to really protect a woman's rights to land.

The first clause was to cater for the situation where, at the time of marriage, a single woman or a single man owns a piece of land. The problem arises with the common practice here in which a man assumes ownership of any land that belongs to a woman he marries. One day this single woman owns land in her own right, the next day she gets married and the land now belongs to her husband. Now, we said, it is time to protect this woman. You know, most women in Uganda never own land. It is estimated that somewhere between 7 and 10 percent of

Ugandan women own land. Actually, this land ownership by women is mainly in Buganda. Somehow Buganda has become more enlightened than other regions on this matter, to such an extent that some fathers have willed their land to their daughters. And, of course, some women who have money, like me, buy land.

In this first clause we categorically declared that if a person owns a piece of land when he or she marries, that person continues to own that land after the marriage. Straightforward enough.

The second clause pertained to monogamous marriages. In this situation, the matrimonial home and the land that is used for sustenance of the family were to be co-owned by the husband and the wife. We did not include the bigger piece of land that the family could have had because, we thought, that would have made this provision very difficult to pass. After all, this could be a big farm. We left out the land used for farming where the family earned a lot of money. That land would continue to be owned by the man. So we limited this co-ownership to the matrimonial home and the land surrounding it that produced the family's livelihood. You know, this was not really much. Just the family home where the couple lived as a married couple and the land used for the family's food supply and surplus to sell to secure necessities for the family. Truly, this was not really too much to ask. That's why I was so disappointed when our efforts failed. We were not asking much, only a little for the mothers of Uganda.

The third clause was for those people in a polygamous marriage. In Uganda men are permitted to have more than one wife. In this polygamous marriage, each of the wives, whether 2, 3, or 4, is living in her own matrimonial home and having a piece of land that is used for the sustenance of that woman and her children. In this situation, each woman would co-own with her husband her home and that piece of land.

Clause 4 was similar to clause 3. In this case the wives all live in the same house with their husband, each having a separate bedroom. What we did here was to recognise that these situations exist and we catered for them. We were saying that we wanted protection for these women, too. Therefore, this husband and his wives would co-own the matrimonial home and the land together.

As you can see, these four clauses contain some basic principles. After I read them in Parliament, we debated them. It was not so easy. I based my argument on Article 33, 5 and clauses 6. Let me put them here again because the arguments here are so very important.

> (5) Without prejudice to article 32 of the Constitution, women shall have the right to affirmative action for the purpose of redressing the imbalances created by history, tradition or custom.
>
> (6) Laws, cultures, customs or traditions which are against the dignity, welfare or interest of women or which undermine their status, are prohibited by this Constitution.

My argument was that by custom and tradition women had been denied land. We were now setting out to correct those imbalances by using affirmative action. It is time to correct this imbalance. It is time for women to co-own this land that is the centre of their existence, the land that they have faithfully tilled for the benefit of their families.

Another argument I used was based on Article 237 in Chapter 15 of the Constitution, which states, 'Land in Uganda belongs to the citizens of Uganda'. I said, either women are Ugandan citizens, in which case land belongs to this female half of the population along with the male half, or they are not citizens. But the question then arises, how can land belong to women except to have the law state that they own it together with their husbands? Then I said, since we women are citizens and since Parliament is making a law to translate these concrete provisions of the Constitution into laws that will protect people, then we must accept co-ownership because it makes the constitutional provisions a reality.

One of the problems that I encountered concerned a constitutional provision (under human rights) which says that no person shall be deprived of his or her property without adequate compensation (Article 26). Somebody said, 'Matembe, the amendment you are bringing here is in contravention of the Constitution. How can you take away this land from this man and give it to his wife to share without compensation, the compensation as required by the Constitution?'

I said, 'I don't refer to registered land. It is only the registered land that is registered in a particular name. So, if it is registered in a particular name, then the provision you are referring to applies. But most of customary land holding is not registered and it is not in anyone's name.'

So they agreed since we are talking about the land held customarily, and it is not indicated with this kind of land who owns it, that this co-ownership provision will not contravene the Constitution. So I got support from members of Parliament.

So now, as I argued for these clauses, basing my arguments on the Constitution, I called on the members to realise that the challenge at this time was to translate the Constitution into action. This was the time to implement the constitutional provisions as far as women's rights were concerned. This was the time. Now. Either the Constitution was to remain a paper document or it was to become a reality for Ugandans.

Other women leaders spoke up in support of this amendment. When things were moving nicely, nicely, the Minister of Gender, Hon. Janet Mukwaya, stood up and argued for the amendment. Vice-President Kazibwe also spoke in favour. So this amendment was passed. Now, when it went through, the Speaker of the House said, 'Okay, Hon. Matembe, we have passed this amendment in principle. The four principles which are expounded in these clauses have been passed by this House. But the language needs improvement. You need to go and 'massage' the language to make it more appropriate and legal. In principle, these provisions have passed. Rewrite them and bring them back and we shall give the amendment an article number and put it in the Land Act.' The Speaker said all this.

After that, of course we were very happy. The news of the passage of the amendment on co-ownership appeared in the press. The headlines announced, 'The Matembe amendment has passed'. Very good! Of course, the debate on other provisions continued. I met with the legal draftsman. I told him what was needed, and he drafted the provisions in proper legal language very nicely, and we waited.

Now when the debate on the Bill came to the final day, there were many small details to resolve. It was quite a laborious process, really exhausting, to clear up all those small matters, and we were facing a serious deadline. Remember that the Constitution had set a deadline which we were working to meet. We debated all morning and into the afternoon, without taking any break. People were noticeably tired as we went through all those provisions that had been postponed, that needed attention.

When we finally came to my amendment, the Speaker called my name. He said, 'Hon. Matembe, what about your amendment?' This was the time for me to read those four clauses that had been massaged into proper legal language. Earlier that day I had given copies of the clauses to the Speaker, the Minister, and the Chairperson of the committee. I stood up to read those four clauses in the amendment, one by one, but as soon as I stood up, the members of the House said, 'Ah, that one was passed'. When they said that, the Speaker said, 'So we have finished'. I did not read the clauses and the Speaker declared the Bill passed.

The story of what happened in these proceedings must be told. By that time I did not know that the amendment must be read into the microphone in order to be recorded in Hansard (the official parliamentary record). When the clauses are not read in this way, they don't appear in Hansard. When I stood up to read the amendment, I had not been given the microphone. And when members shouted, 'That was passed,' those words were not spoken into the microphone either, so they did not appear in the Hansard. The Speaker was the one with the microphone. Therefore, there was no record of the amendment on the co-ownership clauses in the Hansard.

The next step for the Land Bill was with the draftsman who was responsible for drafting what would be the Land Act.

Whatever was recorded in Hansard was what he drafted into the law. Now imagine the situation. We walked out of the House thinking that our amendment had passed, when in fact it would not be in the Land Act, since it was not read into the microphone so as to be recorded in Hansard.

After about three weeks the Land Act was printed and received the President's assent. When it came out we found that the provision on consent was there but the co-ownership provisions were not included in the Act. We were so shocked. How could this be? There was no immediate answer as to what had happened to our amendment until I found out the problem myself, that since the provisions were not read into the microphone, there was no record of them in the Hansard. So we lost like that. It was indeed an extremely sad moment. Very sad indeed.

Yes, we lost out on this amendment, these four clauses that were to guarantee women a place to belong. Immediately we made attempts to correct what we considered a great injustice. Women MPs and other women activists who had worked so hard on this matter shouted angrily in the media and in the House, 'Where is the Matembe amendment? We want it in there'. Some funny, funny things went on. One day when he was addressing a public meeting, the minister actually had the audacity to say that the amendment was missing because Matembe was not there that day in the House. What an absurd thing to say! Of course, I was there. How could I be absent on that critical day when I had spent so many sleepless nights strategising and planning how to secure co-ownership rights for women? I was really so mad about the whole situation.

Eventually, I explained to the women and to the Uganda Land Alliance what had happened. The women MPs attempted to bring this amendment back to Parliament. After all, the principles had been passed and that action had been recorded in the Hansard. So, we argued, since the principles were passed, why don't we, on the basis of these principles, integrate these clauses into the Act? But we appealed to deaf ears, and, in the end, we lost completely.

I want to make one thing clear. If this had not been an amendment to give women their due rights, if this had had to do with things that the male MPs consider important, Parliament would have found a way to bring the matter back for more review. They would have said, this is just a technicality, and the provisions would have found their way into that law.

You can be sure that we didn't give up easily. The donors were also extremely unhappy. They were on the neck of the Minister. Yes, together with the Land Alliance which was still active, and the donors, we pursued this matter. Representatives from the Land Alliance, and representatives from DFID (Department for International Development), the main donor agency on the Land Act, and the Minister met in my office, and we agreed that the law should be amended to cater for the co-ownership clause. The Land Alliance was still active and gave their support. We reviewed and agreed on these specific clauses on co-ownership, and the Minister got them drafted. We were aware of a good amount of political will in Parliament to see that these provisions were included in the Land Act.

At the same time this activity was going on, the President was making public statements that he did not support the idea of the co-ownership of land. At a national gathering held in Rukungiri to mark International Women's Day, the President criticised the principle of land co-ownership and called for its rejection by the people. In fact, this was a function held after the Land Act had been passed, and women had learned that the co-ownership clause was missing. Many women, and particularly women in Mbarara and Rukungiri, had planned to demonstrate against the omission of the amendment, but the Minister of Gender had persuaded them not to demonstrate, but to raise their concern to the President. However, some women at the function carried placards saying 'No land, No votes'. Mark you, this was about two years before the presidential elections. After the President had publicly criticised the amendment and called for its rejection, he promised that he was nevertheless prepared to have a discussion with the women over this matter, to see how best women's interests could be protected.

But where is the meeting? Now that even the presidential elections are over, and women gave the President their overwhelming support, they no longer have anything to bargain with on the question of co-ownership of land. Women have really lost out.

It was clear that, following the President's lead, other top government officials, including, sad to say, some women politicians in key posts, were also speaking against these provisions. Soon we realised that this second chance to include these provisions in the Land Act was slipping away.

Some important people began to say, 'This co-ownership is going to destabilise marriage'. And I heard again, 'Matembe is trying to destabilise marriage'. Here was that accusation again that I was a marriage breaker, when in fact my own marriage was a success story of unity and stability. The suggestion was made to send these provisions to the Law on Domestic Relations, 'since it concerns husbands and wives'. Since anyone who knows anything knows the Domestic Relations Bill is dead, dead, dead, this was the same as killing the co-ownership clauses forever. What an easy way out. What an easy betrayal of the mothers of Uganda!

You can see the tactics used by these male conspirators. The men had achieved what they wanted for themselves in the Land Act. The Baganda got their share. The Banyoro got their share. And after the women lost out, except for the provision on spousal consent, none of these men was ready to come our way with support. This defeat was so bad. With the Land Bill being formulated and debated with the serious intent to solve problems with land policy caused by history, this was the time to bring justice and fairness for all. As with so many things, the women were left out again. Justice for women? Not this time? But when?

So what does it mean to have this so-called, 'women-friendly' Constitution? Five years down the road of its implementation, women have no land, there is no domestic relations law to protect women, and so women continue to be homeless, only holding homes at the will of men. What has happened to my dream? What has happened to women's sacrifices and efforts? God, for how long will women of Uganda remain in misery and jeopardy?

CHAPTER 8

Past, Present and Future

Duringmylong political career, I have come to a certain
conclusion, that in Uganda, Matembe has come to
mean 'women,' and that Matembe's voice is somehow heard
as 'women's voice.' When people read that statement, they
might want to accuse me of the worst kind of egotism. 'Who
does this woman think she is?' some might ask. From my own
perspective, I see this role I play not as ego, but as a heavy,
heavy responsibility. No hour goes by, no day passes, without
me asking myself, what do I need to be doing for women now?
Who should I be lobbying? How can I mobilise women to
organise a challenge to the status quo so that we can change
the system? What other women (and men) can I persuade to
join me in this work?

Hardly a week passes without a woman or two or more
bringing their problems to me. Many times I am really angry,
in fact enraged, about society's inability to see and respond to
these injustices and the violence that continues to be unleashed
on women. The burden of women's problems at times weighs
very heavy on my heart.

When the Land Bill was being debated in Parliament, I found
it nearly impossible to sleep. I would be wide-awake thinking
about the opportunity we had, and wondering what strategies
I should be making and what tactics I should be using. When
I couldn't sleep, my husband asked me what was wrong. I told
him that I was extremely worried about getting land for women.
He asked me if I thought it was my responsibility to get land
for women. To tell the truth, I did think it was my responsibility.

I was taking the lead role in this matter. I didn't want to fail Uganda's women at this most critical moment. Would I be smart enough? Would there be enough support? What did I have to do, what did I have to say, so at last women in Uganda could sleep peacefully in their beds because they *belonged* somewhere, they *belonged* in their homes, and no one could chase them away. In spite of all our efforts, the Land Bill became the Land Act, and women had little to celebrate and much to cry over.

During the Land Bill debate, women activists decided not to ask for much. We really wanted something, so we didn't ask for much. Good enough, the consent provision was passed and is part of the Land Act that is now law. Of course, when we think about that provision, we wonder whether it really matters whether there is a law that says that a woman must give her consent before the family home and land can be sold. What if her husband really wants to sell the family plot, can't he intimidate his wife, can't he threaten her or beat her until she 'consents' to sell this property? Will there be anyone on the scene to protect the woman who refuses to give her consent? Will the man's family be an overwhelming force against this vulnerable woman saying 'no.'

I have mentioned about how tired I get sometimes from the responsibility I carry. I was re-elected to my seat in Parliament in the 1996 elections, but the campaign was a tough one. I have to admit that it was disappointing to see all the forces that opposed my candidacy, including many women. Having worked so hard to achieve this gender-sensitive and gender-responsive Constitution for women, I had not expected to be confronted with such an ugly and tough opposition. It was quite shocking to me to see fellow women activists leading a venomous attack against me to make sure I was not elected to Parliament.

I saw the term in Parliament following those elections as a time for me to participate in the implementation of the Constitution. I thought this was the opportunity for me to go to Parliament to enact laws, gender-sensitive laws, that would bring the Constitution into action for women. The Constitution was clearly not enough in itself. The provisions needed to be operationalised through the enactment of laws. That was going to be the role of the next Parliament, hence the need for me to offer my candidature. Yes, I have to admit that I was appalled by, and I felt betrayed by, the actions and words of the very women who had benefited from my hard work. Thank God, my God is always there for me at times of need. He was there to see me through this period of vicious personal attacks. The people of Mbarara said no to the opposition, and voted me in with 50 percent of the vote against the 50 percent received by my two opponents.

To tell the truth, afterwards I was really exhausted, but it was more than being physically tired. I felt tired in body and spirit. I felt unappreciated. Didn't people recognise how I had thrown myself wholeheartedly into all the women's causes? How could they oppose me when I was running for the 'women's seat,' the seat for the district representative for women who would sit in Parliament? Surely, no one represented women better than I did. Surely, nobody accomplished more for women than I did.

When the election was over, I began to seriously question whether all this work was worth what I put into it. I asked myself, is what I do really worth the effort, the exhaustion, the backache – my back was giving me constant pain. That's when I began to think that I needed a break. During the next year, I went to UK for treatment for this chronic back problem, which included an intensive programme of therapy. While I was residing there, I also joined the MA programme at the University of Warwick. Through this whole period I felt tired and worn out, and quite fed-up with the struggle for women's liberation. I was aware that I needed a new sense of direction. After all, what did I want after realising my dream? Had I not achieved what I set out to do, to study law, to become a parliamentarian and make good laws for women? Is there any more fundamental law than the Constitution? Surely, ten years of gender activism, culminating in the enactment of this good Constitution was satisfying enough for me. So, I prayed to God to give me a new sense of direction and I patiently (oh, maybe not so patiently) waited.

When I returned to Uganda after my MA course, I felt like I had quit. I felt it in my very bones. In fact, I spent some time not talking about gender issues, and not addressing any public gatherings as I had always done. Soon the press was speculating about me. 'Matembe has quit.' 'Where is she?' 'She's not talking.' 'She's lost.' And the most interesting, 'Shame on her.' But what was this all about? Surely, I needed time off, a period of rest, recuperation and renewal. I was pondering deeply (praying) about what to do next. And what happened next? I heard the announcement that I had been appointed Minister for Ethics and Integrity.

Having this new post was like a fresh beginning. When I went to take up that assignment, I could feel myself being revitalised by this interesting new challenge. As usual, I threw myself into this job with energy and enthusiasm. Yes, it was wonderful to feel like Matembe again. Part of what made this assignment appealing was that this was a cause, a cause similar to what I had actually committed myself to long ago. Another good thing about this job was that fighting corruption is about changing attitudes, which had been a central part of what I had been doing in the struggle for gender equality. Certainly, the experience I had had in the previous struggle, and the skills I had developed in that work would be valuable in mobilising people around this new cause.

You know, Ugandans are not naturally unethical people. We used not to be like this. In the past, we were good people. We were behaving well. Corruption of the kind we know today was not there. How do we understand what is happening these days? Are present conditions directly related to our painful years of division, hatred and bad governance? Surely, Ugandans can move forward together to solve this problem. I visualise what is needed as a programme of rewinding. Our minds and value systems that were shattered and broken by our dark period need a new direction. It's like rebuilding and rewinding the thinking, the actions, the excuses that have caused our problems in this area of corruption.

Now, why was I chosen for this position, the Minister for Ethics and Integrity in this new ministry? I think it was because of my outspokenness. Once I'm convinced of a line, I'll go out there and talk about it, without fear or favour. I think maybe the President knew that once he put Matembe there, if she sees that anybody is corrupt, she will have to talk about it, and she will not fear these people. Certainly, President Museveni knew that I have an independence of mind, that I call a spade a spade, and that I speak the truth without mincing my words.

I was quickly convinced of something else. When the President appointed me, that act persuaded me to believe that he was really committed to fighting corruption. I had no doubt this was true. After all, here I was, Matembe, the woman with the big mouth. Surely, if he wanted to hide some corrupt practices, he wouldn't choose me to take up this job. He knew I wouldn't keep quiet about what I saw. In fact, I thought, if he called me to tell me what to say or do, and I knew these things were wrong, I would tell him, 'No, sir, I'm not going along with this one.' I was sure that he knew that. I concluded, he's committed and he needs help.

So now I was the Minister for Ethics and Integrity. Not only was this a new ministry, but this ministry had a first time minister as its head. Our government has no training programme for new ministers. I couldn't go to Makerere or Kyambogo and take a two-week course called 'How to be a Minister.' I have to say that at the beginning I couldn't tell where myself ended and Minister Matembe began. Of course you have to pay attention to the formal minister part: the protocol, the security, having your own driver, and attending cabinet meetings with the President and the other top people. I found that the most challenging part for me as a government insider was having to watch the words I said.

I have to admit that from time to time I had thought about the possibility of being a minister. I had really not wanted to be in the cabinet very much, but, I thought, maybe at the end of my political career, I would like to be a minister, shall I say, so as 'to improve my CV.' Ego talking? Because of all the things I had been doing, many people tended to salute me like a minister, for example, when I travelled to other countries as a representative for the government of Uganda. Then I would hear people saying, this is the minister Matembe, and I would have to correct them, saying, no, no, no, I'm not a minister. It seems that I had the reputation without the credentials of a minister. When I would tell people, no I'm not a minister, they would say, how is that possible, why are you not a minister? And so sometimes I thought, well, why not? But while other people out there were impatiently waiting for me to be a minister, I was not bothered.

The main reason I preferred to be where I was, as a backbencher, was to keep my independence of mind. I really enjoyed my freedom. It was important for me to be able to express what I thought when a situation arose. I wanted to express my view in my own direct way based on my own convictions, without any hindrance. Yes, I wanted to talk freely. I believed that my outspokenness was one of my main strengths, although I admit that it also got me into hot water at times. Even if the papers wrote, even if they misquoted me, I would still get out in public and talk. But then I was not talking on behalf of the government. I was talking for women, and I generally didn't hear women say, stop saying those things, they are not good for us.

However, I thought giving up some of my freedom in my job as minister would be okay if I could make a worthwhile contribution. I saw getting to the Cabinet as a step forward in the realisation of gender equality. Whereas outside the Cabinet, you can talk and not be able to influence action, as a Cabinet Minister you have both a right to talk at the highest level of government and a right to take decisions and actions too.

I had some other thoughts. I know that I am not an easy person. I am a perfectionist, I'm somebody who wants action, and I'm a workaholic. What was I going to do if people in my ministry didn't do things on time or if they made lots of excuses for inaction? In this position, I must move to challenge corruption. Would people working in the Ministry cause me to fail? I don't want to fail. I don't expect to fail. As a member of Parliament, I talk, I work, I move where I want, I do what I like. Maybe with the bureaucracy, I will not manage.

I recall that working in ACFODE was very satisfying. With the NGOs there is little or no bureaucracy, no protocol, no bureaucrats. I call the personal secretary. I call the messenger. I call the members. These interactions are easy. There is no such thing as first writing to the Permanent Secretary, or to the Head of Department, or to another minister or to the Personal Secretary of another minister. I was wondering if in this position I would fall out with everybody. I had at one time discussed these things with the President. I had told him that I was satisfied with what I was doing. Interestingly enough, he appointed me without even asking me.

Now, with this new position, I moved out of the civil society area into the executive. I moved from gender to ethics and integrity. One thing I thought was, now women have me in the Cabinet. This is now their place, women's place. Yes, the women of Uganda have their voice in the Cabinet. There is always a lot of criticism of women in high positions, suggesting that they don't relate with 'ordinary women,' whatever that means.

I thought, now I will be a different woman from those other women. Over the years women had wished me to become a minister. If Miria was the minister, they would say, this would become our ministry. So finally I arrived there, though not in the Gender Ministry, but in this newly created Ministry of Ethics and Integrity, where, by the way, I feel women have a very big role to play. I was sure that women were going to come and join me, and we would create this ministry together. But where were they? I didn't see them. I organised workshops, bringing together people to help me design a programme and chart a way forward for this new ministry. Did the women activists turn up? Apparently, they were busy here and there. So, what was going on here?

There is one woman who has been my companion in the gender struggle and my good friend for many years. One day I rang her and said, 'We must have lunch together. I want to have lunch with you so I can see how you can assist me in this new ministry. You were so excited about my getting this position. You even participated in lobbying for my appointment. Having reached here, I now ask, where are you?' Even this friend was nowhere. Strange, isn't it?

When I have said these things to some colleagues, they said, 'It's not us. It's you who should be calling us, not the other way around.' Now, I'm learning that maybe these women in high positions are not really ignoring fellow women, but they are just isolated. I don't yet know how to sort out this issue but it is a real problem for women in high-level positions. The problem is isolation. You find you are completely alone. For instance, I was telling these women activists that when they no longer invite me for women's conferences, I'm no longer informed about the critical matters that affect women. It seems that I am no longer in the network of what is happening in the gender field. I'm still out there in public, with my big mouth, speaking on corruption, but I appear to be there alone. I don't see women. When I'm being bashed and abused, and shouted at, out there fighting corruption, I don't see any shoulder to lean on. The women I have worked with – after all, these are my people – and the younger ones I have mentored, I thought once I reach there, they would come and we would move forward together. Big problem, isn't it?

So what am I to do? I'm no longer actively in the gender network and the women that I have worked with are not located where I am now located. So the question is, how are they supposed to support me, because I must succeed. When I succeed in my work, the women of Uganda will have succeeded. But how can I succeed without their support? From where, from whom, do I draw my strength? How can I be so busy with government work and at the same time be able to maintain my links with the women? They see me as too highly placed and too busy, and I see them as deserting me, isolating me. How can women continue to empower each other, because in order for any of us to succeed, we need each other's support.

Women must be empowered. I'm thinking now about the ACFODE motto, 'Breaking through, Building Up, and Binding.' Who am I binding with now? Am I not abandoned? And aren't they going to be on the other side and criticize me, 'What is she doing about this?' Shouldn't they call in once in a while asking, how are you moving on such and such? What are you doing on this? So how do my former women colleagues and I communicate? How do we work together now? In fact, I'm just struggling to learn. I call someone and say to her, 'Shame on you. How can you desert me? You don't even know my office. What kind of support is that?' But it seems somehow that it's something I haven't fully grasped yet, that when you get in these positions of power, people approach you very differently. You have left them. You are alone there. You are such a big person. You are too busy – that's the main thing I hear them say. She is too busy for me so I won't call and bother her. But being a big person and not having contact with your former colleagues, it's not right.

But, wait a minute. Does something similar happen to men or is their situation much different from that of women? The men have clubs where they meet after work, yes, sports clubs, drinking places, health clubs, the golf course. Through these venues, men in high-level positions keep linkages with their fellow men. But women, what about family responsibilities, yes, the double workload? Where is the time for socialising with women colleagues when a woman is rushing home to attend to domestic chores? You see, my fellow women colleagues, we need to understand the situation, the environment in which we work, the male-dominated, male-designed (with men in mind) world of work, where women are trying to fit in. All these factors lead to the isolation and loneliness I have been describing in high-level positions, where women are concerned. These women, like myself, need you and your support. I am searching for a way of resolving this dilemma of how women at those top levels can stay connected with their sisters located in different places, so that all these women can draw strength from each other for the advancement of their cause.

Now my second problem is that I'm curtailed in my public speaking because of the press in Uganda. They take one statement out of context and make it a headline. They trivialise what I say. The important message is lost. The people who were not there to hear what I said get a false picture. I hope nobody believes anything that the press writes about me. Most of it is far from the truth, and I am more often misquoted than quoted accurately.

Actually, there is something constraining me more than the media, and that is the position I'm holding, this government position. Being a minister. When you talk, whatever you say is a policy. So this one is preventing me from my natural expression of what I think. This situation is quite stressful, because I would like to continue expressing myself from my personal conviction, from what I believe. But now here I am. I'm a government minister. Some of these situations where in the past I would have operated from my personal conviction, these days the government makes the decisions on them, decisions I may not totally agree with. And, of course, it is necessary for me to go along with those decisions. Once I go along with them, I am prevented from expressing my personal views and convictions. The principle of collective responsibility binds me, sometimes in a stranglehold. There are times when I don't know when to talk and how to express myself. Nevertheless, I enjoy this present challenge and I am committed to move on it. Who knows, just as we got some breakthroughs on gender equality, so shall we, on corruption.

What Others Say *(The voice of Matembe, the man)*

Nancy Dorsey interviewed Mr N. Matembe on Makerere University campus in September 2001

At the time I met Miria in 1974, I had just returned from a year's course in brewing at Heriot Watt University. My cousin met me at the airport in Entebbe, and as we moved to Kampala, he indicated that his sister was getting married very soon. There would be a number of parties connected to the wedding, and these parties would give me a chance to see people after my absence.

At the bachelors' party, I put on my bell-bottom trousers and one of my favourite shirts, a casual shirt. I still remember that shirt that was red and black with a very good design. The party was not far from Port Bell where I was living. At the party, there was a lot of greeting and talking and dancing. As I was dancing, I spotted a young, rather shy looking lady seated with friends and relatives. After some time, I picked her to dance. I like to dance and people say I am a good dancer. I thought that maybe she would notice and admire my way of dancing.

The party went on and I picked her to dance again. Eventually I asked one of my relatives in Runyankole, *Ogu omwishiki murungi nooha?* which means, 'Who is this beautiful girl?' I was told about her family connections and that she was at Makerere studying law. Later, I learned that, as I was doing research on her, she was also doing on me. I was told that she asked, 'Who is this man dancing nicely? He is casual and he appears to be free.' A cousin of Miria (who later was to serve as the matron at our wedding) told her all about me, how I went to Ntare School, then to Makerere, and just recently to study in Scotland. The party concluded and some friends of mine gave her a lift back to Makerere.

The next day was the wedding day, which started at the church. Afterwards, we went to the reception, which was followed by an after, party somewhere in Entebbe. I had a new camera with me that I had purchased in Scotland. There were not many cameras like it in the country at that time. It had an automatic flash, which meant that the light flashed every time I took a picture. It was quite an attraction. I started taking photographs of this interesting young woman, at the church, at the reception and then at the party. She would send a very wide smile my way and it appeared to me that she liked the attention I was giving her. *(Laughter)*

During the activities surrounding that wedding, Miria and I got acquainted with each other. We talked a lot and danced a lot. We both love to dance and are known as good dancers. That was the beginning of a very active courtship where I would visit her at Makerere every chance I could get. I was living at Port Bell near Uganda Breweries where I worked. I had a nice two bed roomed house and I would bring her back there now and then to visit. At first Miria was not ready to have a deep, deep relationship. We talked and joked and learned about each other. People who knew us, both friends and family members, were encouraging this relationship. Many of those friends are still alive and they like to remind me of those days.

We settled into a pattern whereby we spent a lot of time together. After about three or four months – it was less than six months – I thought I should propose to her. When I did, she told me I was in a rush. I said I was not in a rush, but that it was time for her to introduce me to her parents. After some time, she took me to meet her parents, as the tradition goes. Everyone except the father appeared to approve of our getting married. One uncle, Mzee Tabaro, was very much in favour of me marrying Miria. He was well educated himself, one of the outstanding opinion leaders in Mbarara District. He thought that Miria should choose someone with a high level of education like myself. He sort of intervened with the family on my behalf.

Following that resistance from the father, I thought I should give this lady reassurance that I would not be a difficult man to live with. Right from my time at the university (Makerere), right from my time in Scotland, I wanted to marry an intelligent, educated woman, someone who could talk with me about the things that interested me.

At Makerere, I studied chemistry and bio-chemistry although my background from secondary school was mathematics, physics, and so forth. Right from Senior 1, I was part of a group of boys who took their studies very seriously. We had a reputation for being able to answer any question on our special subjects. We all had nicknames. My name in the school up to the university was 'Calculus,' indicating that I didn't have any problems with maths.

In deciding to marry an independent, educated woman, I was challenging traditions in my community. I felt that once you are educated, you don't just fall below your level. You know, at that time university graduates were few in number. Most men who graduated from Makerere were marrying nurses and teachers, primary teachers, not even secondary teachers. When I look back, I think there were very few of those people slightly ahead of me in school, plus my group, who chose to marry the women graduates. It was only the group that followed us that started to pick graduates to marry.

During my undergraduate days at Makerere, I remember going with my friends to visit girls at Mary Stuart Hall, which students called 'the box.' Among these fellows there was always a fear, 'Shall we be able to manage these girls who are as smart as we are?' For me, I didn't see any problem with that one. I made a choice in that direction and that choice came to be reflected in our dealings after Miria and I were married. I had decided to support her fully in what she was doing, and she gave me full support as well.

After we married, Miria remained on campus at the Faculty of Law while I was working and living in Port Bell. Of course, she would come to our home there on weekends. You know, because the brewing process is continuous, a brewery doesn't ever shut down. That meant that sometimes I had to work night shift. That was the time when, instead of staying home by herself, Miria would come and keep me company on my shift.

Our first son was born during Miria's last year at Makerere. I assured her, 'You can continue studying while we share the responsibility of looking after the boy.' With my background in chemistry and so on, it was easy to mix formula and clean the bottles and other utensils. It was no problem to feed the baby and change nappies, whatever had to be done. Then in the evening I would take him to campus for breastfeeding, then take him back home and see that he was comfortable. I'm a very practical man.

Of course, when people came to visit and found me doing all these things, the questions flew around. Miria's uncle who had spoken on my behalf during the introductions to her family gave us support. In fact, he gave me a heifer in appreciation of what I was doing. He said, 'I have not come across men in Uganda, and I don't think there are many in Africa, who are doing what you are doing.' Perhaps this arrangement was a landmark in some way, and this set-up gave Miria comfort to really concentrate on her studies.

Up to now, I continue thinking whether Miria would be what she is today if she had married a different man. I don't know whether my name 'Matembe' has contributed to who she is, whether it is a good name. Would we be having Hon. Koburunga, Minister of Ethics and Integrity? What I am saying is that we struck the right sort of relationship, the right sort of thinking in terms of support, in terms of straight forwardness, in terms of personal development, so that Miria could reach her full potential. I don't know whether this could have happened with another man. Anyway, we can't really know the answer to that.

Even after we had arranged the give-away, Miria's father appeared not to be convinced that the time had come for Miria to marry. There were several exchanges between my father and my father-in-law. Of course, at that time the groom and the bride didn't normally talk during the proceedings. You only sat in your chair and waited as the exchange went on. However, I decided to do something quite extraordinary for the groom coming to marry. I stood up in the tent (set up for the give-away ceremony) and made some comments directly to Miria, but speaking through the Bible. I told the clergyman present that I was going to read from the Bible. He said, 'Eeh, you are reading from the Bible. That is good.' And Miria's uncle who later gave us the heifer said, 'These are the things that I was telling you about, that seem extraordinary, but are actually normal when people are educated.' So I picked the verse, Revelation 2, verse 10 and addressed it to Miria. This verse says, 'Be faithful to me, and I will give you the crown of life.'

At the time I did not know that as time went on, the crown in life that I referred to would be the support I gave her, the freedom to become who she is now. To me, that crown of life means that she has been able to become successful according to what she had on her mind. From the time she was a child, she wanted to become a lawyer. So, right from the give-away ceremony I was assuring her that I would support her to follow her dream.

So, Miria finished her studies, and of course we held a party to celebrate her graduation. We continued living in Port Bell. I could see Miria's determination to give me full support. If she felt lonely in the house, she would come and find me at the brewery working my shift, even going with me into the cold room while I checked temperatures. Sometimes she would stay with me until it was time for me to leave, or we would talk on the company intercom system, Miria at home and me at work. At that time it was not common in Uganda for employees to work all night or to work 8 hour shifts at their companies. At first our friends and family could not quite understand that I sometimes worked from 6.00 am to 2.00 p.m. or from 2.00 p.m. to 10.00 a.m. or from 10.00 p.m. to 6.00 p.m.

Of course, sometimes we would have family squabbles. You cannot have roses all the time. However, when we would have a quarrel or a misunderstanding, we would think again about how we started, and then somehow we would mend. The interesting thing is that the domestic squabbles and quarrelling did not erode the support we gave each other. During any of these misunderstandings, I found it very helpful to keep a positive attitude and not to come home with a gloomy face.

When we look at what is happening these days, Miria being appointed as a Minister in the President's cabinet, these accomplishments are in part possible because of the mutual support in our marriage. Many men have found it difficult to be married to politicians. They are not able to cope with such an arrangement. In our case, this goes back to what my mind was set on when I was thinking about getting married. I wanted to marry a woman who would be my equal. I thought that whatever level my wife reached, whatever high level she might attain, her career would not make any difference in our relationship in real terms. In our dealings, I never found a problem in this. If she had to do her work, and then eventually found me in bed, that was OK. This attitude of mine has gone a long way to strengthen our marriage. Miria has been free to do her own work without interference or criticism from me. You know the normal relationship between men and women, between husbands and wives in Uganda – 'Where have you been,' the man asks. 'Why didn't you come to have lunch with me? Why are you late?'

In our marriage it is the same with me. If I go drinking with friends, she would not say, you have delayed, or you have come too late, or something like that. With this agreement of ours behind her, Miria had that room to be herself. Of course, I faced the criticism of other men who wondered why I wasn't being 'a real man.'

Miria was not only involved in government, but she also worked in women's organisations, ACFODE being the main one. One time I had an interesting visit from Dr Ankrah of ACFODE. Miria informed me that her friend wanted to talk to me. I had heard about this woman but had not yet met her, and this would be Dr Ankrah's first visit to our home. When she came, we sat in the sitting room and had a cup of tea, just the two of us.

First, she asked me whether I had heard about ACFODE. I told her that Miria had talked about it. Then she asked me how I felt about the organisation. She went on to find out whether I supported ACFODE. I answered, 'How do you want me to show my support?'

Then she said, 'Suppose Miria becomes deeply involved in ACFODE. How would you feel?'

I told her I wouldn't have any problem.

She said, 'Are you sure?'

I said, 'Yes, I'm sure.' She actually asked me three times if I was sure. I think she wasn't convinced I could give my full support so quickly.

I decided to give her a background of the way Miria and I had stayed together. I described how we had started, and that our marriage had gone on well, in spite of the normal quarrels and misunderstandings. I told her that I would not interfere with what God had planned for Miria. I also praised Miria's attitude toward my advancement, including coming to visit me during my long shifts at work. One might say it was love and affection driving the whole action, the whole approach. Dr Ankrah said that was wonderful and offered me membership in ACFODE, saying that they didn't mind having men, especially husbands, join this organisation. That is when I joined ACFODE, becoming one of the first male members, and I always supported their activities.

I heard that afterwards Dr Ankrah talked to many women about our interview and told them that she had found a man who was apparently not a Ugandan *(laughter)* because he appeared not to be thinking and acting like Ugandan men she knew (she's an American married to a Ghanaian). I think the Ankrahs must also be supporting each other well in their marriage. This brings me back to the question I raised earlier, about whether Miria would be who she is today if she had chosen a different man, whether she would have had the support.

Miria showed her support for me in another way. You know, in African societies we are not used to giving little gifts like flowers or a card on special occasions. I saw this done in Britain, for example, when some extraordinary thing happened – a promotion, a birthday, or something like that. On many occasions I would see a card from Miria saying a few nice words to me. She did this even during Amin's time when things were so bad, when we had only a little money, when everyone's morale was down. These small gestures were encouraging both of us to continue on through those hard times.

When I came back from Scotland, I was a very good cook. During my time abroad I had learned how to cook European dishes very well. So I would surprise her by preparing food, good food, a variety of food that we both liked. She knew how to prepare African meals but I was able to cook many different kinds of food and to do it quickly. 'Quickly' is certainly different from how much of the local foods is cooked.

Miria was eager to enter into active politics but that was not possible until 1986 when the NRM government came in. I should describe how she and I were situated when the NRA captured Kampala in January 1986. Miria had just given birth to Grace, the last of our four boys, in Mulago. Her pregnancy had some major complications, including a caesarian delivery, and her doctor kept her in the hospital about a month. The battle for Kampala was going on right in that part of the city. In fact, the fighting separated the other three boys and me from their mother, and she was certainly in danger from the battle. Her situation really made her doubt whether I was giving her the support she needed. Actually, she didn't fully understand that crossing from our home in Port Bell on one side of the fighting to the other side where she was in Mulago was really dangerous for me and almost impossible.

This is now the background of what I want to talk about. When the NRM really settled in, Miria went to great lengths to see whether I would mind if she joined the Resistance Councils (RCs). I said, 'Why are you asking that?'

And she said, 'You never know. I want to ask.'

And I said, 'I have no problem with that one.' She then went from one level to the next until she was at the peak of Kampala municipality (RC5). Since she was not from the Central Region, her political rise was really unique. Whenever I would meet my friends, I would describe how Miria had ventured into local politics and was doing well. Now people started taking a step back. It seemed they didn't quite understand. They would say, 'What is wrong, Matembe? You are in the house, and you're saying that madam is very important.' At times I would want to add that I also helped cook. *(laughter)*

As time passed, some of these friends and relatives would start disassociating themselves from me. They didn't understand me having that type of relationship. They stopped coming to see me, because when they came, she was often not around. You know, traditionally our wives are the ones to go behind the kitchen, pick something and put it on the table. They would find it strange for me to go to the fridge, take out a drink and give it to them. They were really uncomfortable. It wasn't just men that couldn't cope with this arrangement, but even women friends, and wives of friends. That situation was even worse when Miria became a minister. Now, when they came to visit, the gate was manned by police officers.

So, after her success in the RCs, Miria opted for being a member of the NRC. She literally asked for my permission to go upcountry to campaign. Since I had agreed when we married that I would support her in doing what she chose to do, this was also not a problem.

One year President Museveni came to the opening of a trade fair at the Show Grounds in Kampala. He visited the display that Uganda Breweries had set up, and I had the honour of taking him around our show. At some point, he stopped, took me by the hand and said to the people in his entourage, 'Gentlemen, let us stop here for one minute. I want to introduce this man. This is Matembe, the husband of Matembe.' Then everybody laughed. This was clearly a very nice compliment, and it made me feel very good, very proud. Everyone there interpreted the statement to mean that this man was Matembe, who had a wife who was also Matembe. This statement featured in the papers.

Now, for fun, people, especially close friends, would change from calling me Nekemia, and would call me 'the husband of Matembe.' In Kampala Club, for example, when we came in together side by side, people would point at us, and say, 'Now you look at the husband of Matembe with Matembe.' It was obvious that this was good fun and not for demoralising me. So we had support from our friends. Of course, there are some friends who don't look at things that way, and they would say, 'How can you betray *real* men?'

By the way, before I arrived home to tell Miria about the President's remark at the Show Grounds, she had already heard about it on the radio. I certainly did not feel put down. What the remark showed to me was that the President knew Miria well, in a particular forum, in a particular way because of her work in politics. Also the President was not stopping at every display, and he was not introducing everyone he knew. He chose to introduce me, to recognise me, to acknowledge me, and I think he was pointing out that I was giving her support, that we had a good, strong marriage, which could be joked about in good humour. I felt the President's respect for me and for Miria in this incident.

Recently, at a dinner at State House which Miria and I attended, as the President was walking around to greet people, he stopped to talk to me. After the usual greeting, he said in Runyankole, *Yebare kumbasiza muhara wa Rukoza*, which means, 'Thank you for managing the daughter of Rukoza for me.' To me this meant that sometimes she may give him a challenge, and he was joking good-naturedly about it. Everyone around us burst into laughter.

The Vice President, Specioza Kazibwe, has also said some nice things to me. She has always had a positive attitude towards me. We were together recently at a ceremony to inaugurate a school. When she was giving her remarks, she looked over at where I was sitting and said, 'This man is great, and we know him as our husband.' This kind of comment pleases Miria, as it indicates that I have not only given Miria the support she deserves, but I have extended my support to other powerful women as well. I would add that the VP is probably praising our kind of marriage as well.

Now when you look at the recent campaign, I gave Miria support as usual. One place where she was campaigning, she was being bashed for not being married properly and for wanting to break up other people's marriages, and so on. Just at that time, the four boys and I showed up. This was a place far from Mbarara town that could only be reached through very rough roads. When she saw us, she was very surprised. She paused in her talk, and I think she was saying to herself that God had now answered these people. It seems that just at that time she was being asked,

'How good is your marriage?' The boys and I went to the platform and I greeted the people. And of course I asked them for their votes.

I remember another incident, this time in the 1996 elections, when one candidate was being sponsored to unseat Miria. This rally took place near the border between Tanzania and Uganda. At that time all the candidates were there to give addresses at the college where the rally was held. Apparently, before I arrived, the two other candidates had hinted that this woman (Miria) did not have a marriage, that her marriage had broken down a long time ago. And then I showed up. She came to greet me, and then told the crowd, 'That one who is saying I don't have a home, tell me who is this one? This is my husband.' Her supporters were very happy about that one. And my arrival there really helped her.

The people in Bushenyi where I come from are always trying to convince her to come and represent them. They say, 'You are our woman. You married here. Why don't you come and represent us here?' Her courage and determination are recognised there..

When Miria ran for Parliament this last time, in 2001, I had extra time because I had already retired. The thing, which some people could not believe was that together, the two of us, established a campaign office on her behalf. We divided the constituency in sections, and then we had two teams to campaign. She would go one place with one team and I would go to a different place with the other team. The stories in the papers said that Matembe was campaigning for his wife, that he had taken leave to do it – they didn't understand that I was retired.

Recently, at the swearing in ceremony for the ministers, the President pointed out that I had gone to the district to look for votes for Matembe. And, in fact, I was campaigning in his county, Nyabushozi County. The people there look at us as special people. They like me, and when I talk, they appear not to see the difference between Miria and me. That is why she doesn't have to be there when I am there. That makes the situation very interesting because you find the rural women addressing me with confidence and assuring me that the votes will be there.

CHAPTER 9

⬦⬦⬦

Conclusion

In concluding my story, I want to say that I consider myself blessed, yes, very blessed indeed. Those people who do not relate to God on a personal basis might call what I am talking about luck or coincidence, but I call it being blessed. I wonder how many people have had their dreams realised during their lifetimes? How many people have had the opportunity to tell their life stories like I am doing here? Well, I am one of those blessed ones.

I had a dream, a childhood dream, to become a lawyer and to plead for women. My dream was later extended to include becoming a member of Parliament, and to participate in making laws to liberate women from what enslaves them. At the age of 48, I have realised those dreams of my heart and I have been able to tell the story about those dreams and their fulfillment. It is hard for me to believe, but these things are true. Of course, I have experienced frustrations and challenges as well as happiness on the journey to the realisation of my dreams. It is a great joy to sit back and recapture all these moments in my life as I have been writing this story.

Right now I want to return to one very special moment that will remain in my memory forever, the day, 8 October 1995, when, as a member of the Constituent Assembly, I received a copy of the Constitution of Uganda from the hands of the President. This was the long awaited day, the day of the promulgation of the Constitution, 'the People's Constitution' that was expected to usher in a new era, an era of popular democracy, an era of equality and equity between sexes, an era of peace, unity and development. Yes, the Constitution which I had been fully involved in creating.

On this historic national day to celebrate the constitutional rebirth of the country, a very solemn and impressive ceremony at the International Conference Centre brought together Ugandans from all walks of life. All the Constituent Assembly delegates were there. Many people dressed in their traditional attire. I rarely put on my Kinyankore traditional dress because it is much too cumbersome for the speed at which I live my life. However, on that day I happily and proudly wore such a dress. Indeed, I felt and looked (so I was told) very dignified as I prepared to receive the Constitution of Uganda on behalf of the women of Mbarara. I dressed in the traditional way as women do back in my home district during their most important functions. Mark you, every part of the country was represented there on that special day.

After the ceremony for the promulgation of the Constitution for the whole nation was completed, the day's proceedings took a more personal turn as each Constituent Assembly delegate, one by one, walked proudly to the platform to receive a copy of this historic document on behalf of her or his people. Nobody can know the feelings of joy, accomplishment and satisfaction I carried with me to the platform. I felt I was truly walking the journey to freedom.

As I received my own personal copy of this document, I felt so inspired. I thought about the story of Simeon in the second chapter of Luke in the Bible. Simeon had been told that he would not die until he had a chance to see the Messiah who was promised to liberate humanity from misery and suffering. When the parents of Jesus brought their baby into the temple, and Simeon held him in his hands, he said, 'God, you can take your servant in peace.' That is exactly the kind of sentiment I felt when I received a copy of the Uganda Constitution with all the provisions for the protection and promotion of women's rights. I felt I had realised my dream for liberating the women of Uganda. I thought that if I died at that moment, I would die happy and in peace.

You know, I find life very interesting. Surely, life is worth living. Today is a moment of happiness, and tomorrow a moment of frustration and sadness. As well as remembering this day of great happiness and satisfaction, I can also recall the times of disappointment and pain. One such instance was during the 1996 election campaign when I was treated so badly. By that time I thought I had been ridiculed and bashed in every imaginable way. Surely, there was nothing more that people could do to me. But here I was, being attacked as if I was some kind of monster who was doing some great damage to society! Me, Miria Matembe, the dedicated advocate for women, being accused of doing great damage to women and families! How was this possible? I have to admit that the attack got to me, so much so that I seriously thought about quitting the women's struggle.

In fact, I almost quit. But then, how could I quit? The Land Bill was there to debate, the Land Bill which presented new possibilities for women. It was time to go to battle again. How disappointing it was when that battle ended in only a partial victory (the consent provision). The disappointment of not getting the co-ownership provision seemed at the time to be the last blow. After that defeat, I might have been expected to quit the political race.

Well, you know what. I did not quit. I had another go at the parliamentary race in 2001. I again contested my usual women district seat, against the loud calls from many elites in Kampala, both men and women, for Matembe to quit contesting for that seat. The rural women and the people of Mbarara ignored those calls to throw me aside. It seems they appreciated my work, particularly so my spirited fight on the Land Bill. They returned me to Parliament with an overwhelming majority of 82 percent. Wow, what an energiser! Now, you tell me. How can I quit? Does anybody who knows me well really expect me to quit? I tell you I am not quitting! I am hanging on, the major reason being that, perhaps one day, Parliament will take their responsibility to women seriously, Parliament will take up the Law of Domestic Relations. Here is another chance to pass legislation that will guarantee women land and property, that will guarantee women a permanent home in which they can live their lives securely and freely. Surely, when Ugandans think seriously about this issue, that is what they want for their hardest, most dedicated workers, for the mothers of Uganda's children.

I do not expect to live to see the total liberation of women in Uganda, but wherever I can, and as long as I live, I shall continue to struggle to move one more step ahead.

In closing, I wish to make a heartfelt appeal to the women of Uganda to stay by my side. Let us move forward together to break through the gates of liberty. You see, it is necessary to break through the gates, for no guard at the gates is prepared to open them for us. I know all too well that the remaining journey is long, and the road is narrow, steep and slippery. But along this rough road, women of Uganda shall have to walk, step by step, metre by metre, even mile by mile, until we achieve a triumphant entry in through the gates of liberty.

May God bless us on our journey to freedom.

Amen.

References

Byanyima, W. Karagwa, 1992, 'Women in Political Struggle in Uganda', in Jill M. Bystydzienski, (ed) *Women Transforming Politics: Worldwide Strategies for Empowerment*: Indian University Press.

Mukholi D. 1995, *Uganda's Fourth Constitution: History, Politics and the Law*, Kampala: Fountain Publishers.

Museveni, Yoweri Kaguta, 1995, Address on the Occasion of the State Opening of the 9th Session of the NRC.

Rwabwoogo, Mugisha, 1991, in the *New Vision*, June12.

Tamale, Sylvia, 1999, *When Hens Begin to Crow: Gender and Parliamentary Politics in Uganda*, Kampala: Fountain Publishers.

Tripp, Ali Mari, 2000, *Women and Politics in Uganda*, James Currey Publishers.

Uganda Constitutional Commission, 1992, Sources of People's Views.

Waliggo, Rev Fr John Mary, 1996, 'Did Women get a Raw Deal in the New Constitution? *Arise Magazine No. 17*, June-July.

Index